Palgrave Studies in European Union Politics

Edited by: **Michelle Egan**, American University, USA, **Neill Nugent**, Visiting Professor, College of Europe, Bruges and Honorary Professor, University of Salford, UK, and **William Paterson OBE**, University of Aston, UK.

Editorial Board: **Christopher Hill**, Cambridge, UK, **Simon Hix**, London School of Economics, UK, **Mark Pollack**, Temple University, USA, **Kalypso Nicolaïdis**, Oxford, UK, **Morten Egeberg**, University of Oslo, Norway, **Amy Verdun**, University of Victoria, Canada, **Claudio M. Radaelli**, University of Exeter, UK, **Frank Schimmelfennig**, Swiss Federal Institute of Technology, Switzerland.

Following on the sustained success of the acclaimed *European Union Series*, which essentially publishes research-based textbooks, *Palgrave Studies in European Union Politics* publishes cutting-edge research-driven monographs.

The remit of the series is broadly defined, both in terms of subject and academic discipline. All topics of significance concerning the nature and operation of the European Union potentially fall within the scope of the series. The series is multidisciplinary to reflect the growing importance of the EU as a political, economic and social phenomenon.

Titles include:

Oriol Costa and Knud Erik Jørgensen (*editors*)
THE INFLUENCE OF INTERNATIONAL INSTITUTIONS ON THE EU
When Multilateralism Hits Brussels

Falk Daviter
POLICY FRAMING IN THE EUROPEAN UNION

Renaud Dehousse (*editor*)
THE 'COMMUNITY METHOD'
Obstinate or Obsolete?

Kenneth Dyson and Angelos Sepos (*editors*)
WHICH EUROPE?
The Politics of Differentiated Integration

Michelle Egan, Neill Nugent and William E. Paterson (*editors*)
RESEARCH AGENDAS IN EU STUDIES
Stalking the Elephant

Theofanis Exadaktylos and Claudio M. Radaelli (*editors*)
RESEARCH DESIGN IN EUROPEAN STUDIES
Establishing Causality in Europeanization

Jack Hayward and Rüdiger Wurzel (*editors*)
EUROPEAN DISUNION
Between Sovereignty and Solidarity

Wolfram Kaiser and Jan-Henrik Meyer (*editors*)
SOCIETAL ACTORS IN EUROPEAN INTEGRATION

Christian Kaunert and Sarah Leonard (*editors*)
EUROPEAN SECURITY, TERRORISM AND INTELLIGENCE
Tackling New Security Challenges in Europe

Christian Kaunert and Kamil Zwolski
The EU AS A GLOBAL SECURITY ACTOR
A Comprehensive Analysis beyond CFSP and JHA

Finn Laursen (*editor*)
DESIGNING THE EUROPEAN UNION
From Paris to Lisbon

Karl-Oskar Lindgren and Thomas Persson
PARTICIPATORY GOVERNANCE IN THE EU
Enhancing or Endangering Democracy and Efficiency?

Daniel Naurin and Helen Wallace (*editors*)
UNVEILING THE COUNCIL OF THE EUROPEAN UNION
Games Governments Play in Brussels

Dimitris Papadimitriou and Paul Copeland (*editors*)
THE EU's LISBON STRATEGY
Evaluating Success, Understanding Failure

Emmanuelle Schon-Quinlivan
REFORMING THE EUROPEAN COMMISSION

Roger Scully and Richard Wyn Jones (*editors*)
EUROPE, REGIONS AND EUROPEAN REGIONALISM

Yves Tiberghien (*editor*)
LEADERSHIP IN GLOBAL INSTITUTION BUILDING
Minerva's Rule

Asle Toje
AFTER THE POST-COLD WAR
The European Union as a Small Power

Liubomir K. Topaloff
POLITICAL PARTIES AND EUROSCEPTICISM

Richard G. Whitman and Stefan Wolff (*editors*)
THE EUROPEAN NEIGHBOURHOOD POLICY IN PERSPECTIVE
Context, Implementation and Impact

Richard G. Whitman (*editor*)
NORMATIVE POWER EUROPE
Empirical and Theoretical Perspectives

Sarah Wolff
THE MEDITERRANEAN DIMENSION OF THE EUROPEAN UNION'S INTERNAL SECURITY

Jan Wouters, Hans Bruyninckx, Sudeshna Basu and Simon Schunz (*editors*)
THE EUROPEAN UNION AND MULTILATERAL GOVERNANCE
Assessing EU Participation in United Nations Human Rights and Environmental Fora

---

Palgrave Studies in European Union Politics
Series Standing Order ISBN 978–1–403–99511–7 (hardback) and
ISBN 978–1–403–99512–4 (paperback)
(*outside North America only*)

You can receive future titles in this series as they are published by placing a standing order. Please contact your bookseller or, in case of difficulty, write to us at the address below with your name and address, the title of the series and one of the ISBNs quoted above.

Customer Services Department, Macmillan Distribution Ltd, Houndmills, Basingstoke, Hampshire RG21 6XS, UK.

The EU as a Global Security Actor

A Comprehensive Analysis Beyond CFSP and JHA

Christian Kaunert
Senior Lecturer in International Relations and Politics, University of Dundee, and Marie Curie Senior Research Fellow, European University Institute, Florence, Italy

and

Kamil Zwolski
Lecturer in Global Politics and Policy, University of Southampton, UK

© Christian Kaunert and Kamil Zwolski 2013

All rights reserved. No reproduction, copy or transmission of this publication may be made without written permission.

No portion of this publication may be reproduced, copied or transmitted save with written permission or in accordance with the provisions of the Copyright, Designs and Patents Act 1988, or under the terms of any licence permitting limited copying issued by the Copyright Licensing Agency, Saffron House, 6–10 Kirby Street, London EC1N 8TS.

Any person who does any unauthorized act in relation to this publication may be liable to criminal prosecution and civil claims for damages.

The authors have asserted their rights to be identified as the authors of this work in accordance with the Copyright, Designs and Patents Act 1988.

First published 2013 by
PALGRAVE MACMILLAN

Palgrave Macmillan in the UK is an imprint of Macmillan Publishers Limited, registered in England, company number 785998, of Houndmills, Basingstoke, Hampshire RG21 6XS.

Palgrave Macmillan in the US is a division of St Martin's Press LLC, 175 Fifth Avenue, New York, NY 10010.

Palgrave Macmillan is the global academic imprint of the above companies and has companies and representatives throughout the world.

Palgrave® and Macmillan® are registered trademarks in the United States, the United Kingdom, Europe and other countries.

ISBN 978–0–230–37867–4

This book is printed on paper suitable for recycling and made from fully managed and sustained forest sources. Logging, pulping and manufacturing processes are expected to conform to the environmental regulations of the country of origin.

A catalogue record for this book is available from the British Library.

A catalog record for this book is available from the Library of Congress.

10 9 8 7 6 5 4 3 2 1
22 21 20 19 18 17 16 15 14 13

Printed and bound in Great Britain by
CPI Antony Rowe, Chippenham and Eastbourne

Contents

List of Illustrations	vi
Preface	vii
Acknowledgements	viii
List of Abbreviations	ix
Introduction	1
1 The EU as a Comprehensive Security Actor: Towards a Theoretical Framework	19
2 The Historical Evolution of the CFSP and JHA	50
3 The EU and Climate Security	68
4 The EU and Counter-Terrorism	88
5 The EU and Refugees	116
6 The EU and Non-proliferation: The Case of Russia	144
7 The EU and Somali Piracy	167
Conclusion	192
Notes	210
Bibliography	211
Index	240

Illustrations

Figures

1.1	Instruments for the EU's international security policy	45
4.1	September 11 – The EU at a normative crossroad	109
7.1	The EU as an international security actor in the case of maritime piracy: three categories of instruments	178

Tables

1.1	The instruments of integration and the criteria of actorness	46
6.1	ISTC and STCU statistics covering the years 1994–2003	156
7.1	EU counter-piracy and long-term, preventive resources	179

Preface

This book is about European security, both conceptually and empirically. It is based on many discussions that the authors of this book have shared through vivid intellectual exchanges. We are grateful to a great number of people – family members, friends and colleagues – who have helped through the various stages of the writing of this book. Without these very special people, the writing of this book would have been impossible.

The findings in this book are based on research generously supported by scholarships and grants received from numerous institutions, including the University of Salford, the University Association for Contemporary European Studies (UACES), Manchester Metropolitan University and Regent's College London in the United Kingdom. In addition, Christian Kaunert wishes to thank the University of Salford for its support, as well as the European Commission for funding his Marie Curie Intra-European Fellowship (within the Seventh European Community Framework Programme) at the European University Institute in Florence, Italy. While writing this book, we also benefited enormously from the comments and insights of numerous experts in the field. The support and expertise of UACES have also been outstanding. Christian Kaunert would also like to thank the Institut Barcelona d'Estudis Internacionals (IBEI) for its support during his research fellowship while he had the good fortune to be on sabbatical from the University of Salford in 2010, as well as the Collegio Carlo Alberto in Turin, Italy, which supported him in 2012. All of these institutions have supported us in this research project.

Moreover, throughout the entire publication process, the entire team at Palgrave Macmillan provided extremely useful comments and suggestions. The support provided by Amber Stone-Galilee at Palgrave Macmillan was exceptional and very much appreciated. The thoughtful and exceptionally useful comments by the series editors of the Palgrave Studies in European Union Politics series, Neill Nugent, William E. Paterson, M. Egeberg, A. Verdun, C. Radaelli, F. Schimmelfennig, C. Hill, S. Hix, M. Pollack, K. Nicolaidis and Michelle Egan, were very much appreciated. Finally, we thank the anonymous reviewers for their helpful comments and suggestions.

Acknowledgements

The authors acknowledge their debt to those many people who have helped and influenced the approach and findings presented in this book. Parts of the research presented in this book have been disseminated in a number of articles, under a licence to publish agreement without a transfer of copyright, including the following: Zwolski, K. and Kaunert, C. (2011) 'The EU and Climate Security: A Case of Successful Norm Entrepreneurship?', *European Security*, 20(1); Kaunert, C. and Zwolski, K. (2012) 'Somalia versus Captain "Hook": Assessing the EU's Security Actorness in Countering Piracy off the Horn of Africa', *Cambridge Review of International Affairs*, iFirst, DOI:10.1080/09557571.2012.678295; Kaunert, C. (2007) '"Without the Power of Purse or Sword": The European Arrest Warrant and the Role of the Commission', *Journal of European Integration*, 29(4); Kaunert, C. (2009) 'Liberty versus Security?: EU Asylum Policy and the European Commission', *Journal of Contemporary European Research*, 5(2); Kaunert, C. and Léonard, S. (2011) 'Counter-Terrorism in the European Neighbourhood Policy', *Terrorism and Political Violence*, 23(2); Kaunert, C. and S. Léonard (2012) 'The Development of the EU Asylum Policy: Venue-Shopping in Perspective', *Journal of European Public Policy*, iFirst, DOI:10.1080/13501763.2012.677191; Zwolski, K. (2011) 'The External Dimension of the EU's Non-proliferation Policy: Overcoming Inter-institutional Competition', *European Foreign Affairs Review*, 16(3); Zwolski, K. (2011) 'Unrecognised and Unwelcome? The Role of the EU in Preventing the Proliferation of CBRN Weapons, Materials and Knowledge', *Perspectives on European Politics and Society*, 12(4); Zwolski, K. (2012) 'The EU as an International Security Actor after Lisbon: Finally a Green Light for a Holistic Approach?', *Cooperation and Conflict*, 47(3); and Zwolski, K. (2012) 'The EU and a Holistic Security Approach after Lisbon: Competing Norms and the Power of the Dominant Discourse', *Journal of European Public Policy*, 19(7).

Abbreviations

AFSJ	Area of Freedom, Security and Justice
AMISOM	African Union Mission in Somalia
AU	African Union
BMP	Best Management Practices
CAP	Common Agricultural Policy
CBRN	chemical, biological, radiological and nuclear
CEE	Central and Eastern European
CEAS	Common European Asylum System
CFSP	Common Foreign and Security Policy
CMR	Critical Maritime Routes
CPA	Cotonou Partnership Agreement
CSDP	Common Security and Defence Policy
CSI	Container Security Initiative
CTF	Combined Task Force
CTR	Cooperative Threat Reduction
DG	Directorate General
DG EuropeAid	Directorate General EuropeAid Cooperation Office
DG Relex	Directorate General External Relations
EASO	European Asylum Support Office
EAW	European Arrest Warrant
EC	European Community
ECJ	European Court of Justice
ECSC	European Coal and Steel Community
EDA	European Defence Agency
EEAS	European External Action Service
EEC	European Economic Community
EERA	European Energy Research Alliance
EFP	European foreign policy
EP	European Parliament
EPC	European Political Cooperation
ERF	European Refugee Fund
ESDP	European Security and Defence Policy
ESS	European Security Strategy
EU	European Union
EUMC	European Union Military Committee

EUMS	European Union Military Staff
EUNAVFOR	European Union Naval Force
EUSC	European Union Satellite Centre
EUTM	European Union Training Mission
FAC	Foreign Affairs Committee
FHQ	Force Headquarter
FPA	foreign policy analysis
GAERC	General Affairs and External Relations Council
GDP	gross domestic product
GHG	green-house gases
GLOBE	Global Legislators Organisation for a Balanced Environment
HR	High Representative
IES	Institute for Environmental Security
IfS	Instrument for Stability
IMO	International Maritime Organization
INSC	Instrument for Nuclear Safety Cooperation
IOM	International Organisation for Migration
IPCC	Intergovernmental Panel on Climate Change
IR	International Relations
ISTC	International Science and Technology Centre
JHA	Justice and Home Affairs
JNA	Joint Needs Assessment
MAD	mutual assured destruction
MEP	Member of the European Parliament
MLAT	Mutual Legal Assistance Treaty
MMT	Mission Monitoring Team
MSCHOA	Maritime Security Centre: Horn of Africa
NNWS	non-nuclear weapon states
NPT	Non-Proliferation Treaty
NWS	nuclear weapon states
OHQ	Operational Headquarter
OSCE	Organisation for Security and Cooperation in Europe
PDBTS	Policy Dialogue on Borders and Transport Security
PEP	Protected Entry Procedure
PNR	Passenger Name Record
PSC	Political and Security Committee
QMV	qualified majority voting
R&D	research and development
RAF	Red Army Fraction
RDP	Reconstruction and Development Programme

ReCAAP	Regional Cooperation Agreement on Combating Piracy and Armed Robbery
RPP	Regional Protection Programme
RRM	Rapid Reaction Mechanism
SALW	Small Arms and Light Weapons
SEA	Single European Act
SHAPE	Supreme Headquarters, Allied Powers Europe
SIS	Schengen Information System
STCU	Science and Technology Centre in Ukraine
TACIS	Technical Aid to the Commonwealth of Independent States
TEEC	Treaty Establishing the European Community
TEU	Treaty of the European Union
TFEU	Treaty on the Functioning of the European Union
TFG	Transitional Federal Government
TPC	Transit Processing Centres
UN	United Nations
UNDP	United Nations Development Programme
UNFCCC	United Nations Framework Convention on Climate Change
UNHCR	United Nations High Commissioner for Refugees
UNSC	United Nations Security Council
VPD	vessel protection detachment
WEU	Western European Union
WMDs	weapons of mass destruction
WNIS	Western Newly Independent States

Introduction

What constitutes security in the 21st century? The former United Nations (UN) Secretary General Kofi Annan states the obvious when he contrasts the perception of security threats of a New York investor passing Ground Zero on a daily basis with that of a Malawian orphan who has lost his parents to AIDS. Further, the fears of an Indonesian fisherman, who has lost his family to a tsunami, are also likely to differ from the security concerns of a villager threatened by bombing raids in Darfur (Annan, 2005). Over the last two decades, age-old problems, such as poverty, pandemic diseases and environmental disasters, together with new ones, such as climate change, have become increasingly integrated on the international security agenda; this reflects the growing understanding of their role not only as the main causes of death in many regions of the world but also as multipliers of more traditional, military threats. In this context, an increasing body of scholarship has recognised the European Union (EU) as a security actor, which is well equipped to tackle these complex security challenges, due to the multidimensional (Bretherton and Vogler, 2006) or structural (Keukeleire and MacNaughtan, 2008) character of its policies. Yet, at the same time, a rather narrow approach to security has been prevailing in scholarly works analysing the EU's security policy at the international level. It manifests itself in a strong focus on the Common Foreign and Security Policy (CFSP) and particularly the Common Security and Defence Policy (CSDP).

In recent years, issues such as energy security, environmental and climate security, underdevelopment, health and pandemic diseases, population movements and economic security have become important matters of international security (McInnes, 2008; Thomas, 2008; Dalby, 2009; Smith, 2010). Furthermore, more traditional security challenges, such as terrorism and the proliferation of weapons of mass destruction (WMDs), have evolved and changed character (Walton and Gray, 2007; Wirtz, 2007; Rogers, 2008; Busch and Joyner, 2009). This complex international security agenda requires a comprehensive, multi-dimensional approach. Military power remains an important, but insufficient, instrument to address the security challenges of the contemporary world. While the EU, consisting today of 27 Member States and a number of common institutions, attempts to develop itself as an actor in international security policy, the institutional architecture of EU international security policy is not a finished product; rather, it is a work in progress, with the Lisbon Treaty bringing some important innovations in this respect (Whitman and Juncos, 2009; Missiroli, 2010; Vanhoonacker and Reslow, 2010).

However, does the growing quantity and quality of EU institutions translate into a more effective role as an international security actor? What specific resources does the EU have to address contemporary security challenges? Is it recognised by other international actors for its efforts? This book examines the role of the EU in international security. In other words, this book aims to investigate the extent to which the EU has developed as an organisation playing a role in international security policy. Given the sustained interest of governments in the development of this most dynamic dimension of the EU, this book generates significant policy-relevant findings that will have an important impact on both academic and governmental debates. This book provides crucial new insights into several important aspects of the EU's role in international security. It is therefore of value to those academics interested in the strengthening of cross-disciplinary ties between the field of EU studies and International Relations (IR) and security studies.

There are two main reasons why undertaking this exercise is important. Firstly, on many occasions, the EU has expressed the ambition of becoming a global security actor. At the beginning of the 1970s, European states successfully established a modest framework for political cooperation, namely European Political Cooperation (EPC). They were careful to avoid any association of the EPC with the European Economic Community (EEC).[1] It took more than 20 years for European states to take this political cooperation to the next level, by its inclusion as one of the pillars of the newly established EU, in the form of the CFSP (Whitman, 1998a, 2002; Nuttall, 2000; Smith, 2002; Smith, 2004). Towards the end of the 1990s, partially as a result of the EU's inability to handle conflicts in the Balkans, the CSDP[2] was established as a framework to enhance EU crisis response capacities (Howorth, 2007;

Keukeleire and MacNaughtan, 2008). In the last decade, the most prominent manifestation of this ambition took the form of the European Security Strategy (ESS) (Council, 2003a; Biscop and Andersson, 2007). In this document, approved at the level of heads of state and government working together in the European Council, the EU states that 'Europe should be ready to share in the responsibility for global security and in building a better world' (Council, 2003a: 1). Over the last decade, the EU has also progressed in its development of certain institutional capacities to match its ambitions in international security policy. For example, in 1999, the Western European Union (WEU) was incorporated into the EU's institutional structure. This allowed the EU to develop its own, autonomous military capabilities, within the framework of the aforementioned CSDP. Recognising a strong link between development and security, the EU developed another important instrument. In 2007, the Rapid Reaction Mechanism (RRM) was replaced with the Instrument for Stability (IfS), which is 'designed to provide the Union with a new strategic tool to address a number of global security and development challenges' (European Commission, 2007a: 3).

Furthermore, the former third pillar, Justice and Home Affairs (JHA), or the Area of Freedom, Security and Justice (AFSJ), as it has been called since the Amsterdam Treaty (1997), experienced very significant growth in the late 1990s and the early part of the new millennium (Kaunert, 2005, 2007, 2009a, 2010a, 2010b, 2010c). Thus, the EU is making strong inroads into areas of security, especially internal security matters, traditionally reserved for states. Monar (1999) underlines the fact that there has been no other example of a policy area making its way so quickly and comprehensively to the centre of the treaties and to the top of the EU's policy-making agenda. After major treaty revisions in Maastricht, Amsterdam, Nice and finally the Lisbon Treaty, which entered into force on 1 December 2009, as well as an increased political impetus through the European Council Summits in Tampere (1999), the Hague (2004) and Stockholm (2009), the area of security appears as one of the most promising policy fields for integration in the EU in the foreseeable future. This process has become even more significant after the terrorist attacks on 11 September 2001 in the United States, on 11 March 2004 in Madrid and on 7 July 2005 in London. Some scholars have even suggested that these empirical developments and the resulting increasing involvement of the EU in internal security matters have changed EU governance more generally. The rapid development of the AFSJ in recent years has led to an expansion of the scholarly literature on this topic (see Geddes, 2000; Guiraudon, 2000; Guild, 2002; Boswell, 2003a, 2003b,

2008; Mitsilegas et al., 2003; Occhipinti, 2003; Balzacq and Carrera, 2005, 2006; Friedrichs, 2005; Bures, 2006; Kaunert, 2007, 2009a, 2010c; Bossong, 2008). However, with its focus on policy outputs and the role of the main EU institutions, this literature has tended to largely overlook the role of the EU in international security. Furthermore, the existing literature has tended to privilege a formal account of EU institutions over a comprehensive assessment of EU security activities. This means that the role of the EU in international security in practice remains vastly under-researched. This is very problematic given the increasing importance of both the AFSJ and CFSP in the EU and the role of the EU in international security more broadly. Consequently, this book is crucial in order to fill this gap in the scholarship.

Secondly, it is important to examine the role of the EU as an international security actor because there is an important gap in the existing literature. This book suggests that, in order to assess the role of the EU as an international security actor in a comprehensive manner, it is important to examine EU institutions and instruments available beyond the CSDP and even the JHA policy framework. The establishment of the CFSP in 1993 and, even more importantly, the introduction of the CSDP in 1999, opened new possibilities for policies to be implemented at the EU level, within the so-called second pillar of the EU. The three-pillar structure of the EU was introduced by the Treaty of the European Union (TEU) in 1993 and was formally abandoned in 2009 by the Lisbon Treaty. Nonetheless, the 'pillarisation' of the EU naturally had an important effect on the academic debate. It created an assumption among scholars that the international security policy of the EU takes place almost exclusively within what used to be the second pillar of the EU (for example, Gärtner, 2003; Hyde-Price, 2004; Longhurst and Zaborowski, 2004; Salmon, 2005; Gänzle and Sens, 2007; Kaldor et al., 2007; Matlary, 2008; Moschini, 2008). When addressing the question of EU international security 'actorness', those scholars (with some exceptions, for example Hintermeier, 2008; Keukeleire and MacNaughtan, 2008) also tend to focus on more traditional security threats, such as regional military conflicts, and omit the so-called non-traditional security challenges, such as migration, pandemic diseases, extreme poverty and environmental security. There is a significant body of studies examining the role of the EU in these policy areas, but it does not relate this knowledge directly to the EU as an international security actor (for example, Bretherton and Vogler, 1999, 2006; McCormick, 2001; Lacasta et al., 2002; Vogler, 2005; Groenleer and Van Schaik, 2007; Schreurs and Tiberghien, 2007). This contributes to a gap between the European studies literature and literature on contemporary security studies. The latter category tends to indicate that the concept of security has broadened and deepened in the last few decades (for example Collins, 2007; Dannreuther, 2007; Williams, 2008; Smith, 2010). Consequently, in order to take into account this development when studying the EU as an international security actor, it is important to look at both traditional and new security issues.

Thus, the aim of this book is to analyse the role of the EU in international security comprehensively. The empirical analysis, which consists of five detailed case studies, including, but going beyond, both the CFSP and JHA frameworks, is guided by a theoretical framework that has been inspired by the literature on the EU as a global actor but has been modified to increase its analytical relevance to the cases considered. As a consequence, the book is able to generate a more sophisticated and accurate understanding of the processes of EU security governance at the international level than that provided by the current literature. However, this is not the only contribution that this book makes. The empirical findings are also used to develop the theoretical framework further and improve its adequacy for understanding EU security governance at the international level. In sum, this book offers an original and much needed contribution to the literature on EU security governance at the global level. At the same time, it seeks to shed new light on EU 'actorness' approaches and to develop them further in order to make this more applicable to actual empirical cases. Finally, going beyond the specific topic investigated here, the book also reflects on European security governance processes in general.

The EU as a global security actor

What debates does this book engage with? Individualist scholars of the 'European Union-as-Actor' approach concentrate on the impact of Europe on world politics (Smith, 2002, 2008; Bretherton and Vogler, 2006). This approach aims to identify what kind of an actor the EU is at the global level, thereby relating this research strand back to the conception by Duchêne (1972) of Europe as a civilian power. The latter stresses the 'soft power' exercised by the EU, which extends its internal virtues and values through politico-economic (Rosecrance, 1998) and normative means (Manners, 2002; Nicolaïdis and Howse, 2003). This approach has significantly contributed to the discipline, particularly to the understanding of the EU's role in global politics. While scholars may not always find a coherent policy outcome in European foreign policy (EFP), it would be empirically careless to neglect the role of the EU on the international stage. Structuralist scholars provide an explanation for Member States' behaviour as actors. These actors are located in a complex set of interdependencies, institutions and structures (Nuttall, 2000; Ginsberg, 2001; Smith, 2004). Member States' behaviour is altered, according to these scholars, as a result of operating in a European institutional context. Institutional structures can include supranational institutions such as the European Commission or the Council Secretariat (White, 2004). The merits of this approach derive from its empirical observation that Member States – though still very significant – are not the only important actors any more. International institutions, especially European institutions, are increasingly gaining in importance. Bruter (1999) suggests that European diplomacy, increasingly, is not confined to a state structure any longer – the external delegations of the EU work to a significant degree like diplomatic missions.

What kind of an actor is the EU at the global level? Duchêne (1973) envisaged the EU as a 'civilian power' and as a 'soft power'. It wields civilian instruments, having renounced the use of force among its members and, thus, encourages others to do likewise. Duchêne did not explicitly offer a clear definition of civilian power, but his understanding of a civilian power seems to suggest that EU foreign policy should focus on the promotion of democracy and human rights, alongside security cooperation. This is in contrast with approaches arguing that the EU should have hard power. Hedley Bull (1982) argued that, due to a serious divergence of interests between the western European countries and America, Europe should take steps towards 'making themselves more self-sufficient in defence or security'. Derived from this debate, many scholars have discussed the concepts of civilian power, military power and normative power (see Manners, 2002, 2006a, 2006b, 2011; Diez, 2005; Orbie, 2008; Sjursen, 2006a, 2006b; Whitman, 2006; Diez and Manners, 2007).

Karen Smith (2008: 1), in her updated volume on the EU's foreign policy, notes that the EU tends to be conceptualised as a 'superpower', 'quiet superpower', 'normative power', post-modern power', 'civilian power', 'civilian model', 'civilising power' and even 'metrosexual power'. After the European Security and Defense Policy (ESDP) had started to take shape in the late 1990s, some scholars argued that 'civilian power Europe' became 'a contradiction in terms' (Bretherton and Vogler, 2006: 42). In response to this challenge, Manners (2002: 238) declared that by 'refocusing away from the debate over either civilian or military power, it is possible to think of the ideational impact of the EU's

Introduction 7

international identity/role as representing normative power'. Manners (2002) bases his conceptualisation on Duchêne (1973). Under the most basic definition of normative power, the EU acts in an 'ethically good way', which involves 'living by example'. His nine substantive normative principles for the EU are: (1) five main principles – peace, liberty, democracy, human rights and rule of law, and (2) four minor contested principles – equality, social solidarity, sustainable development and good governance. The EU has become a normative power due to its many unique characteristics, such as the idea of the 'pooling of sovereignty', the importance of a transnational European Parliament and the pursuit of human rights. Manners (2002) links the emergence of Europe's ideological power to the construction of a specific European identity as part of a process. His argument is certainly one of the most important contemporary scholarly contributions surrounding notions of 'actorness' and the EU. Diez (2005) explores Manner's point further by suggesting that the EU's identity is constructed against an image of others in the outside world (Diez, 2005: 614) – with its other primarily being the United States. The 'civilian/normative power Europe' debate continues to influence scholarship on the EU's international security role, with European military ambitions bearing the risk of undermining the normative character of the EU (Manners, 2006a, 2006b).

In parallel to this debate, scholars have been attempting to conceptualise the scope of the EU's power, sometimes also with strong normative arguments. Notably, in his controversial thesis formulated in the 1970s, Galtung (1973) argued that the European Community was turning into a superpower – and not the kind based on positive values. Instead, the trends at the time led Galtung to believe that the Community was becoming a superpower in the traditional sense (divide and rule), thus necessitating containment if this trend was to be halted and reversed. This vision never materialised, not least because of the overwhelmingly civilian nature of the EU's resources, even 12 years after formally launching the ESDP. The slow progress in developing more traditional power qualities prompted a fresh set of arguments on the EU's role as a 'strategic' power. On the one hand, Biscop (2009) argues that the EU needs a 'grand strategy' that would specify objectives and priorities for the EU's global role. In a similar tone, Howorth (2010: 464) points out that the EU has the potential to achieve greatness, but it will need to adopt 'a more calculated strategic approach and begin at long last to think in terms of "large ends"'. On the other hand, as Toje (2011) convincingly argues, the lack of 'big thinking' in the EU can be better understood if the Union is conceptualised as a small power. This approach could

8 *The EU as a Global Security Actor*

indeed serve as 'the best path to making peace with the inconsistencies associated with the presence, capabilities and patterns of behaviour that characterize the European Union' (Toje, 2011: 57). The arguments depicting the EU as a small power or even as a risk-averse power (Laïdi, 2010) partially stem from a disappointment with the EU's international foreign and security policy performance (see for example Bailes, 2008; Menon, 2009). This, in turn, could be the result of the 'Euro-strategic discourse', which since the late 1990s has been pushing for a strong and strategic international security role for the EU. Rogers (2009: 843–44) argues that 'a growing pan-European complex of bureaucracies and institutions, think tanks, academic establishments and private organizations, appear to have mobilised to take part in a discursive battle to re-articulate European grand strategy'.

This book is not based on the premise that in order to matter in international security policy, the EU must become an assertive strategic power with strong military muscle. Instead, it examines, in a comprehensive manner, what the EU does to address some of the pressing contemporary security challenges. The state of the art on what and how the EU operates in international security policy indicates a diversity of approaches, with a strong focus on the CSDP. This is partially the result of a rather narrow approach to 'security', because 'if one applies a broad approach to security, the set of capabilities that will be considered as important and relevant will differ from an approach that applies a narrow concept of security' (Rieker, 2009: 704). However, this concentration of empirical research on the CSDP also stems from the formal separation of the 'Community' pillar from the 'foreign and security policy' pillar in the Treaty of Maastricht. Consequently, it is not necessarily just a narrow understanding of the 'security' concept which leads to an almost exclusive concentration on just one policy framework but also a natural outcome of the EU's institutional structure between 1993 and 2009 which does so. The first assessments of the EU's role in international security took place even before the St Malo summit of 1998 and the following institutionalisation of the ESDP. Already in 1993, Petersen (1993: 27) had anticipated that the Maastricht Treaty had introduced an 'authentic qualitative change' to the Community's foreign and security policy.

The post-1999 developments in the EU's international security policy have led to the development of scholarly literature along two broad lines. One strand approaches the question of the EU's international security policy as part of the broader assessment of the EU's role in IR; another strand focuses specifically on the emerging ESDP (and now CSDP). In the former strand, the books by White (2001) and Ginsberg (2001) apply specific theoretical frameworks to analysing the EU's role in foreign and security policy. On the one hand, White adopts the framework of foreign policy analysis (FPA), distinguishing between Community foreign policy, Union foreign policy and national foreign policies – all constituting the foreign and security policy of the EU. Ginsberg (2001), on the other hand, adopts Easton's (1979) model of governmental decision-making to evaluate the political impact of the EU on IR. Hazel Smith (2002), in *European Union Foreign Policy: What It Is and What It Does?*, acknowledges that EU security involves areas such as 'reduction of crime, control of the narcotics trade, migration control, environmental protection and the maintenance of liberal democratic systems' (Smith, 2002: 18). Yet she chooses to focus mainly on the military-related aspects of security in EU policy. Sjursen, in two edited volumes on the EU's role in IR (1998, 2004), similarly recognises that 'security' has broadened, and factors such as social and economic inequalities must be integrated when studying the concept. Yet, this more comprehensive approach is only modestly reflected in the empirical analysis, which for the most part deals with intergovernmental cooperation within the CFSP.

In the broader area of the EU's role in IR, two contributions are particularly important. Firstly, *The European Union as a Global Actor* by Bretherton and Vogler (2006) introduces a conceptual framework to assess the nature of the EU's international 'actorness' in areas such as trade, the environment, the CFSP and the CSDP. Secondly, *International Relations and the European Union*, edited by Hill and Smith (2010), has become one of the key resources for those who seek a thorough overview of the EU's activities in foreign and security policy. A distinctive and rather original feature of this volume is a chapter by Wyn Rees introducing the external dimension of the AFSJ. This should not come as a surprise, considering the rapid expansion of European integration in internal security matters, including the growing 'externalisation' of AFSJ policies. In response to these empirical developments, the external dimension of the AFSJ has developed into a distinctive research theme (Kaunert, 2005, 2007, 2009a, 2010a, 2010b, 2010c, 2010d; Léonard, 2009, 2010a, 2010b; Kaunert and Léonard, 2010, 2011a, 2011b; MacKenzie, 2010). This has also led authors, who, in principle, are mainly concerned with the EU's foreign and security policy, to look at the AFSJ. One of the more recent examples in this respect is the volume by Keukeleire and MacNaughtan (2008) titled *The Foreign Policy of the European Union* and Karen Smith (2008) in *European Union Foreign Policy in a Changing World*.

In addition, a significant body of scholarship focuses more narrowly on the defence and security policy of the EU, mainly in the context of the ESDP (and now the CSDP). Howorth's (2007) volume *Security and Defence Policy in the European Union* is one of the most comprehensive assessments of the ESDP, as is Anderson's (2008) *Crafting EU Security Policy: In Pursuit of a European Identity*. While it is important to underline that European security scholars have increasingly recognised the fact that the 'security' concept has broadened over the last few decades, incorporating such a broadened understanding into the empirical analysis of the EU's security 'actorness' seems difficult. Gänzle and Sens (2007), in *The Changing Politics of European Security: Europe Alone?*, elaborate on how 'security' has evolved after the Cold War. Yet, the contributors to this edited volume choose not to look in greater detail at the role of the EU in addressing these issues, which would have required a significant move beyond the CSDP. Furthermore, some scholars (Biscop, 2009; Howorth, 2010) point out that although the EU has a variety of instruments at its disposal, it lacks an overarching strategic vision to utilise them in a coherent manner. A similar type of difficulty can be recognised in a strand of research on the EU and human security.[3] Matlary (2008), in her article 'Much Ado about Little: The EU and Human Security', focuses exclusively on the CFSP and the CSDP, which by themselves seem ill-equipped to tackle the security concerns that have been identified in the UN Development Programme (UNDP) report.

Originality and innovative nature of the book

This book is innovative and original for several reasons, including: (1) the novel theoretical conceptualisation of the EU's global security role, (2) the theoretical contribution of the findings to the literature of EU security governance and (3) the empirical importance of the five cases within this book. Firstly, this book suggests a novel conceptualisation of the EU as an international security actor. As discussed before, the majority of scholarly research on the EU and international security tends to adopt a limited approach, by focusing almost exclusively on the CFSP/CSDP. This book offers a broadened conceptualisation of the EU as an international security actor, which also includes JHA policy and even goes beyond both frameworks. This original contribution is important, because the way in which EU international security policy is conceptualised inevitably affects the conclusions about the level of the EU's international security 'actorness'.

In addition to this conceptual contribution, the empirical components of this book offer an original contribution to the study of EU policy in the area of five contemporary security challenges. The literature on EU policy in the area of environment and climate change is thriving (for example McCormick, 2001; Lacasta, et al., 2002; Vogler, 2005; Bretherton and Vogler, 2006; Groenleer and Van Shaik, 2007; Schreurs and Tiberghien, 2007; Parker and Karlsson, 2010; Wurzel and Connelly, 2010). This book, through conceptualising climate change as a contemporary security challenge, brings the analysis of EU security 'actorness' closer to scholarly work on contemporary security studies. The problem of piracy off the coast of Somalia only emerged as a pressing international issue in 2008. The EU deployed its military operation at the end of 2008. Thus, this book offers one of the first comprehensive assessments of EU policy in this area. EU policy on the non-proliferation of WMDs from Russia and the former Soviet Union did not attract a lot of scholarly attention, even though this potential threat was at the top of the US security policy agenda in the 1990s, and then again attracted international attention in the aftermath of the 9/11 terrorist attacks. Asylum and migration are amongst the most contentious political issues in Europe and have become important topics of contemporary security politics in Europe, both in the 'real world' of policies and in the scholarly literature on the subject (Bigo, 1998a, 1998b, 2001, 2002; Huysmans, 2000, 2006; Guild, 2003a, 2003b, 2009). Finally, this book also investigates one of the most important security challenges for the EU since the 9/11 attacks on the United States – terrorism. Empirical developments seem to point to an ever-increasing role of terrorism on the security agenda of the EU. Europol's *Terrorism Situation and Trend Report* (Europol, 2011) from 2010 confirms this trend. Thus, this book offers a comprehensive analysis of the most important EU security policies.

While this book aims to provide a comprehensive picture of EU security activities at the international level, it also seeks to demonstrate the various linkages and interactions between these policies from a theoretically informed but substantively empirical perspective. This further allows for considerable policy relevance. Given its scope, this book aims to provide the baseline for future research by academics from different disciplines who are interested in this field. It will therefore be of value for those academics interested in interdisciplinary work at the intersection between the areas of EU governance and IR/security studies, Criminology and Law.

Methodology

The methodology of this book is based on the philosophical assumption that all concepts constituting the everyday vocabulary of an IR scholar, such as states and international security, are socially constructed. Thus, in terms of ontological choices, this book is based on social constructivism (Adler, 2003). Further, this book adheres to scientific realism in terms of epistemological choices (Wendt, 1999). Scientific realist epistemology acknowledges the fact that the EU does not exist entirely independently of a shared understanding about its existence. Nonetheless, there are important material factors that constitute the EU, such as its external borders, a common currency and common institutions. In this sense, the EU as a social kind shares the quality of self-organisation with natural kinds, with only the degree of self-organisation differentiating the two. While natural kinds are entirely self-organised (they exist solely because of their material structure), social kinds need to be constituted (recognised) by an external structure.

In addition, this book is structured around case study research design (Burnham et al., 2004). In order to answer the main research question, that is 'to which extent has the EU developed as an international security actor', five case studies were selected. They represent different kinds of contemporary security challenges, ranging from the so-called non-traditional ones to more traditional challenges, requiring a combination of military and non-military responses. The following cases have been selected: (1) climate change; (2) migration and refugees; (3) terrorism; (4) non-proliferation of WMDs; and (5) counter-piracy off the coast of Somalia. Each case is explained in more detail below in the structure of this book.

This research project has been executed according to the principle of methodological triangulation. In other words, different methodologies have been used to collect the data on which the book is based. Firstly, an exhaustive review of the secondary literature on the topic was carried out in order to devise the research question. Then, it was established that the methods best suited to this research project were documentary analysis and semi-structured elite interviews. As this book aims to analyse the role of the EU in international security, EU official documents are of primary importance for the topic investigated. They include documents from the European Commission (for example communications, legislative proposals and decisions), the European Council (for example European Council conclusions), the Council of Ministers (for example directives and Council Conclusions) and the European Parliament (for example parliamentary committee reports). Semi-structured elite interviews have also been conducted for this research project. It was decided to conduct interviews of the elites involved in the EU decision-shaping and decision-making processes for several reasons. First of all, they usefully complement documentary analysis as official documents do not record all the information relevant to the research. The additional information provided by the interviews also helps interpreting the documents under analysis. External funding in the form of a Scholarship of the University Association for Contemporary European Studies (£2450), was secured by one of the authors of this book for conducting two rounds of interviews in Brussels. The first round of interviews took place between 29 March and 17 April 2009. The second round took place between 18 May and 24 June 2009. Additional interviews were conducted in 2010 and 2011. The majority of the Brussels-based interviews were conducted in EU institutions, most notably in the European Commission and the Council Secretariat. A few interviews were also conducted in NGOs, such as think tanks concerned with environmental security. Apart from interviews conducted in Brussels, a number of interviews were conducted over the phone and via e-mail. These included, for example, interviews with non-proliferation experts in the United States, Sweden and Germany. An interview was also conducted with a Turkish navy officer involved in countering piracy off the coast of Somalia.

Structure of the book

The book is divided into seven chapters. Chapter 1 develops the theoretical framework that will guide the subsequent empirical analysis. The starting point of this theoretical enquiry is the question of the comprehensive approach to analysing the EU's role in international security. Although scholars adopt different approaches to examining the role of the EU as an actor in international security policy, this chapter outlines some common limitations that have been identified in the majority of the work analysed. The chapter also identifies and addresses some of the key obstacles, which have been preventing scholars from adopting such a comprehensive approach. The second part of the theoretical framework concerns the question of the EU's 'actorness' in IR, as conceptualised by scholars such as Sjöstedt (1977), Jupille and Carporaso (1998) and Bretherton and Vogler (1999, 2006). There are several reasons for this choice. First of all, a framework centred on EU 'actorness' is arguably the most appropriate since the research project aims to investigate the extent of the EU's 'actorness' in international security. The work by Jupille and Caporaso (1998) and Bretherton and Vogler (1999, 2006) seems to open very promising avenues for research on the linkages between the EU's global role and international security and the ways in which those are established. Even more important for this book, the works by Jupille and Caporaso (1998) and Bretherton and Vogler (1999, 2006) have arguably become a reference point for analysing EU 'actorness' in different regions of the world, including in Europe, as will be shown later. The chapter demonstrates that the framework is well-equipped to analyse contemporary security threats, albeit in a modified form. In addition, the framework also incorporates findings from the existing literature on contemporary security studies, in order to increase its analytical powers.

Chapter 2 examines the institutional structure associated with the CFSP and the AFSJ in their historical perspective. This is crucial, given that this book adopts a broadened perspective on the question of the EU's international security role, which also includes the external policies of the AFSJ. It is particularly relevant given the fact that both external and internal security policies of the EU historically evolved under a single institutional framework, that is EPC, up until the Maastricht Treaty. In the first part, this chapter provides a historical overview of both CFSP and AFSJ, including their common roots under the EPC and their subsequent separation under the Maastricht Treaty. In the second part, this chapter assesses the current institutional and decision-making frameworks of these two policy-areas, as reformed by the Lisbon Treaty.

Chapter 3 analyses the EU's actions with regard to climate change, which represents an important 'non-traditional' security challenge. Why are these actions important? As a scientific phenomenon, for the first time, climate change was discussed by a Swedish scientist Svante Arrhenius in 1896. Almost 100 years later, in 1988, the international community appreciated the severity of the potential consequences of climate change by establishing the Intergovernmental Panel on Climate Change (IPCC). This led to climate change becoming one of the top issues on the contemporary political agenda. However, it was only in the last decade that practitioners and academics began thinking about the security consequences of climate change (Barnett, 2003, 2007; Hough, 2004; Floyd, 2008; Dalby, 2009; Trombetta, 2009). This discussion was significantly influenced by a few high-impact scientific reports on climate change and its consequences for international security and stability (Haldén, 2007; IPCC, 2007; Stern, 2007; WBGU, 2007). The non-traditional character of climate change as a security risk stems from the fact that even though it may have 'hard' security consequences (that is conflicts over scarce resources and massive migration leading to clashes between populations), there is no 'hard' security response to it. Assuming that human beings contribute to climate change, the only solution to this problem lies in international cooperation (for example the reduction of green-house gases (GHGs)) and scientific progress on the one hand, and adaptation on the other hand.

Chapter 4 analyses the EU's actions with regard to another, somewhat more traditional, security threat, terrorism, whereby empirical developments certainly seem to point to an ever-increasing role of terrorism on the security agenda. Why are these actions important? On 7 July 2005, four young Islamist suicide-bombers attacked London's transport system, killing 52 members of the public and injuring several hundred more. The perpetrators were British, the children of Pakistani immigrants. The London bombings were the first attacks on UK soil to be carried out as part of the global jihad, which was, of course, preceded by the horrific attacks on the United States on 11 September 2001, and on Spain on 11 March 2004 (Kaunert et al., 2012). Despite setbacks, militants continue to plan attacks, as evidenced by the 2007 suicide attack on Glasgow airport. On 14 May 2010, a young girl, Roshonara Choudhry, radicalised by Al Qaeda and antagonised by the War in Iraq, stabbed the British MP Stephen Timms almost fatally. In October 2010, warnings against terrorist attacks were issued in France, Germany and other European countries, and, subsequently, bomb packages sent from Yemen, designed to go off on a US-bound aircraft, were intercepted. This confirms the sentiments of the *EU Terrorism Situation and Trend Report* (Europol, 2011), published by Europol in 2011. In this document, Islamist terrorism is still underlined as the biggest threat to most EU Member States. The report suggests that the threat emanating from Islamist terrorism is driven by developments in countries such as Afghanistan, the Afghanistan/Pakistan border area, Iraq, Somalia and Yemen. For EU Member States, Al Qaeda has increasingly emerged as the most dangerous terrorist organisation. The danger it represents mainly relates to its specific organisation and structure, which make European cooperation crucial in order to tackle it (Hoffman, 2006; Wilkinson, 2006). Its structure is that of a large transnational movement or network, rather than a traditional 'terrorist' organisation, which makes it dangerous even after the demise of Osama Bin Laden in May 2011. It is more difficult to establish good intelligence in a mono-national setting. Yet, how well placed is the EU in tackling this prominent security threat? Amongst scholars of EU counter-terrorism, there are diverging opinions as to the extent to which EU competences matter in the fight against the global terrorist threat (Reinares, 2000; den Boer and Monar, 2002; Dubois, 2002; Occhipinti, 2003; Friedrichs, 2005; Gregory, 2005; Kaunert, 2005, 2007, 2009a, 2010a, 2010b, 2010c; Bures, 2006, 2011; Deflem, 2006; Zimmermann, 2006; Mitsilegas and Gilmore, 2007; Spence, 2007; Bossong, 2008; Müller-Wille, 2008; Kaunert et al., 2012). On the one hand, the EU is characterised as a 'paper tiger' (Bures, 2006: 57) and thus an ineffective counter-terrorism actor. On the other hand, scholars point out that the EU has taken great strides towards increasing integration and encouraging co-operation between Member States since 9/11 (Zimmermann, 2006; Kaunert, 2007, 2010a, 2010b, 2010c).

Chapter 5 examines the EU's actions with regard to refugees, an issue which has increasingly given rise to intense political debates, and which is, in many ways, somewhat similar to the issue of climate change. Why are these actions important? Increasingly, asylum and migration are being seen as a significant security threat, which has supposedly influenced the first phase of the Common European Asylum System (Bigo, 1996, 1998a, 1998b, 1998c, 2002; Guild, 1999, 2002, 2003a, 2003b, 2004; Guiraudon, 2000, 2003; Huysmans, 2000, 2004). Policy developments after 9/11 have prompted a series of scholars (Huysmans, 2000; Kostakopolou, 2000; Ceyhan and Tsoukala, 2002; Karyotis, 2003; Faist, 2004) to argue that migration has been constructed as a security threat in Europe. These scholars often draw upon the Copenhagen School's securitisation theory and argue that migration issues have been securitised in the EU. However, this fear could be counter-intuitive. The European Commission is especially well known for its legalistic approach to policy problems, always following the letter of the law; in fact, the Commission is often derided for being technocratic. It thus seems counter-intuitive that the Commission would 'securitise' the EU Asylum Policy. Moreover, this goes against several academic arguments that have often been made about asylum cooperation in Europe (Freeman, 1998; Joppke, 1998, 2001; Lavenex, 1998, 1999, 2001a, 2001b, 2004, 2006; Geddes, 2000, 2001; Guiraudon, 2000, 2003; Stetter, 2000, 2007; Thielemann, 2001a, 2001b, 2004, 2005, 2006; Occhipinti, 2003; Boswell, 2003a, 2003b, 2008; Thielemann and Dewan, 2006). Refugees in this book represent another category of the so-called non-traditional security risks, with similarities to climate security, albeit with a strong difference, most notably the fact that the construction of refugees as a security threat has, for the most part, been resisted by EU institutions, such as the European Commission. Firstly, this chapter investigates the institutional arrangements and legal competences of the EU to develop policies in the area of global migration and refugees.

Of particular importance here is the question of whether the EU has used its competences to depict refugees and migrants as a security threat at all. Secondly, this chapter examines EU resources with respect to the development of the security dimension of global migration, which remains notoriously difficult to develop. Finally, this chapter investigates the extent to which the EU has been recognised as an actor in this policy area, despite the fact that security constructions of refugees do not remain shared.

Chapter 6 examines the EU's actions with regard to the proliferation of WMDs, which may potentially represent the greatest, existential danger to humanity. This was particularly the case during the Cold War, with the culminating moment being the Cuban Missile Crisis. In the post Cold-War period, and particularly after the 9/11 attacks, one of the main concerns is the danger of an unauthorised access to CBRN (chemical, biological, radiological and nuclear) materials. Terrorist organisations acquiring such materials represent a significant threat to states and societies. However, as in the case of climate change, there is no effective 'hard' security response to this potential threat. The only appropriate action requires international cooperation within various international institutions and regimes, such as the G8 Global Partnership and the Non-Proliferation Treaty (NPT), in order to safeguard the existing stockpiles of WMDs and to systematically reduce their numbers. This book focuses primarily on the territories of the former Soviet Union, most notably Russia, which possess the largest stockpile of WMDs, including chemical weapons. Undertaking this task is important, because there have not been many comprehensive assessments analysing EU activities aiming to prevent the proliferation from Russia. Denza (2005: 293) notes that 'the international effort and the European Union's contribution to that particular exercise in containment deserves greater acknowledgement than it has received'. At the same time, the threat from this geographical region has been substantial, particularly throughout the 1990s. Turpen and Finlay (2009: 304) argue that 'Moscow's ability to exercise adequate command and control and to prevent unauthorised access into its WMD complex became frequently challenged'.

Chapter 7 evaluates the EU's actions with regard to maritime piracy off the Somali coast, which can be considered one of the most 'traditional' security challenges in the typology developed in this book. In fact, piracy is one of the oldest international security problems, particularly in Southeast Asia, where 'pirate traditions go back virtually uninterrupted to the fifth century' (Murphy, 2009: 72). Maritime piracy has also been widely popularised by Hollywood movie productions, yet its contemporary version has little to do with popular images. This is particularly the case with maritime piracy off the coast of Somalia, where piratical gangs are best described as organised criminals, hijacking vessels and crews for ransom and contributing to organised crime in Somalia. This has a further spill-over effect on international efforts to restore Somalia as a functioning state. Despite international mobilisation under the leading role of numerous global and regional institutions, Somali pirates continue to threaten maritime transport in the Horn of Africa and increasingly further away from the African coast. In 2010, 49 vessels and 1016 crew members were taken hostage by organised Somali gangs, which amounted to 92 per cent of all ship seizures that year. In February 2011, four American hostages were killed. The piracy off the coast of Somalia constitutes an example of a challenge, which must be tackled through a variety of means, including short-term, military action. Finally, the conclusion brings together the various findings of the study and highlights the various contributions made by this book to the existing literature.

1
The EU as a Comprehensive Security Actor: Towards a Theoretical Framework

The purpose of this book is to investigate the role of the European Union (EU) as an international security actor in a *comprehensive* manner. This entails including the so-called 'new' security problems into the analysis, as well as different short- to long-term instruments at the EU's disposal, which are only rarely taken account of in these types of analyses (Zwolski, 2012a). However, this poses challenges that need to be addressed, such as (a) the difficulty in delimiting security from non-security policies of the EU, due to the contested nature of the security concept; (b) different perceptions of security among Member States, even if there is agreement on security strategies at the EU level; (c) the arguable lack of an overarching 'grand strategy' or a 'strategic vision', which would help to make better use of the diversity of security instruments at the EU's disposal; and (d) a connected challenge of assuring consistency in developing and conducting the EU's international security policy. All these factors hamper an effort to adopt a comprehensive approach, and thus they have to be addressed. Nonetheless, they do not prevent scholars from attempting a more encompassing analysis. In fact, considering the very complex and multi-dimensional nature of the EU's external security governance, it is only such a comprehensive approach which can offer a more accurate image of the EU as an actor in international security.

A comprehensive approach to the EU's security policy constitutes only one of the conceptual building blocks of this book. Another is the concept of 'actorness' and the question of the EU as an international actor. Is it possible for a non-state entity without central government such as the EU to be an actor in international relations (IR)? Scholars have been trying to understand the role of the European Economic Community (EEC) on the international stage since the 1970s. This book draws on this scholarship in order to provide the conceptual context for defining the main characteristics of EU 'actorness'. Consequently, the second part of this chapter demonstrates various approaches to studying the EEC as an actor in this early scholarship. It is suggested that, whilst more general IR literature tended to limit the analysis to mainly identifying the EEC as a non-state, supranational actor, there was another body of scholarship emerging at the time, which attempted to assess the 'actorness' of the EEC and later the EU. This latter scholarship led to the development of, first, theoretical frameworks for analysing the EEC as a *sui generis* actor. Two features of these theoretical frameworks are of particular significance. First, they have conceptualised the EEC and later the EU as *sui generis* entities, not as states or intergovernmental organisations. Second, even frameworks that were developed in the 1970s for studying the EEC as an actor are still widely utilised (with modifications) by scholars analysing the role of the EU in the 21st century. The third and the fourth sections of this chapter, drawing on previous discussions, introduce the framework for studying empirically the role of the EU as an international security actor. This framework is applied in the remainder of this book, assessing empirically the extent to which the EU has developed as an international security actor in five contemporary security challenges.

The EU and international security: towards a comprehensive approach

Many recent instances of the EU's international security policy illustrate the importance of adopting a comprehensive approach when assessing the EU as an international security actor. On the one hand, an explicit conceptualisation of climate change as a security challenge reinforces the 'human security' approach often present in the EU's official documents and narratives. Similarly, the EU is faced with illegal immigration and terrorism as non-state-based forms of security problems. All these challenges provide a compelling case for scholars to include 'new' security problems when analysing the EU security policy. On the other hand, the EU's response to maritime piracy off the coast of Somalia serves as a confirmation that security instruments in the policy apparatus of the EU are located within the Common Security and Defence Policy (CSDP), but also outside this policy framework; they include, for example, a range of external assistance instruments that enable to address security problems in the medium- and longterm, such as the Instrument for Stability (IfS) and European Development Fund.

The EU as a Comprehensive Security Actor: Towards a Theoretical Framework 21

Furthermore, improved law-enforcement mechanisms and increased judicial cooperation indicate the importance of Area of Freedom, Security and Justice (AFSJ) regulatory mechanisms which contribute to the EU's international security role.

There is a growing body of scholarship that incorporates this broadened approach to studying the EU security policy, moving beyond traditional security problems and the CSDP. For example, Cottey (2007: 192–216), Keukeleire and MacNaughtan (2008: 249–52) and Hintermeier (2008: 666–67) not only include more traditional security threats into their empirical analysis but also examine the EU's role in addressing 'new' security challenges, such as climate change and HIV/AIDS, more in line with contemporary security studies literature (Collins, 2007; Williams, 2008). Further, scholars increasingly take into account non-CSDP, security-focused instruments and policies of the EU. Notably, Kirchner (2006: 962–63) argues that states have lost the monopoly on providing security and have emerged as one type of participants in a cooperative system. In this cooperative system, according to Marsh and Mackenstein (2005: 15), the EEC emerged as an international security actor, by contributing to the Western European zone of peace and by establishing a dense network of economic and humanitarian agreements with the rest of the world. This role was recognised by the Norwegian Nobel prize committee in 2012 by awarding the EU with the Nobel Peace Prize. In addition to the literature on the EU as an international security actor, a comprehensive approach to the EU security policy dominates the scholarship on the AFSJ. Notably, Kaunert has been arguing about the strong role of the European Commission as a 'policy entrepreneur' in the AFSJ policy-making (Kaunert, 2005, 2007, 2009a, 2010a, 2010b, 2010c). Agencies such as Europol and Frontex are also increasingly recognised for their role in the EU's security (Léonard, 2009, 2010b, 2010c), including the external dimension (Germond, 2010).

Undoubtedly, there is more to the EU's international security profile than the relatively recent CSDP framework and capacities or even Justice and Home Affairs (JHA). Indeed, the EU's security policy is multidimensional, seemingly well equipped to tackle contemporary security challenges in a comprehensive manner. However, if the EU is actively broadening its view of security and utilising a wide range of measures in responding to contemporary security problems, why is it so difficult to take a systematic account of all these measures? Scholarship adopting such an all-encompassing stance is still in the minority, with the prevailing approach reflecting the post-Maastricht division into economic and international security policies, until recently embedded in the first and second pillars of the EU. The authors argue that there are significant stumbling blocks preventing a more systematic, comprehensive analysis, which include the following: (a) conceptual difficulties in delimiting security from non-security policies; (b) real differences in threat perceptions across the EU; (c) the arguable lack of an overarching strategic vision behind the range of EU's short- and long-term security measures; (d) the problem of utilising all those measures in a consistent manner.

The EU and 'new' security problems

The European Security Strategy (ESS) – a document drafted by former High Representative (HR) Javier Solana and approved by the European Council in 2003 – provides for a broad understanding of security (Council, 2003a). It not only identifies more traditional security threats such as weapons of mass destruction (WMDs) but also points to global warming and poverty as the possible causes of conflict (Biscop, 2008: 8–13). These non-traditional or 'new' security issues have been further elevated in the Report on the Implementation of the ESS in 2008 (European Council, 2008). In this document, energy security and climate change are identified as global challenges and key threats, alongside the proliferation of WMDs, organised crime and terrorism (European Council, 2008: 3–6).

The EU's broad approach to international security reflects the widening (new security threats) and deepening (new referent objects of security) of the international security agenda (Williams, 2008: 7–9). Problems previously overshadowed by a nuclear rivalry between major powers and labelled as 'low politics' have become recognised for their impact on the security of millions beyond the Western world (Annan, 2005). This process has been facilitated by the shift away from an exclusive focus on 'present' existential threats towards a more probabilistic approach, focusing on diffuse risks (McInnes, 2008: 276). Thus, security studies experts are not dismissing more traditional security threats but they also incorporate the analysis of the nexus between security and health (Elbe, 2007; McInnes, 2008), poverty (Thomas, 2008) and climate change (Barnett, 2003; De Wilde, 2008; Dalby, 2009; Zwolski and Kaunert, 2011).

In its official narrative, the EU often subscribes to the concept of human security (European Council, 2006; European Council, 2008: 10; European Commission, 2010a: 6), institutionalised in the United Nations Development Programme's (UNDP) Human Development Report from 1994 (UNDP, 1994: 22–46). Human security entails moving beyond territorial defence and national interests to include universal concerns such as unemployment, drugs, crime, pollution and human rights violations (UNDP, 1994: 22). However, human security does not entail ignoring more traditional security problems such as terrorism. It simply points to the obvious fact that the experience of insecurity is relative. As Kofi Annan observes:

> Ask a New York investment banker who walks past Ground Zero every day on her way to work what today's biggest threat is. Then ask an illiterate 12-year-old orphan in Malawi who lost his parents to AIDS. You will get two very different answers. Invite an Indonesian fisherman mourning the loss of his entire family and the destruction of his village from the recent, devastating tsunami to tell you what he fears most. Then ask a villager in Darfur, stalked by murderous militias and fearful of bombing raids. Their answers, too, are likely to diverge.
>
> (Annan, 2005)

Yet, McDonald (2002: 286) argues that international actors do not rationally 'choose' any given approach to international security. Instead, 'issues such as history, culture and identity shape what is rational, appropriate and possible'. Consequently, 'human security' frames the positions of actors for which it is relevant, instead of actors purposefully adhering to 'human security' as the 'right' security narrative for them. If the EU's international identity is pacifist, principled, consensus-based, network-based, open and contra-Westphalian (Manners and Whitman, 2003: 398–99), then 'human security' appears to fit well.

In particular, human security underpins the EU's commitment to link security objectives with the development policy. An ongoing process whereby the EU incorporates security considerations into its development policy, as well as development concerns into its security strategies, is reflected by the growing body of scholarship on the so-called security–development nexus in the EU policy (for example, Bagoyoko and Gibert, 2009; Hadfield, 2007; Hout, 2010; Youngs, 2008; Zwolski, 2012b). In terms of security, the aforementioned ESS and the Report on the Implementation of the ESS draw strong links between security and development, famously arguing that, indeed, security is the precondition for development. The EU Programme for the Prevention of Violent Conflicts, approved by the 2001 Göteborg European Council, places strong emphasis on strengthening short- and long-term preventive instruments for the EU. This Programme served as an important basis for the Commission when designing the new set of external assistance instruments in 2004, and particularly when putting together the proposal for the IfS. The Commission noted that Community-financing instruments make a 'major contribution' to conflict prevention and to the development of the Union as a global player (European Commission, 2004a: 11).

On the development end, the Cotonou Partnership Agreement (CPA) with African, Pacific and Caribbean countries from 2000 (revised in 2005 and 2010) has a significant political and even security component. In contrast to previous agreements (Lomé and Yaoundé Conventions), the CPA reflects an increasingly political approach of the EU to developing regions in general and to Africa in particular (Gänzle, 2009: 39). The 2005 revision contains explicit references to security objectives, such as the fight against terrorism and the non-proliferation of WMDs, making the reduction of poverty the primary but not exclusive goal of the agreement (Hadfield, 2007). This combination of development goals with security objectives in the CPA is consistent with the EU's overall approach to development, codified in the European Consensus on Development from 2006. The Consensus underlines the complementary nature of security and development objectives in the EU's relations with third countries, because they both contribute to 'creating a secure environment and breaking the vicious cycle of poverty, war, environmental degradation and failing economic, social and political structures' (European Council, 2006: 7).

The broad, human-focused approach to security has important consequences for research regardless of the extent to which the EU rationally chooses its approach to international security or the extent to which the EU is 'chosen' on the basis of its particular history, identity and culture. On the one hand, it is important to incorporate this broader security agenda when studying the EU as an international security actor. On the other hand, at least two problems arise with the EU's 'human security' approach; these include (a) delimiting security from non-security problems and (b) the challenge of vertical consistency (between Member States and the EU).

Incorporating 'new' security problems into the research agenda

An obvious challenge concerns the boundaries of 'security' in the EU's international policy. As one of Solana's former advisors rightly points out: 'It is in the DNA of our organisation to define security problems broadly' (CON-E, 2009). Yet, this presents the challenge of delimiting security from non-security policies of the Union. If climate change, AIDS and poverty are included in the EU's security agenda, which specific policy actions can be assessed in the context of the EU's role as a security actor and which actions fall merely under environmental, health and development policies?

This seemingly trivial choice bears considerable consequences for the analysis, because the extent to which the EU can be considered a security actor depends largely on the definition of security (Kirchner, 2006: 952; Rieker, 2009: 704). Thus, Biscop (2008: 12) argues that the ESS should have been named a foreign policy strategy and that the label 'security' must be reserved for issues posing an effective threat of violence. This critique echoes the more general dilemma concerning human security: 'How to delimit the concept, and how to judge which insecurities to honour when conflicting concerns are at stake' (Buzan and Hansen, 2009: 204).

The European Consensus on Development exemplifies this dilemma, emphasising the correlation between development and security and the necessity for the EU to pursue both values in its external policy. At the same time, the document fails to specify which objectives will be given priority when values conflict with each other. For example, the EU wants to prioritise local ownership (a popular Euro-catchphrase), but at the same time it wants to press authoritarian regimes for democracy (Youngs, 2008: 421). This dilemma also points to another subtle distinction in the EU's approach to security, between the strand relating to instability, conflict and insecurity in developing countries (which are the most vulnerable to 'new' security problems) and the EU's own security concerns. While both understandings of security are amply addressed in the ESS and other strategic documents, the second strand remains contested and raises questions about the EU's real intentions in Africa and elsewhere (Youngs, 2008: 422).

From a normative perspective, NGOs raise concerns about increasing skewing of global aid spending to satisfy military and security interests. Oxfam in its recent report notes that donors increasingly focus aid on areas of their security concern. For example, since 2002, 'one-third of all development aid to the 48 states labelled "fragile" by the OECD has gone to just three countries: Iraq, Afghanistan and Pakistan' (Oxfam, 2011: 2). Although the majority of European aid remains ring-fenced for Africa, some increases in funding have obvious security objectives, including resources for controls against illegal migration, anti-terrorism cooperation assistance and security patrol initiatives in the Mediterranean (Youngs, 2008: 431).

The less obvious challenge to incorporating 'new' security problems into the research agenda concerns vertical consistency (between national and EU policies) (Nuttall, 2005: 106). The high level of vertical consistency entails that Member States comply with the policies agreed upon at the EU level. For example, the case of climate security demonstrates that all Member States have, in principle, approved the move towards developing the security dimension of climate change in the EU policy (see Chapter 3). Yet, this principled acceptance of the climate security narrative by all Member States at the EU level does not preclude significant differences at national levels. If the international identity of the EU is pacifist, principled, consensus-based, network-based, open and contra-Westphalian (Manners and Whitman, 2003: 398–99), the identities of Member States vary considerably. These identities, forming particular security cultures, are shaped by such factors as (a) internal cultural cohesion; (b) interactions with neighbours; (c) defeat and occupation; (d) threat perception; (e) past martial or imperial ambitions and traditions; (f) impermeability and durability of national borders (Howorth, 2007: 178).

Consequently, countries of Central and Eastern Europe (CEE) attribute relatively less importance to 'new' security challenges due to their distinctive historical experiences and their ongoing insecurities concerning Russia's foreign policy intentions. In the case of Poland, this traditional view is reinforced by the dominance of right-wing political parties and the influence of nationalistic media outlets (Zwolski, 2009). As a result, for the most part, CEE countries do not play an active role in the Steering Group on Climate Change and International Security. This is how one CEE state representative explains this absence: 'The EU, under "climate security" label, does not do anything new. Thus, it does not really matter whether my country is part of the Steering Group, because we basically do the same things' (PermRep, 2009).

It is not only CEE countries which often differ in their perceptions of 'new' security problems from older EU Member States. Following the approval of the Joint Report on Climate Change and International Security by the European Council in March 2008, the Council Secretariat drafted the follow-up report with some more specific recommendations (Council, 2008a). It was thus expected in the Council Secretariat that it would be the December 2008 European Council discussing these recommendations. Instead, the French Presidency did not find room for this agenda item, submitting it instead to the December 2008 Agriculture and Fisheries Council, which merely acknowledged the document (Council, 2008b: 49).

These two roadblocks to incorporating 'new' security problems into the research on the EU as an international security actor must be acknowledged, but cannot prevent a more holistic research agenda. Although the security concept will remain contested, the move towards widening and deepening its understanding is fairly well established in security studies and in the practice of many states and non-state actors. The security consequences of climate change and pandemic diseases have been acknowledged by the UN Security Council, which further fosters the focus on non-state referent objects, such as societies and individuals. The EU subscribes to this broader view of security (including the concern with human security) and this must be taken into account when studying the EU's role in security policy.

Similarly, the diverging perceptions of security problems and differing accents in national security strategies will remain part of the security landscape in the EU in the foreseeable future. However important these differences are, they did not prevent Member States from approving strategic documents at the EU level, which institutionalise a broadened approach to security, acknowledging the relevance of 'new' security problems. Some of the most important among these are the Joint Report on 'Climate Change and International Security', the EES and the Report on the Implementation of the EES.

Moving beyond the CSDP

International security policy of the EU has traditionally been associated almost exclusively with the European Security and Defence Policy (ESDP), rebranded the CSDP in the Lisbon Treaty. The establishment of the ESDP and the deployment of the first EU missions attracted scholarly attention, contributing to the fact that the analysis of various aspects of the ESDP constitutes the bulk of scholarly work on the EU's international security policy (for example, Duke, 2000; Deighton, 2002; Howorth, 2007; Menon, 2009). There is a good reason for this; the speed at which the ESDP has acquired its shape and the number of operations deployed up to date are remarkable and can be surprising, even if missions are relatively modest (Toje, 2011: 51). When evaluating the first five years of the ESDP, Solana pointed to the paradox that while it remains difficult for the Member States to cooperate on security and defence, the cooperation in these areas advanced rapidly since 1999 (Solana, 2004: 5).

This book suggests that the CSDP does not represent the whole body of the EU's international security role; non-CSDP instruments and policies have to be included in the analysis. In this context, Hintermeier (2008: 667) notes that the EU's approach to security is based on two liberal institutionalist principles, that is (a) political integration, economic interdependence and multilateral cooperation, which weaken the anarchical system of states, and (b) the principle of democratic peace. More specifically, the EU pursues its security objectives through integration and enlargement, promotion of liberal values, promotion of sustainable development, effective multilateralism and strengthening international law. These objectives are pursued by the EU through a variety of economic, political and also, recently, civilian and military CSDP means (Hintermeier, 2008: 670–73). Among measures that are both economic and political in nature, one of the most important is the range of external financial and technical assistance instruments that have traditionally been at the disposal of the European Commission and that recently were partially incorporated into the European External Action Service (EEAS).

The most prominent of these financial instruments is the IfS, which former member of the European Parliament (MEP) Angelica Beer (also European Parliament's rapporteur on the IfS) defined as an attempt to 'define the Grey Zone between the Council's CFSP, ESDP and the Commission's development policy', with the potential to 'encourage active conflict prevention' (Beer, 2006: 34). This instrument, building on the Rapid Reaction Mechanism (RRM), allows the EU not only to respond rapidly to crisis situations but also to develop longer-term, capacity-building projects. The regulation for the IfS allocated it the budget of €2062 for the years 2007–2013 (European Parliament and the Council, 2006: 10).

The first component of the IfS, defined in article 3 of the regulation, concerns the provisions for assistance in response to situations of crisis or emerging crisis, which fulfils the primary aim of the IfS. The second component, regulated by article 4, concerns the provisions for providing assistance in the context of stable conditions for cooperation. Only about 23 per cent of the overall IfS budget was allocated for 'article 4' types of projects, which may be developed in three security areas: (a) threats to law and order, to the security and safety of individuals, to critical infrastructure and to public health; (b) risk mitigation and preparedness relating to chemical, biological, radiological and nuclear materials or agents; and (c) pre- and post-crisis capacity building. Of these areas, non-proliferation was given priority; this enabled the European Commission to continue developing capacity-building non-proliferation programmes, primarily in Russia, further building on its already extensive experience in this area (see Chapter 5). The European Community started providing Russia with non-proliferation assistance already at the beginning of the 1990s, first through the programme called the Technical Assistance for the Commonwealth of Independent States (TACIS), and since 2007 through the Instrument for Nuclear Safety Cooperation (INSC) and the IfS (Höhl et al., 2003; Anthony, 2004; Müller, 2007; Zwolski, 2011a, 2011b).

Similarly, non-CSDP instruments and policies have to be taken into account when investigating the EU's response to maritime piracy off the coast of Somalia. This response consists mainly of the CSDP's first naval operation European Union Naval Force (EUNAVFOR) 'Atalanta', but other (medium- to long-term) efforts are also important. However, the case of non-proliferation policy, counter-piracy measures and other security policies of the EU also indicate some obstacles hampering a more comprehensive research agenda. The first concerns the question of the EU's grand strategy and the extent to which these diverging instruments are deployed purposefully, reflecting clearly defined and codified strategic objectives of the EU. The second concerns consistency between different institutions and policies.

Incorporating non-CSDP policies into the research agenda

Biscop (2009) argues that the ESS and the Report on the Implementation of the ESS provide only a partial strategy. These documents set guidelines for the EU's international conduct, underlining the preventive, holistic and multilateral character of the EU's action, but they do not explain what exactly the EU should do. This lack of clearly specified objectives and priorities, according to Biscop, is particularly problematic in the wake of Lisbon Treaty institutional reforms, NATO's new Strategic Concept and the growing political role of BRIC countries (Biscop, 2009: 3). Howorth (2010) further underscores these concerns, arguing that 'the EU should adopt a more calculated strategic approach and begin at long last to think in terms of "large goals"' (Howorth, 2010: 464). Only then, Howorth argues, can the EU make the best use of the wide range of crisis management instruments that it has at its disposal.

The empirical analysis in this book demonstrates that the EU is able to draw on a vast array of resources when addressing, for example, organised crime, such as maritime piracy. However, even though the EU presents its political and economic efforts in Somalia as part of its 'comprehensive approach', listing them together with EUNAVFOR 'Atalanta', these longer-term measures do not serve explicitly the purpose of countering piracy. Instead, they are part of the EU's pre-programmed development policies in Somalia, as well as its multilateral policy aiming to strengthen the Somali Transitional Federal Government. The 'grand strategy' or 'strategic vision', in this case, could contribute to a clearer identification of a set of relevant policies that the EU deploys in specific security situations. This would prevent the impression of randomness in international security policy of the EU.

The second obstacle hindering a more systematic inclusion of non-CSDP instruments and policies into the analysis of the EU as an international security actor concerns the traditional problem of institutional and horizontal inconsistency – the challenge closely related to the one discussed above. In Nuttall's (2005) categorisation, horizontal consistency entails that different EU policies are aligned and support each other. Institutional consistency, on the other hand, is traditionally concerned with the degree to which the Council and the Commission have been coordinating their policies and supporting each other's actions. The Lisbon Treaty introduces important changes in this respect, discussed further in this section.

The problem of assuring inter-pillar consistency in the international security policy of the EU has attracted significant scholarly attention, and rightly so (Tietje, 1997; Missiroli, 2001, 2010; Dijkstra, 2009; Van Elsuwege, 2010; Zwolski, 2011b). The growing profile of the European Commission in IR, particularly through its Directorate General for External Relations (DG Relex), coincided with the international role of the Council, including its Secretariat. Notably, the Council Secretariat has been steadily growing in quantitative (number of officials) and qualitative (number of policies) terms (Hayes-Renshaw and Wallace, 2006: 101), thus increasing the risk of overlapping competences between the first and the second pillar of the EU.

The Lisbon Treaty addressed this very problem, opening up opportunity for a more holistic approach to researching an international security policy of the EU. On the personal level, it merged the post of the High Representative with that of the Vice President of the European Commission, in order to 'ensure the consistency of the Union's external action' (Council, 2008c: 35). On the bureaucratic level, the Lisbon Treaty provided for the establishment of the EEAS, which brings together DG Relex and the part of the Council Secretariat responsible for foreign and security policy. The EEAS, which also includes Member States' representatives, assist the High Representative.

These and other reforms not only provide opportunity for a more consistent international security policy of the EU but they also create a new set of challenges. On the personal level, the new permanent President of the European Council is entrusted with ensuring 'the external representation of the Union on issues concerning its common foreign and security policy' (Council, 2008c: 30). Depending on personalities, the perception of interests and the interpretation of the EU law, this can lead to tensions with the High Representative. On the bureaucratic level, the EEAS consists of three different bodies with different institutional cultures. It will become fully effective only when old institutional loyalties are replaced with the new ethos (Whitman, 2011: 12).

The underdeveloped strategic vision, together with the difficult task of assuring consistency in the EU's external action, has been to a large extent preventing a comprehensive approach to studying the EU's international security policy. However, regardless of the pace of the progress in these areas, this book argues that it is important to incorporate the analysis of all the relevant policies and instruments when assessing the EU's role in international security. Some of them, for example the development and political assistance in Somalia, may not be directed at the security threat in question (such as maritime piracy). Nonetheless, they may still be contributing to addressing the problem indirectly and over a longer term.

Of course, a more assertive strategic vision for the EU is in order, not least to supplement the institutional reforms instigated by the Lisbon Treaty and to make better use of the diversity of resources in the EU's security apparatus. Yet, as Toje (2011) convincingly argues, the lack of 'big thinking' in the EU can be better understood if the Union is conceptualised as a small power. This approach can indeed serve as 'the best path to making peace with the inconsistencies associated with the presence, capabilities and patterns of behaviour that characterize the European Union' (Toje, 2011: 57). Finally, the abandonment of the pillar structure in the Lisbon Treaty and institutional reforms concerning the EU's foreign and security policy create conditions for improved consistency in the EU's external action. Furthermore, these reforms offer an opportunity for further research concerning all three types of consistencies: between Member States and the EU, between different EU policies and between different EU institutions.

International 'actorness' beyond the nation state

The question of 'actorness' in IR is of crucial importance for this book, because the way in which it is conceptualised determines whether the EU can be considered an actor. If states were the only units in IR which can be conceptualised as actors, then a non-state entity, such as the EU, could not be included in this analysis. As a result, the EU could be best studied as 27 nation states attempting to agree together on common policies within intergovernmental bodies of the EU, that is the European Council and the Council of the EU (Bretherton and Vogler, 2006). In practice, the analysis would almost exclusively focus on examining the policies of the most powerful states of the EU, that is Germany, France and the United Kingdom (Hoffman, 2000; Hyde-Price, 2004; Sherman and Sussex, 2004; Peters, 2010). There are, for example, Realist scholars who argue that 'despite forces of globalization and the growth of transnational terrorism, politics still takes place within territorial boundaries of the nation state' (Sherman, 2004: 23). Nevertheless, if states are not the only actors in IR, then the conceptual challenge arises with regard to analysing the role of the EU, which is neither a state nor an intergovernmental organisation. A significant body of scholarly work has attempted to conceptualise the EEC and later the EU as international actors. Yet, before proceeding to discuss the EU, the following section addresses the broader question of 'actorness' in IR.

Actorness in international relations

Traditionally, sovereign states have been considered the main or even for some the only actors in IR. However, two dimensions of this state-centrism must be distinguished. On the one hand, from an empirical perspective, sovereign states are a relatively recent phenomenon, with their origins dating back to the 17th century, and particularly to the Peace Treaties of Westphalia of 1648. On the other hand, from a theoretical perspective, states have been at the centre of analysis of the major approach to IR, namely Realism. This section first outlines the conceptual characteristics of the nation state as the main actor in IR. Then, it identifies important challenges to this state-centric view, and how these challenges have been conceptualised by alternative theoretical approaches to IR, thus challenging the dominant position of Realism in this respect.

Empirically, the Westphalian Treaties concluded the Thirty Years' War, recognising that the idea of the united Catholic empire was unachievable and that Protestants and Catholics had to coexist. Conceptually, these treaties mark the first crucial step in the process of establishing modern statehood. The Westphalian system, which established the 'normative structure or constitution of the modern world order' (McGrew, 2008: 23), gave birth to three interlinked basic elements of states, that is territoriality, sovereignty and autonomy. Territoriality refers to the principle that humankind is organised into communities with fixed borders. Sovereignty refers to the principle that 'within its borders the state or government has an entitlement to supreme, unqualified, and exclusive political and legal authority' (McGrew, 2008: 23). Autonomy refers to the principle of self-determination, granting states the freedom of political, social and economic activities within their borders. For Realists, states are the fundamental units of political analysis; in other words, this theory is based on a state-centric assumption.

This dominant state-centric perspective came increasingly under strain after 1945, when a new, more interdependent world began to emerge. Keohane and Nye (1974) in the 1970s identified the main characteristics of this world to be transnationalism and complex interdependence, giving rise to the third generation of liberal institutionalism. Lamy (2008) notes that this new interdependent world has four characteristics: (a) increasing linkage between state and non-state actors; (b) new international political agenda, blurring the distinction between high and low politics; (c) new channels of communication between actors; and (d) the diminishing role of the military as the tool of states. One of the most important non-state actors to emerge in this context of transnationalism and complex interdependence was the EEC. Cosgrove and Twitchett (1970: 48) were among the first scholars to recognise the EEC's role in world economy: '[I]n the long run the United States' early nurturing of the E.E.C. might well be against its national interests. She has already begun to feel the impact of the Community's economic strength – an impact which is more likely to grow than decrease'.

Furthermore, the world in the 1970s, according to Marsh and Mackenstein (2005), also created conditions allowing the EEC to enhance its role as a non-state security actor. First, according to those authors, the very system of liberal institutionalism, as defined by Keohane and Nye, which meant the EEC was increasingly identified as an important economic power, also allowed the EEC to strengthen its influence in international security policy. Second, the development of the 'mutually assured destruction' (MAD) doctrine and other technological advancements drastically sidelined the role of conventional military capabilities in the Cold War rivalry. Third, the emergence of new economic centres of power and the relative decline of the United States, as evidenced by the Vietnam War and the collapse of the Breton Woods system, have challenged the bi-polar system. Fourth, the strategy of détente, initiated by Kissinger and Nixon at the beginning of the 1970s, was of particular significance for the conceptualisation of the EEC as a developing security actor. This new strategy was partially based on the recognition that there were new important centres of power, most notably in China, Western Europe and Japan. All of these developments allowed the EEC to enhance its position as a non-state actor on the international stage; this, in turn, attracted scholars to try to understand the nature of EEC 'actorness'. Yet, the categorisation of the EEC and later the EU as actors has proved to be a challenging task. Nonetheless, as the scholarship in the next section demonstrates, the EU can be considered an actor and its 'actorness' can be evaluated.

The EEC and the EU as *sui generis* actors

When approaching the question of the EU's role in IR, scholars, according to White (2004), tend to focus either on agency or structure, or they try to combine both approaches. The 'EU as an actor' approach, according to this author, by focusing on agency, concentrates on the impact of Europe on world politics. Within this category, important attempts have been undertaken to characterise the role of the EU at the international level. Some of these attempts include conceptualising the EU as (a) a civilian power (Duchêne, 1972); (b) an international identity (Whitman, 1998b); (c) international presence (Allen and Smith, 1990); and (d) a superpower in the making which soon will have to be contained (Galtung, 1973). Although generating a wealthy amount of empirical data, this approach, according to White, has two limitations: (a) it focuses on outcomes rather than on the process of EU foreign policy formulation and (b) it is based on the assumption that the EU is a single actor; this, according to White, ignores the fact that the EU is a complex organisation with multiple realities. Alternatively, according to this author, structure-driven structuralist approaches, such as neo-realism and neo-liberalism, tend to downplay the role of agency at the expense of the international system. Approaches such as Europeanisation and social constructivism, as White (2004) notes, attempt to bring agency and structure together into one framework.

Such a defined conceptual map of the scholarship on the EU's external relations, as demonstrated in this section, is not entirely accurate. Most notably, the two limitations of the 'EU as an actor' approach are arguably problematic. The discussion in this section demonstrates that scholars applying the 'EU as an actor' framework are far from ignoring the complexity of EU decision-making processes. Through the careful selection of criteria to assess EU 'actorness', scholars often attempt to capture the *sui generis*, complex nature of EU policy-making. Similarly, this book, when building on this scholarship, aims to demonstrate just how complex and multi-dimensional an actor the EU is. Furthermore, the 'EU as an actor' approach does not *a priori* have to discriminate the processes at the expense of outcomes. This book considers the processes an important part of the analysis. As such, the processes of the EU security policy-making constitute an important part of the empirical component of this book.

The argument in this section unfolds in the following manner. First, it is demonstrated that the IR literature had in the 1970s already recognised the EEC as a new actor in IR, but in a rather superficial manner. Second, it is demonstrated that a more thorough approach to understanding EEC 'actorness' emerged at the same time, providing significant tools and concepts for assessing the role of the EEC and subsequently the EU as an actor at the international level. In the IR literature, the EEC became recognised as an actor mainly at the beginning of the 1970s. Pryce (1972: 194) notes that '[u]ntil recently, relatively little attention has been paid to the political aspects of the Community's external relations (...)'. However, this early literature, for the most part, does not attempt to develop a specific framework to analyse the nature and the role of this new non-state phenomenon (Calvocoressi, 1977). Instead, it tends to focus on the non-state and partially supranational character of the EEC. Reynolds (1971), for example, underlines the fact that the EEC, Euratom and the European Coal and Steel Community (ECSC) were international actors. He notes: 'Not merely does their existence, whether action is being taken or not, very much affect the behaviour both of their members and of other states outside, but they do directly engage in international activity' (Reynolds, 1971: 30). Although important, the contribution of the IR literature is limited by the unprecedented character of the EEC's nature of 'actorness'. Some scholars have attempted to compare the EEC with other regional organisations, such as NATO, within the broader category of interstate governmental organisations (Frankel, 1979). Others, for example Young (1972), have developed a category of 'mixed actors', in which 'several qualitatively different types of actor interact in the absence of any settled pattern of dominance-submission' (Young, 1972: 136).

Whilst this IR literature went as far as to recognise the EEC as an actor and attempted to identify some original characteristics of this organisation, another body of literature, focused primarily on EEC 'actorness', started to emerge in parallel. In fact, this latter literature sought to assess the extent to which the EEC emerged as an international actor; to this end, scholars began to develop special conceptual tools. Notably, Cosgrove and Twitchett (1970) developed a framework for assessing the degree of 'actorness' of the EEC and the United Nations.

More specifically, they developed '[t]hree mutually interdependent tests, or rather guide lines, for determining an international organisation's capacity to act on the global scene' (Cosgrove and Twitchett, 1970: 12). More recent literature on EU 'actorness', for the most part, refers to these 'tests' as criteria of 'actorness'. According to Cosgrove and Twitchett (1970), the level of 'actorness' of an international unit can be measured by (a) the degree to which central institutions can undertake autonomous decisions; (b) the degree to which the organisation has an impact on inter-state relations; and (c) the degree to which Member (and to some extent non-member) States consider the organisation important when formulating their foreign policies. These three 'tests', more or less, correspond to criteria of 'actorness' which are defined in more recent scholarship as autonomy, impact and coherence, respectively.

Sjöstedt (1977) was dissatisfied with the methodology proposed by Cosgrove and Twitchett (1970), arguing that those authors 'at best tried to solve the problem on an *ad hoc* basis without any ambition of finding a generally valid specified definition of actor' (Sjöstedt, 1977: 5). As a result, according to Sjöstedt (1977), theoretical instruments available for determining the degree of the EEC's 'actorness' were only few and as such were crude. This is why the author, in his book *The External Role of the European Community*, develops a complex framework for assessing the degree of 'actorness' in IR. As a starting point, Sjöstedt (1977) notes that attempting to establish whether the EEC is an actor is an incorrect exercise. Instead, he suggests that 'the capacity of being an actor is most appropriately conceived of as a variable property which the Community may possess to a greater or lesser extent' (Sjöstedt, 1977: 14). This book incorporates this argument by analysing 'the extent' to which the EU has developed as an international security actor.

Based on this assumption, Sjöstedt has developed threshold conditions and a list of necessary qualities for an entity to qualify as an international actor. According to this author, any unit, in order to be considered at all an actor, must possess autonomy, which is composed of two elements: (a) the unit must be discernible from its external environment, thus having a minimal degree of separateness, and (b) the unit must also have a minimal degree of cohesion. Once these conditions are met, a unit can be considered to have actor capability. In his analysis, the author assumes as a starting point that the EEC meets these basic conditions. Once the EEC can be considered to be autonomous, the next step in Sjöstedt's framework is to assess the degree of actor capability. To this end, the author has identified a set of structural prerequisites, which in other words are 'a set of variable properties'

(Sjötstedt, 1977: 16). Again, the more recent literature addresses these prerequisites as criteria of 'actorness'. In Sjötstedt's typology, they are grouped into three categories: (a) basic requirements, such as a set of goals; (b) decision-making and monitoring facilities; and (c) action-performance instruments, allowing an actor to behave externally. This book integrates the structural prerequisites identified by Sjötstedt into a set of criteria of 'actorness', which are discussed in detail in the third section of this chapter.

The structural prerequisites allowing to be determined as the degree of actor capability, and thus focused on agency, represent, according to Bretherton and Vogler (1999, 2006), only one side of the agency/structure debate. Those authors, in their important contribution, *The European Union as a Global Actor*, argue that, in order to assess the EU's 'actorness', it is important to combine the behavioural criteria with the structural approach, which also requires 'the perceptions and actions of third parties' to be taken into consideration (Bretherton and Vogler, 2006: 22). According to those authors, these structural components 'contribute significantly to the shared understandings that frame the policy environment, shaping practices of Member State governments, EU officials and third parties alike' (Bretherton and Vogler, 2006: 22). With regard to assessing actor capability, Bretherton and Vogler draw on the structural prerequisites developed by Sjötstedt (1977), but they simplify these prerequisites into four criteria: (a) a shared commitment to a set of values; (b) domestic legitimation of decision processes regarding external policy; (c) the ability to identify priorities and formulate policies (including the consistency and coherence of EU external relations); and (d) the availability of, and capacity to utilise, policy instruments, such as diplomacy, economic tools and military means. The scholarship on EU international 'actorness' has widely utilised these criteria, adapting and modifying them, in order to suit most effectively individual case studies. It is important to examine these applications in greater detail because they provide an important background for the theoretical framework developed in this book; this task is undertaken in the next section.

The present section has introduced the concept of 'actorness' in IR. In particular, it has demonstrated how a state-centric, realist view was challenged in the 1970s by novel approaches such as transnationalism and complex interdependence. These new approaches aimed to highlight the fact that actors other than states were growing in numbers and importance. Identifying the role of the EEC as an emerging actor has been important for scholars in defining this new reality. Some of the conditions enabling the EEC to develop its position as an international actor have also been outlined. Moreover, within this context, the section has discussed the early conceptualisations of the EEC as an actor. It has been suggested that, whereas the general IR literature tended to acknowledge the emerging 'actorness' of the EEC, it was literature focusing more specifically on the external role of the EEC which attempted to advance the concept of 'actorness', through developing theoretical tools to assess it. Based on the core contributions discussed in this section, scholars have begun to develop further and apply these theoretical tools in their own work, by utilising case study research design. The theoretical framework developed in this chapter integrates findings of this growing body of scholarly work.

Applying criteria of actorness to case study research design

The 'EU as an actor' approach has grown in popularity over the last few decades. This fact reflects the quantitative (the number of Member States) and the qualitative (the number of policies) growth of the EU. In particular, scholars have been adopting this approach in single or multiple case studies, investigating the EU's role in various policy areas (Larsen, 2002; Groenleer and Van Shaik, 2007; Beyer, 2008; Dryburgh, 2008; Kaunert, 2010; Zwolski, 2011a). When developing their theoretical framework, researchers have particularly drawn on two studies, discussed in the previous section – studies by Sjöstedt (1977) and Bretherton and Vogler (1999, 2006). This book also draws on the conceptualisation of 'actorness' as developed by those authors. However, it modifies their criteria of 'actorness', in order to take into account some important contributions by other scholars. These more recent contributions are discussed in this section.

One of the most important recent contributions to understanding and assessing the EU as an international actor has been the work of Jupille and Caporaso (1998), who defined the EU's role in external relations as follows: 'The EU can be thought of as an evolving entity, composed of numerous issue areas and policy networks, neither a full-blown polity nor a system of sovereign states, which displays varying degrees of "actorhood" across issues and time' (Jupille and Caporaso, 1998: 214). This understanding, shared in this book, explicitly underlines the complexity and multiple realities of EU decision-making. However, how can such a complex entity be assessed? To this end, the authors propose adopting criteria of 'actorness' which are observable, continuously variable and abstract. For their case study, analysing the role of the EU in environmental politics, the authors incorporate the following criteria

The EU as a Comprehensive Security Actor: Towards a Theoretical Framework 39

for assessing EU 'actorness': (a) international political and legal recognition; (b) authority, which refers to the EU's legal competence to act in a given subject matter; (c) autonomy, which refers to distinctiveness, or independence, from other actors, most notably states; and (d) cohesion, which captures the degree to which Member States can reach consensus on common policies.

This particular framework has proved to be popular among scholars researching EU 'actorness' at the international level. For example, Groenleer and Van Shaik (2007) adopted it to analyse the role of the EU in establishing the International Criminal Court and in negotiations leading to the signature of the Kyoto Protocol. These authors adapted the original framework not only to investigate the extent to which the EU is an international actor but also to explain why EU 'actorness' emerges and under what circumstances it is more likely to occur. In this regard, they propose an 'institutional perspective that not only focuses on formal rules, but also attends to informal practices and routines based on shared social norms and values' (Groenleer and Van Shaik, 2007: 972). Whilst these additional questions are interesting, they go beyond the scope of this book. The aim of this book is to assess the degree to which the EU has developed as an international security actor. Consequently, the theoretical framework incorporates criteria of 'actorness' as defined by Jupille and Caporaso (1998), although with a few modifications. In addition to recognising autonomy and authority, the theoretical framework for this book also incorporates capabilities as an important indicator of the EU's international security 'actorness'. These modifications are discussed at length in the third section of this chapter, which defines criteria for assessing the EU as an actor in international security policy. In this section, it is of primary importance to demonstrate how criteria of 'actorness' established in this book relate to the existing scholarship.

In this context, the conceptualisation of EU 'actorness' developed by Bretherton and Vogler (1999, 2006) has influenced the framework underpinning many contributions that analyse the EU's role in various policy areas. For example, Larsen (2002), in his article examining the military dimension of EU 'actorness', adopts social constructivist ontology, arguing that 'actorness of a particular social unit is not an essentialist category that is given by certain objective material elements. Rather, the grouping achieves its actorness as a result of its members and its surroundings articulating this grouping as an actor in a particular social field' (Larsen, 2002: 287). He also adopts a social constructivist epistemology, incorporating discourse analysis into his methodology. According to Larsen, a social constructivist approach to 'actorness' focuses on two elements: (a) whether and how a unit and its members constitute themselves as an actor and (b) whether and how the outside world constitutes this entity as an actor. It can be argued that Larsen has applied a version of constructivism which is closer to post-structuralism, whilst this book adopts a more conventional understanding of this approach (Buzan and Hansen, 2009). The methodology for this book, established in Introduction, explains that the element of constitution is of critical importance in the social world. Yet, drawing on Wendt (1999), it is also explained that material factors (the internal structure) cannot be neglected when analysing the international 'actorness' of an entity. As a result, the empirical part of this book investigates not only the internal structure of the EU but also the extent to which it is recognised by other actors in particular policy areas.

However, in his other contribution, analysing the foreign policy of Denmark within the EU context, Larsen (2003) develops a more 'complete' actorness framework. Inspired again by Bretherton and Vogler (1999, 2006), the author identifies five criteria of actorness: (a) a conception of itself as an actor; (b) a particular framework of meaning within which an action takes place; (c) consistent and concrete policies; (d) some kind of administrative/diplomatic apparatus; and (e) resources and policy instruments. Dryburgh (2008) finds this framework particularly useful for studying the EU's policy towards Iran. She notes that '[w]hile Bretherton and Vogler's criteria are a useful means of evaluating the actorness of the EU at the institutional level, they present difficulties within individual policy areas (...)' (Dryburgh, 2008: 256). As a consequence, Dryburgh applies a simplified version of Larsen's framework to her case study analysis; her list of criteria includes (a) articulations of 'actorness'; (b) consistent and concrete policies; (c) a diplomatic/administrative apparatus; and (d) resources and policy instruments. In addition, Dryburgh includes third-party perceptions of the EU's 'actorness' as an important criterion in a social constructivist perspective. According to her, ' "actorness" must be understood as a social construct between the agents involved, based on shared understandings of the EU as an actor, as having a role to play. The agents involved are both external to the EU, and internal – the Member States' (Dryburgh, 2008: 257). Indeed, the recognition of the EU as an actor constitutes an important criterion for assessing the degree of EU 'actorness' at the international level. In order for the EU to be considered an important actor in a particular security policy area, it must be recognised by other actors. The next section of this chapter establishing criteria of 'actorness' addresses the question of recognition at greater length. Whilst Dryburgh (2008) has attempted to make her framework relatively parsimonious, Beyer (2008) has chosen to develop a scheme that is even more differentiated than that of Bretherton and Vogler. In order to analyse EU policy in counterterrorism, Beyer (2008) has developed a scheme consisting of the following components: (a) 'structure', including coherence, one voice and addressability; (b) 'actor', including participation in global governance and external recognition in international law; and (c) 'effect', including the existence of strategies, the capacity to act internally and externally, and intended effects. Many of these elements are integrated into the framework developed in this book; they are discussed in detail later in this chapter. However, the 'one voice: addressability' criterion is problematic. The EU is a complex actor, defined more accurately as a multi-level governance system rather than a unified polity with a single 'foreign policy' centre. Even the Lisbon Treaty is not capable of changing this reality, although Member States have attempted to bring more unity to the Union's external relations, by strengthening the post of the High Representative (Zwolski, 2011a, 2011b, 2012a, 2012b). Furthermore, the question of addressability is also problematic in the case of nation states. For instance, who can the EU 'call' if it wants to speak to the United States on the subject of climate change? It could be the President, but it could equally be Congress. The following section establishes the framework for this book, identifying three criteria of 'actorness': the scope of integration, capabilities and recognition.

Scope, capabilities and recognition: a framework for analysis

The three criteria of 'actorness' identified in this section are closely interlinked and often depend on each other to be fully fulfilled. The scholarship on the EU as an international actor acknowledges this relationship. For example, Cosgrove and Twitchett (1970: 12) note that their three tests (remotely corresponding to the criteria of autonomy, impact and coherence) 'are not clear cut and have a close functional relationship with each other: which comes first or is of primary significance is difficult, if not impossible, to gauge'. Jupille and Caporaso (1998: 220), when commenting on their criteria of 'actorness', observe that 'these indicators form a coherent ensemble, depending one on another for full meaning'. Similarly, Groenleer and Van Shaik (2007) underline the interconnectedness of the criteria that they have adopted in their research. The remainder of this section introduces the scope of integration, capabilities and recognition as three criteria of 'actorness' constituting the framework adopted in this book to assess the role of the EU in international security.

Scope

The scope of integration, identified as the first criterion of 'actorness', is defined as 'the procedures according to which policy decisions are taken focusing on the involvement of supranational bodies and Council voting rules' (Börzel, 2005: 220). The scope is informed by two criteria of 'actorness' identified by Jupille and Caporaso (1998): autonomy and authority. Autonomy implies a degree of distinctiveness (or independence) of the EU from its Member States. Assessing independence defined in this way is a difficult exercise because of the 'pervasive intermingling of levels of political authority' (Jupille and Caporaso, 1998: 218). However, the authors explain that what is meant by autonomy is institutional distinctiveness: 'An international organization, to be an actor, should have a distinctive institutional apparatus, even if it is grounded in, or intermingles with, domestic political institutions' (1998: 217). The existence of the distinctive institutional apparatus in the EU is beyond question. What requires further empirical investigation is the involvement of supranational bodies in security challenges discussed in the remainder of this book. Supranational bodies are further operationalised as central bureaucracies, including the European Commission, Council Secretariat and the EEAS. The extent to which these bodies are involved in a given security policy issue determines the scope of integration in this area. Furthermore, the scope of integration is informed by the Council voting rules, which can be broadened to include the authority of the EU in a given policy area. Jupille and Caporaso (1998: 216) define authority as the EU's legal competence to act in a given subject matter. Legal competence to act is a minimum condition for the EU to be considered an actor. Qualified majority voting (QMV), rather than the requirement of unanimity in the Council, enhances the scope of integration in a given security policy area.

Capabilities

Following the categorisation introduced by Hill (1998), the EU's capabilities in this book are considered to consist of three components: resources, instruments and cohesiveness. Resources include the use and threat of force, diplomacy, economic carrots and sticks. They can also comprise of civilian resources such as training and monitory missions in third countries. Instruments are established on the basis of the provisions of the treaties to enhance the EU's effectiveness as an international security actor. For example, the Treaty of Maastricht introduced common positions and joint actions as new instruments of diplomacy for the EU. There are other important instruments for the EU's international security policy, the IfS, enabling the EU to provide a timely assistance in situations of a crisis. Of course, what matters in each case study representing a security policy challenge is not mere existence of these instruments, but the ability of the EU to deploy them effectively. This requires cohesiveness, which is defined as 'the capacity to reach a collective decision and to stick to it' (Hill, 1998: 23).

Hill discussed the capabilities of the EU in the context of his famous 'capability–expectations gap' argument, in which he contrasted the capabilities of the EU with internal and external expectations, constituted of the ambitions and demands of the EU's external behaviour (Hill, 1998: 23). Hill concluded in 1998 that although inside-EU expectations were lowered compared with 1993 when he originally developed the argument about the gap (Hill, 1993), there was still an imbalance between what others wanted the EU to do/be and what the EU was actually capable of delivering. The new set of expectations concerning the international role of the EU started to emerge in the late 1990s, following the perceived EU's failure to resolve the Yugoslav Wars and the subsequent institutionalisation of the ESDP. Rogers (2009: 831) argues that new expectations have been fostered by 'a growing coalition of "euro-strategists"', which consists of EU institutions (including agencies such as the Institute for Security Studies), think-tanks and security/defence institutes and the work of academic departments. This book does not start with the presumption that the EU *should* be a global security power; thus, it must meet the criteria that are associated with the global power status. Instead, the purpose is to re-assess what the EU does in international security policy by adopting a comprehensive perspective.

Recognition

Recognition provides an important social constructivist element to this set of behavioural criteria. It implies that in order to be an international security actor, the EU must be recognised by other states and non-state actors. Jupille and Caporaso (1998: 215) specify that '[t]his criterion should be seen as a minimum condition that adds little substantive understanding of any given entity, but simply registers it on the analytical radar. Recognition by others allows for presence in global politics, which, not surprisingly is the sine qua non of global actorhood.' The authors further break down this criterion into *de jure* recognition (diplomatic recognition under international law or formal membership in international organisations) and *de facto* recognition (whenever a third party interacts with the EU rather than/in addition to Member States). Importantly, recognition reflects the constitutive nature of social kinds, such as sovereignty, states and non-state actors (Wendt, 1999). This means that the EU is partially constituted of material forces (for example, its institutions and capabilities) and partially of shared ideas of others (entities and individuals) about its nature. The framework of this book adheres to an understanding of recognition as meaning that 'whenever a third party interacts with the Union, rather than, or in addition to, going to one or more EU Member State(s), the criterion of recognition has been satisfied' (Jupille and Caporaso, 1998: 216).

Different threats – different responses: positive and negative instruments

The criteria for 'actorness' constitute an important, but insufficient, component of a framework which aspires to provide structure for the comprehensive analysis of the EU as an international security actor. Most importantly, they say little about their relative importance for different categories of security problems discussed in the empirical part of this book. Are supranational institutions equally important for conducting an anti-piracy naval operation off the Somali coast and for developing effective counter-terrorism measures? Conversely, are capabilities as important for EU policies on migration as they are for assisting third countries in adaptation to climate change? In order to take account of these divergences, it is important to distinguish between negative and positive instruments of integration. Students of the EU's common market will find this distinction familiar, because it has been almost exclusively applied in the domain of economic policy. Whereas negative integration refers mainly to the removal of barriers to the free movement of people, capital, products and services, positive integration entails adopting common standards and active harmonisation of the European market. Jachtenfuchs (2010: 209) notes that the EU has been much stronger in negative integration, illustrating his argument with the examples of the EU's lack of distributive powers and intergovernmental common, foreign and security policies. He even argues that in spite of significant progress of integration in the AFSJ, what emerges in this policy area is 'a new form of embedding the member states' monopoly of force into a dense institutional structure which has policy-making authority in the issues at stake but leaves sovereignty to the member states' (Jachtenfuchs, 2010: 210).

Regardless of this pattern of European integration leaning towards negative integration (embedded in the principle of mutual recognition), a high degree of international security 'actorness' can only be achieved by positive integration instruments. These are further divided into two sub-categories: (a) regulation and (b) capacity building and intervention. In the first case, the EU constrains the actions of the Member States by harmonising their policies in a given policy issue. In the latter case, the EU utilises its capabilities to achieve a particular external objective. This objective can directly relate to the security challenge in question or can have a long-term character, aiming to 'influence or shape sustainable political, legal, socio-economic, security and mental structures' (Keukeleire and MacNaughtan, 2008: 25). Figure 1.1 demonstrates all three types of integration instruments.

Not surprisingly, different security problems require different instruments. For example, Wagner (2011) demonstrates that in the area of criminal law cooperation, the EU has been applying negative integration measures, relying mainly on mutual recognition between Member States. Most important among these measures is the European Arrest Warrant (EAW), effectively abolishing the traditional institution of extradition within the EU. The EAW relies on mutual recognition that courts in each country provide fair trial and respect the rule of law (Kaunert, 2007: 2010). In practice, even though there is a degree of

```
        ┌─────────────────────────────────────┐
        │ Negative integration instruments    │
        │ ➤ Mutual recognition                │
        └─────────────────────────────────────┘
                          │
                          ▼
        ┌─────────────────────────────────────┐
        │ Positive integration instruments    │
        └─────────────────────────────────────┘
              ↙                       ↘
┌──────────────────────────────┐  ┌──────────────────────────────────┐
│ Regulation                   │  │ Capacity building and intervention│
│ ➤ Harmonisation of policies  │  │ ➤ Short- to long-term utilisation │
│   in a given policy issue    │  │   of capabilities                 │
└──────────────────────────────┘  └──────────────────────────────────┘
```

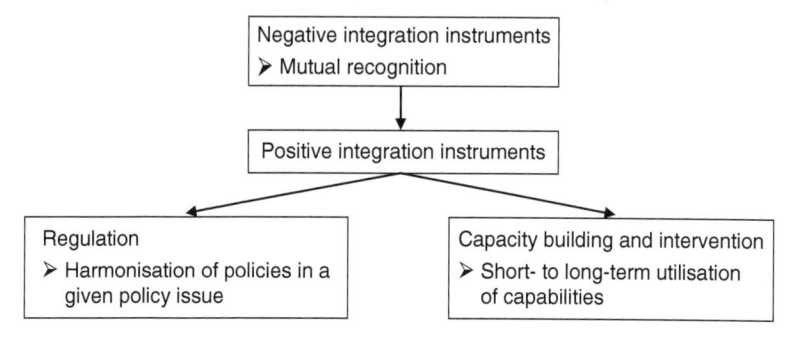

Figure 1.1 Instruments for the EU's international security policy

mistrust towards foreign judicial systems, courts tend to limit non-execution of warrants as much as possible (Wagner, 2011).

Whilst negative integration measures can be appropriate for the EU's internal security, positive measures are necessary in pursuing security objectives externally or with a significant external dimension. All the case studies investigated in this book demonstrate this amply. For example, according to the EU's counter-terrorism strategy, the EU adds value to combating terrorism by (a) strengthening national capabilities; (b) facilitating the exchange of information; (c) developing EU-level capabilities; and (d) promoting international partnership. All these measures require a high scope of integration and some capacity-building instruments. Similarly, problems such as piracy off the coast of Somalia, non-proliferation in Russia and climate security all require significant positive measures in different forms. Table 1.1 summarises the relationship between three instruments of integration and the criteria of 'actorness' identified in the previous section.

Mutual recognition, constituting the most important alternative to positive instruments of integration, does not require significant regulatory measures or extra capabilities. Instead, it is based on mutual trust among Member States. In the case of criminal law cooperation, as discussed above, trust is most prominently expressed through the institution of surrender, which is facilitated by the EAW and which replaced lengthy extradition procedures. In the area of negative economic cooperation (the removal of barriers and mutual recognition), the Commission recognised the importance of mutual trust already in its 1985 White Paper on 'Completing the Internal Market' (Commission, 1985). In fact, Majone (2010) argues that in the EU of 27 or more than 30 countries, negative integration will dominate, with ineffective large redistributive schemes, such as the Common Agricultural Policy (CAP), being increasingly compromised by the dominance of narrow interests. This can well be the case in internal EU politics, but in order to matter

Table 1.1 The instruments of integration and the criteria of actorness

Mutual recognition	Regulation	Capacity building and intervention
Low scope of integration required No capabilities required	High scope of integration required Some capabilities required	Low to high scope of integration required Significant capabilities required

in international security policy the EU has to advance continuously its positive integration instruments.

The first is regulation, which requires a wide scope of integration and some capabilities. A wide scope of integration entails strong involvement of supranational bodies and majority voting rules. On the one hand, in the area of the EU's internal market, regulation and harmonisation have attracted a degree of criticism, mainly because of the risk of unnecessary centralisation (Majone, 2010: 19). On the other hand, regulation and harmonisation can be desirable in the realm of security policy, forcing states to greater cooperation by placing them in the dense network of common institutions and practices. This, in turn, can create greater trust and the 'coordination reflex' (Glarbo, 1999) in policy areas that traditionally have been associated with national competition and even conflict. The second category of positive integration instruments is capacity building and intervention. The involvement of supranational bodies in this case depends on a particular policy action. It can be a CSDP civilian/military operation, which relies almost exclusively on intergovernmental cooperation in the Council, or a more permanent initiative, such as the establishment of institutional structures supporting harmonisation measures. Typically, capacity-building and intervention measures require significant capabilities. This sometimes serves as a basis for criticising the EU's arguably insufficient CSDP resources which forces Europe to rely on American capacities.

Although all three instruments of integration have been separated for analytical purposes, they largely overlap in political practice. Most of the security challenges discussed in the remaining part of this book require the EU to combine mutual recognition and trust with regulation and capacity-building measures. It is only the degree to which each of these measures is appropriate for each case study that differs. For instance, policies developed within the framework of the AFSJ typically rely heavily on mutual recognition and regulation, with some need of capabilities to strengthen the EU's efforts. Counter-terrorism is a good example, with certain resources necessary for the effective operation of EU bodies, including Europol, Eurojust, Frontex and the Monitoring and Information Centre as well as the Situation Centre. In comparison, policies falling mostly within the framework of the Common Foreign and Security Policy (CFSP), or global security problems such as climate change, require significant capabilities. Interventions such as EUNAVFOR 'Atalanta' off the Somali coast are expensive, as are the programmes of non-proliferation assistance to Russia and other regions. Following the 2009 climate Copenhagen Summit, the EU also committed roughly one-third of the fast-track funding for adaptation to climate change in developing countries. However, this does not mean that regulation and harmonisation are irrelevant in the category of problems which require significant capabilities. Importantly, in the CSDP, the harmonisation of national defence planning has been one of the main tasks of the European Defence Agency (EDA). The Lisbon Treaty entrusts the EDA with the 'harmonisation of operational needs and adoption of effective, compatible procurement methods' (Council, 2008c: 54). Consequently, as the rest of this book demonstrates, a comprehensive approach is needed to take account of all the relevant EU policies addressing contemporary security problems in all their complexity.

Conclusion

This chapter has addressed the two key concepts underpinning the main research question, that is the concept of the EU as an international actor and the comprehensive approach to analysing the security 'actorness' of the EU. A brief review of the literature in the Introduction has indicated some limitations in the scholarship on EU security policy at the international level. Thus, explaining and justifying the comprehensive approach adopted in the empirical component of this book constitutes an important building block of this theoretical framework. In particular, it has been explained that the comprehensive approach consists of two parts: (a) moving beyond traditional security threats, also to include the so-called 'non-traditional' security challenges and (b) moving beyond the CSDP and even JHA frameworks to incorporate the whole range of instruments and policies of the EU. However, adopting a comprehensive approach is not as straightforward as it may seem. For this reason, it was also important to identify and address the main obstacles preventing scholars from studying the EU's international security role in a more holistic manner. These include (a) the contested nature of the security concept; (b) different perceptions of security among Member States; (c) the arguable lack of an overarching 'grand strategy' or a 'strategic vision' in the EU; and (d) the problem of assuring consistency in the EU's international security policy.

Once the question of 'comprehensiveness' was addressed, the chapter engaged with debates on 'actorness' at the international level. Notably, favourable conditions for the EEC to emerge and to be recognised as an actor had already developed by 1970, particularly in the context of détente and the conditions which Nye and Keohane described as transnationalism and complex interdependence. After discussing 'actorness' in the context of IR more broadly, the chapter examined how the EEC and subsequently the EU have been conceptualised as actors in the literature. This confirmed that the dominating approach remains that of the EU as a *sui generis* actor, neither a full-blown state nor a typical inter-governmental organisation. The hybrid nature of the EU prompts scholars to look for original ways to assess the nature and scope of the EU in different areas of IR, such as the environment, security and economic relations. This chapter has also established the framework for assessing the 'actorness' of the EU in addressing a range of contemporary security problems that constitute the empirical part of this book. Such a framework concerns analysing the scope of integration, capabilities and recognition of the EU in each case study: climate security in Chapter 3, refugees in Chapter 4, terrorism in Chapter 5, non-proliferation in Chapter 6 and Somali piracy in Chapter 7.

2
The Historical Evolution of the CFSP and JHA

Peterson and Shackleton (2006: 7) in their work on the institutions of the European Union (EU) argue that '[i]f institutions matter, they matter even more in the European Union than in other political systems'. The authors identify a number of reasons for this institutional significance, including the following: (a) EU institutions have a direct impact on Member States and citizens; (b) EU institutions reflect continuity and change, in other words they help to understand better the history of European integration – its past and possible future (Vanhoonacker, 2011: 77); (c) EU institutions enforce intergovernmental bargains agreed by Member States; (d) EU institutions, in contrast to the secretariats of other international organisations, do not merely manage but also have the competences and resources to create policies and provide direction; (e) EU institutions provide the link between Europe and the wider international relations, particularly with the network of international organisations; and (f) EU politics are shaped by both the competition between EU institutions and their interdependence.

This chapter examines the institutional structure associated with the Common Foreign and Security Policy (CFSP) and the Area of Freedom, Security and Justice (AFSJ), including European Political Cooperation (EPC) as their predecessor. There are two main reasons why this analysis is important. First, this book adopts a broadened perspective on the question of the EU's international security role, which further incorporates the external policies of the AFSJ. Although not very common in the relevant literature, this approach is partially justified by the fact that both external and internal security policies of the EU historically evolved under a single institutional framework, that is the EPC. Only in the Maastricht Treaty were these policy areas separated into the second and third pillars of the newly established EU. Second, this book assesses the extent to which the EU developed as an international security actor by identifying a set of criteria, including the scope of integration. This latter criterion, as explained in the previous chapter, refers to the involvement of EU central bureaucracies and Council voting rules in a given international security policy issue. Thus, it is important that these bureaucracies, together with decision-making procedures, are first introduced and explained in greater detail. The two aforementioned reasons are reflected in the structure of this chapter, which consists of two sections. The first section provides a historical overview of the CFSP and the AFSJ as well as their common roots under the EPC and subsequent separation in the Maastricht Treaty. In the second section, this chapter assesses the current institutional and decision-making frameworks of these two policy areas, as reformed by the Lisbon Treaty.

Historical evolution until the Lisbon Treaty

At least two patterns can be identified in the literature on the EU's international policy role (including security), which started to flourish in the 1990s. First, for the most part, scholars have been separating the analysis of EU policies according to the pillar structure. Second, the analysis of the EU's external role and particularly of the EU's performance as an international security actor has traditionally been limited to the CFSP (Knodt and Princen, 2003: 2). This separation and focus on pillar II can to some degree be explained by the empirical developments following the entry into force of the Maastricht Treaty in 1993. However, it is not very helpful when attempting to understand better the role of the EU in international security. Further, from a longer, historical perspective, it overlooks the fact that the CFSP and the AFSJ have common institutional roots embodied in the EPC. This part of the chapter provides an overview of the EU's security policy institutional structure prior to and after the Maastricht Treaty reforms. It is subsequently followed, in the second part, by the analysis of Lisbon Treaty reforms with regard to the CFSP and the AFSJ, which formally abolished the pillar structure in the EU. H. Smith (2002), in her extensive description of the historical background of the institutionalisation of the EU's foreign and security policy, notes that the European Economic Community (EEC) was only successful in launching cooperation in this area at the beginning of the 1970s. The task was uneasy because matters of security and foreign policy are constructed in the history of modern statehood to constitute the core of nation states' competence. Moreover, this task remains difficult over

40 years later, although – as this book demonstrates – integration has progressed at a faster pace in the AFSJ than in the CFSP (Börzel, 2005).

European political cooperation

The beginnings of European cooperation on security policy were modest and exclusively intergovernmental. The first successful step towards the codification of this cooperation took the form of the Luxemburg Report in 1970, requested one year earlier by the EEC's Member States at The Hague Summit (Smith, 2002: 67–71). In this report, six EEC Member States undertook a very cautious attempt to coordinate their international policies. The framework was informal and non-binding, because the report was not ratified by national legislation. Yet, this document 'marked the first successful attempt at foreign policy cooperation by the member states of the European Community' (Smith, 2002: 68). This newly established EPC entailed bi-annual meetings of the foreign ministers of the EEC in a country holding the Presidency. The work for the ministers was prepared by the Political Committee, further divided into working groups. One of the most striking features of the EPC was the strong desire among the EEC's Member States to separate this new, intergovernmental policy forum from the framework of the EEC. Cameron (2007a) notes that this led to some absurd situations, where EEC Member States would finish a meeting on general affairs in Brussels and fly the same day to Copenhagen, which was holding the EPC rotating Presidency, to continue their meeting, but in a new format. This, of course, changed following the Maastricht Treaty reforms, which integrated the EPC into the newly established CFSP.

In terms of internal security cooperation, already in 1975, the Rome European Council established a special group to address the security problem of terrorism in Europe. This so-called Trevi group worked at three levels: Interior Ministers meeting bi-annually, Trevi Senior Officials also meeting twice a year and Trevi working groups, consisting of Justice or Interior Ministry officials, security services and police officials. Again, and related to the fact that the Trevi group operated within the EPC framework, the cooperation on internal security within the EEC was intergovernmental, with Community institutions almost entirely absent from this cooperation. In particular, the European Parliament and the European Court of Justice (ECJ) were excluded and the Commission was occasionally involved. However, this did not prevent the Trevi group from becoming an effective European forum for cooperation on counterterrorism. In fact, Hill (1988: 172) argues that Trevi represented 'the most sophisticated attempt yet at intergovernmental cooperation on anti-terrorist measures'.

The Schengen cooperation

The so-called Schengen cooperation has its origins in the Saarbrücken Agreement of 13 July 1984, in which Chancellor Kohl and President Mitterrand agreed on the gradual abolition of controls at the Franco-German borders. Shortly afterwards, the Benelux countries joined France and Germany in this initiative and the five countries signed the Schengen Agreement on 14 June 1985. This core of five Member States, willing to implement immediately the free movement of persons, came to be considered a 'laboratory' serving as an example for all the EEC Member States. Five years of negotiations were then necessary to adopt the Convention applying the Schengen Agreement concerning the Gradual Abolition of Checks at the Common Borders. This document, drafted mostly by representatives of the national Interior ministries, widely focused on compensatory measures necessary to safeguard internal security after the lifting of checks at the internal borders. Indeed, 128 articles of the 142 article-Convention were dedicated to those compensatory measures (Berthelet, 2003: 220). Their main aim was to strengthen external borders and judicial and police cooperation in order to fight issues as varied as drug trafficking, terrorism and international crime. Finally, a substantial part of the Schengen Convention was concerned with the issue of exchange of information. It was decided to set up a joint information system, called the 'Schengen Information System' (SIS), which would consist of a national section in each of the contracting states and a technical support function. It would contain 'reports on persons and objects for the purposes of border checks and controls and other police and customs checks carried out within the country (...) and (...) for the purposes of issuing visas, the issue of residence permits and the administration of aliens (...)' (Title IV, Chapter 1, Article 92).

The Single European Act

Yet, despite this progress in internal security cooperation, neither the Trevi group nor the Schengen Cooperation was formally recognised in the Single European Act (SEA) from 1987, in contrast with the EPC in the area of foreign and security policy. On the one hand, the SEA was not groundbreaking, because it did not introduce any changes to what EEC Member States had agreed already in the area of foreign and security policy. The scope of cooperation and the procedures were to remain largely the same, that is (a) Member States were to consult each other on foreign policy matters to raise Europe's influence 'through coordination, the convergence of their positions and the implementation of joint action'; (b) Member States, when taking action, should account for the position of their partners; (c) Foreign Ministers and the Commission (fully associated) should meet at least four times a year within the EPC framework; (d) the European Parliament should be informed about the issues discussed; and (e) the Presidency and the Commission should ensure consistency of the EEC's external action and the EPC policy outputs.

On the other hand, the SEA, for the first time, provided an explicit treaty basis for European cooperation on foreign and security policy. This is significant in the context of the early failures of the EEC to cooperate in this policy area, particularly the rejection by the French senate of the European Defence Community (Cameron, 2007a: 24). Furthermore, the SEA not only did codify the system of European foreign and security policy cooperation as it developed in the 1970s and 1980s but also provided important basis for the much more important reform, which was about to take place six years later. The above overview of the main features of the EPC, concluded with its codification in the SEA, points to the key characteristic of this cooperation, namely its intergovernmental character. Although EEC Member States committed to cooperate on foreign and security policy, there was no system of enforcing this cooperation or even ensuring that Member States would comply with what they agreed upon. To reinforce this point, the SEA clarified that nothing in the provisions on the EPC impedes the right of Member States to cooperate closely on security matters within NATO and the Western EU.

The Maastricht Treaty

Importantly, while European cooperation on external security remained largely intergovernmental, internal security cooperation, together with its external dimensions, has become increasingly 'supranationalised', following subsequent treaty reforms, including the Maastricht, the Amsterdam and – most importantly – the Lisbon Treaty. Both internal and external dynamics were at play at the time of preparing the Treaty on the European Union (TEU). Internally, the fall of the Berlin Wall and the unification of Germany provided an impetus to strengthen the political framework in Europe which would facilitate these geopolitical changes. Externally, the collapse of the Soviet Union, the Gulf War and the outbreak of the Yugoslav crisis in 1991 created new expectations about Europe's political role, in addition to ambitious Single Market and monetary union proposals. Eventually, these expectations led to what Hill (1993, 1998) described as the capability–expectations gap, due to the EU's inability to respond coherently and effectively to external pressures.

The TEU did not introduce dramatic changes to the decision-making structure of the EU's international security policy, but it did formally separate external security (CFSP) from internal security Justice and Home Affairs (JHA) policies. Furthermore, both the CFSP and the JHA remained institutionally separate from the EC, a fact which later led to the problem of incoherence and wrangling over competences as some of the main impediments to a more effective EU's role in security policy. EPC became integrated into the second pillar of the EU and was rebranded as CFSP. Its objectives and institutional structure were defined under Title V of the TEU. The language suggested strong commitment on the part of Member States to pursue common foreign policy instead of merely advancing national objectives. For example, the TEU obliged Member States to 'refrain from any action which is contrary to the interests of the Union or likely to impair its effectiveness as a cohesive force in international relations'. Furthermore, the Council was entrusted with ensuring the compliance.

In terms of institutions and instruments, the European Council was entrusted with 'defining the principles of and general guidelines for the common foreign and security policy'. The Council was responsible for implementing policy guidelines set at the summits. Two specific instruments were made available for Ministers working in the Council: common positions (declaratory statements) and joint actions (implying operational action). The EU would be represented externally by the Presidency, which would implement decisions taken in the Council under Title V of the TEU. The European Commission could submit questions to the Council concerning the CFSP, but it also acquired the right to submit proposals vis-à-vis Member States. The European Parliament retained its right to be (merely) consulted. Bureaucratically, the EPC's modest secretariat became integrated into the Council's General Secretariat. Further, the Committee of Permanent Representatives was entrusted with preparing the work for ministers; as a result, the Political Committee became a monitoring body.

In spite of the fact that issues such as migration and terrorism have important external security implications for the EU, JHA became a separate, third pillar under the TEU, regulated by Title VI. This formal separation of the CFSP and JHA has had profound effects on how the EU's role in security policy has become to be perceived and analysed in the literature. As mentioned, first, it led to a clear division of research agendas according to the pillars. Second, the majority of the scholarship analysing the EU's role in international security tends to focus on the CFSP (Knodt and Princen, 2003: 2). The TEU defined areas of cooperation for JHA, many of which had a strong external dimension; thus, there are no conceptual reasons for separating them from an analysis which aims to take account of the EU's international security role. These areas included, for example, the following: (a) asylum policy; (b) rules governing the crossing by persons of the external borders of the Member States and the exercise of controls thereon; (c) immigration policy and policy regarding nationals of third countries; (d) combating fraud on an international scale; and (e) police cooperation for the purposes of preventing and combating terrorism, unlawful drug trafficking and other serious forms of international crime.

In terms of institutions and instruments, the most important innovation introduced by the Maastricht Treaty was that European cooperation on JHA had finally acquired treaty basis. Initially, JHA decision-making structures resembled those established under Title V for the CFSP. The Council was entrusted with adopting joint positions, joint actions and drawing up conventions, which would be subsequently left for Member States to ratify. In most areas, both Member States and the Commission could make proposals, but decisions in the Council were taken unanimously. The European Parliament, as in the case of the CFSP, acquired the right to be consulted. Additionally, a Coordinating Committee was established, consisting of senior officials. Its role was to give opinions to the Council and assist the Council with preparations for the discussions on different areas of cooperation. This overview indicates that although the cooperation in JHA was formalised in the TEU, it started off as an intergovernmental policy area, based on a voluntary cooperation of Member States and a limited official role of the Commission's Directorate General (DG) Justice, Freedom and Security.

The Amsterdam Treaty

As this chapter has already discussed, the EU's cooperation on internal and external security policy originated under a single umbrella of the EPC. Subsequently, the TEU integrated these policies into two intergovernmental pillars of the newly established EU, albeit with similar institutional and decision-making structures. However, as this chapter demonstrates, CFSP and JHA have experienced different levels of integration since 1993. Whereas CFSP has remained intergovernmental, JHA has undergone a significant degree of supranationalisation, which is reflected by the involvement of the European Commission and decision-making rules based on qualified majority voting (QMV) (Börzel, 2005). This process has been gradual, with the Amsterdam Treaty (1997) constituting the first step in revising and consolidating the cooperation of the newly established EU in matters of internal and external security policy.

In relation to CFSP, the Amsterdam Treaty introduced a few reforms supporting the conduct of foreign and security policy by the EU, but without substantially deepening the scope of cooperation in this area. First, it nominated the Secretary General of the Council as the High Representative (HR) for the CFSP, with the role of supporting the Presidency in drafting and implementing decisions as well as representing the EU in conducting dialogue with third parties on behalf of the Council. Second, it established the Policy Planning and Early Warning Unit in the Council Secretariat, with a threefold role: (a) monitoring and analysing developments in areas relevant to the CFSP; (b) providing assessments of the Union's foreign and security policy interests and identifying areas where the CFSP could focus in future; and (c) providing timely assessments and early warning of situations which can have consequences for the EU. The Unit consisted of personnel from the General Secretariat, the Member States, the Commission and the Western EU. Third, the Amsterdam Treaty reformed the so-called troika representing the CFSP outside the EU, which under the Maastricht Treaty consisted of three consecutive Presidencies – the current, the previous one and the one to follow. The reformed troika consisted of the current Presidency, supported by the HR and the Commission. An important reason for this was to ensure greater consistency with the external policies of the EC; the problem of ensuring institutional coherence was a natural outcome of the 'pillarisation' of the EU, and the first bold move to resolve it only came with the Lisbon Treaty, discussed further in this chapter.

The Amsterdam Treaty, whilst introducing rather modest changes to the second-pillar decision-making, has had a more significant impact on the third pillar that was now renamed the Area of Freedom, Security and Justice. Contrary to the Maastricht Treaty, which merely defined the potential areas of cooperation with the aim of supporting the implementation of the Single Market, the Amsterdam Treaty set the goal to 'provide citizens with a high level of safety within an area of freedom, security and justice'. Consequently, achieving the AFSJ has become an end in itself; areas of cooperation include combating crime, in particular terrorism, trafficking in persons and offences against children, illicit drug trafficking and illicit arms trafficking, corruption and fraud.

Although this new approach to internal security cooperation seemed very ambitious, the actual decision-making reforms reflected divisions among Member States as to whether the EU should legislate in the AFSJ. As a result, a number of policy areas have been 'communitarised', that is moved to the first pillar, although with a transitional period. These policy areas included asylum and migration, combating drug addiction and fraud, judicial cooperation in civil matters and customs cooperation. The Amsterdam Treaty further introduced two new legal instruments, that is (a) framework decisions, aiming for 'approximation of the laws and regulations of the Member States' and (b) decisions, for any other purpose consistent with the objectives of the Treaty. Changes were also made to the legislative process, which came to be organised as follows (Simpson, 1999: Peers, 2000: 40; 91–124; De Lobkowicz, 2002: 130; Kaunert, 2005: 466–67): (1) the Council would act unanimously in the consultation procedure with the European Parliament; (2) the legal right of initiative would lie with both the Commission and individual Member States; (3) from 1 May 2004, for the first-pillar competences, that is asylum and migration, the treaty established the sole right of legal initiative for the Commission; (4) the Council could then also decide by unanimity to move towards co-decision with the European Parliament and towards QMV as the decision-making mechanism in the Council; (5) the ECJ, often the engine of integration, initially excluded in its jurisdiction from the area under the Treaty of Maastricht, gained more jurisdiction under Amsterdam but remained still strongly restricted.

However, as one significant drawback in the Treaty of Amsterdam, art 69 consists of three protocols attached to the treaty base (Simpson, 1999: 99). These exempt the United Kingdom and Ireland from all the provisions on asylum and migration (new Title IV), as well as Denmark from involvement in measures under the same title. All these protocols were annexed to both the Treaty of Maastricht and Amsterdam and have thus the legal force of the treaty itself. The United Kingdom demanded this exemption on the grounds of maintaining border controls with other Member States, which practically obliged Ireland to follow suit in order to keep its Common Travel Area (CTA) with the United Kingdom. Both Member States were nonetheless permitted to opt-in to adopting and applying any measure proposed under the title as long as this decision was communicated to the Council Presidency three months after a proposal had been submitted. The Danish position was somewhat different. It requested the legal opt out in response to concerns about a possible ratification failure for the Treaty of Amsterdam after the Treaty of Maastricht had been rejected in its first referendum. Consequently, the protocol exempted Denmark from all legal obligations from Title IV. However, this also meant that, contrary to the United Kingdom and Ireland, Denmark did not receive an opt-in possibility. Thus, Denmark could only unilaterally implement legal decisions by doing this in the form of public international law.

Nonetheless, on the positive side, the Amsterdam Treaty brought the Schengen agreements into the legal framework of the EU for the first time. The legal mechanism of integrating the Schengen acquis was a protocol (Simpson, 1999: 106–7). The 15 Member States of the time would allow the 13 Schengen states to establish closer cooperation between them within the institutional and legal framework of the EU, taking account of the respective opt-out and opt-in protocols of the United Kingdom, Ireland and Denmark. With the integration of the Schengen acquis into the treaties of the EU, it became a legal obligation for all new Member States of the different Enlargement waves of 2004 and 2007 (EU12) to fulfil. The incorporation of Schengen also involved the merging of the Schengen institutions into those of the EU.

Post-Amsterdam developments

Following the Amsterdam Treaty, which provided a rather ambiguous answer to the question as to whether the EU was ready to legislate in the AFSJ, the 1999 Tampere Council Summit aimed to strengthen further European cooperation in this area, without changing treaty provisions. The Summit was the first-ever event at this level entirely dedicated to the AFSJ. Its outcome is interesting because many of the new objectives, as set in Presidency Conclusions, did not have a treaty basis or were only partially founded on the provisions of the Amsterdam Treaty (Kaunert, 2010c). The new objectives of the EU in the AFSJ were grouped into four categories. The first category concerned common migration and asylum policy and included the following: (a) provisions on closer cooperation with countries of origin as part of the comprehensive approach to migration; (b) provisions on Common European Asylum system; (c) provisions on fair treatment of third-country nationals residing legally in the EU; and (d) provisions on better management of migration. The second category concerned a 'Genuine European Area of Justice' and also had only partial basis in the Treaty of Amsterdam. The three objectives of this category were as follows: (a) improving access to justice in Europe; (b) enhancing mutual recognition of judicial decisions; and (c) greater convergence in civil law. The third category covered 'A Unionwide Fight against Crime' and included objectives such as (a) enhancing crime prevention at EU and national levels; (b) stepping-up cooperation against crime; and (c) special action against money laundering. Finally, the fourth category of new objectives concerned the external dimension of the AFSJ and called for the integration of internal security concerns into other policies of the EU. The Tampere Council Summit programme did not directly deepen European integration in the AFSJ; none of the formal rules of cooperation in this area were changed. However, an important aspect of the Summit was that it further strengthened the objective of establishing the AFSJ as the goal in itself, and not merely as a flanking measure for the effective functioning of the Single Market. The autonomous character of the AFSJ became even more urgent and evident following the September 11 terrorist attacks in the United States and the subsequent terrorist attacks in Europe. As a result, the AFSJ has evolved into one of the key driving forces of European integration – a trend which is confirmed in the Lisbon Treaty, discussed later in this chapter.

Whilst the scope of European integration in internal security matters has been steadily undergoing a process of deepening, there is no evidence of a similar trend in the CFSP. Instead, the main feature of European cooperation in this area between the Amsterdam Treaty and the Lisbon Treaty was the modest integration of military cooperation into the second pillar under the European Security and Defence Policy (ESDP). Howorth (2007) argues that there were four underlying drivers behind developing the ESDP: (1) the end of the Cold War and the weakening of American interest in Europe; (2) the normative notion of 'international community', encompassing the right, or even obligation, to deploy interventions when human rights are abused; (3) the outbreak of war in Yugoslavia and subsequent wars; and (4) the urgent need to reform European defence industries. As such, the ESDP is a relatively recent institutional framework of the EU. The impetus for its development came from St Malo in France, where in 1998 British Prime Minister Tony Blair and French President Jacques Chirac declared that 'the Union must have the capacity for autonomous action, backed up by credible military forces, the means to decide to use them, and a readiness to do so, in order to respond to international crises' (Great Britain, 2002). What followed were three important European Council Summits – in Cologne (June 1999), Helsinki (December 1999) and Feira (June 2000) – which gave substance to the ESDP, including setting the Helsinki Headline Goal. The goal was for the EU to establish the European Rapid Reaction Force, capable of deploying 50–60 thousand persons within 60 days for at least one year. This goal was later upgraded through the new Headline Goal 2010, which introduced the idea of smaller and more flexible battle groups.

In terms of institutions and decision-making procedures, the development of the ESDP prompted the establishment of a number of new bodies in the second pillar. First, the Political and Security Committee (PSC) has become the most important preparatory body of the Council, playing a crucial role in the ESDP institutional structure. It is composed of political directors from the foreign ministries of Member States. It meets at least twice a week, but more often if necessary (Howorth, 2007). The PSC worked on an interim basis from 2000 to 2001, when it was transformed into a permanent body. However, the roots of this EU body date back to the 1970s and the creation of the aforementioned Political Committee, as part of the EPC framework (Hayes-Renshaw, 2006). Second, the EU Military Committee (EUMC) has become the highest military body of the EU. It is entrusted with advising and providing recommendations of military nature to the PSC. The EUMC is composed of Member States' Chiefs of Defence, but regular meetings are attended by Member States' Military Representatives. The EUMC plays a central role whenever the Council decides on a CSDP military operation. When such a decision is taken, the EUMC is expected to deliver a consensual advice to the PSC on how the operation should be conducted. The EUMC is supported by the Military Staff, composed of senior officers from EU Member States. This institutional setup confirms the strictly intergovernmental character of the ESDP, which was not undermined in the Lisbon Treaty. Thus, as this section has demonstrated, although European cooperation on both internal and external security emerged under a single intergovernmental framework, it was later separated into two policy areas and experienced diverging paces of integration. The Lisbon Treaty further reinforces this trend, with the AFSJ becoming even more 'supranational', with CFSP remaining intergovernmental.

The CFSP after the Lisbon Treaty

The Lisbon Treaty, which after the prolonged ratification process entered into force in December 2009 (Hoffmann, 2009; Kaunert, 2009b; Kratochvil and Braun, 2009; Tonra, 2009; Zwolski, 2009), introduced potentially significant changes to the institutional structure of the CFSP. Although it is still too early to provide an authoritative assessment of these reforms, this section offers an overview of key changes and makes some observations concerning their implementation to date. In order to understand more effectively the rationale behind Lisbon Treaty reforms, this section begins by restating the main features of the CFSP as defined by the Maastricht and Amsterdam Treaties:

(a) CFSP was introduced as the second pillar of the EU in 1993 in Title V of the Maastricht Treaty, with the system of decision-making different from that existing in the EC;
(b) Ministers of Foreign Affairs, working together in the Council and acting anonymously – General Affairs and External Relations Council (GAERC), chaired by the Presidency – were the main decision-makers, guided by principles set down in the European Council by heads of state and government;
(c) The Maastricht Treaty defined joint actions and common positions as the policy instruments in the CFSP; the Council, in adopting them, was supposed to act on the basis of 'general guidelines' established by the European Council; the Amsterdam Treaty further introduced 'common strategies' as the CFSP instrument;
(d) The Amsterdam Treaty also entrusted the Council's Secretary General with acting as HR for the CFSP. Javier Solana held this post between 1999 and 2009, and his role was to assist the Council on CFSP matters as well as act on behalf of the Council when given such mandate;
(e) The European Commission had a limited role in the CFSP; mainly, it could make proposals on the same basis as individual Member States.

From this summary, it is not difficult to conclude that coherency of the EU's external actions emerged as one of the key challenges hampering the role of the EU as a global actor (Tietje, 1997; Missiroli, 2001; 2010; Dijkstra, 2009; Van Elsuwege, 2010; Zwolski, 2011b). This was caused by the duality of policy frameworks and institutional structures codified in the Maastricht Treaty, with the growing scope of the Community's external activities (Pillar I with the key role of the Commission) separated from the emerging CFSP (Pillar II with the key role of the Council). Member States have long recognised this problem, and the Lisbon Treaty constitutes the boldest effort to date to address the structural causes of incoherence.

At the personal level, the Lisbon Treaty merged the post of the HR for the CFSP with that of the Commissioner for External Relations, into a single post of the HR of the Union for Foreign Affairs and Security Policy. The idea of naming the post simply Union Minister for Foreign Affairs ended with the rejection of the Constitutional Treaty. The new post holder not only chairs Council meetings on foreign affairs (Foreign Affairs Council which was separated from the GAERC) but also is the Vice President of the European Commission. This arrangement aims to tie the two institutions closer together. Furthermore, in order to equip European (foreign) policy with more continuity, the European Council is now chaired by the President elected for two and a half years, instead of the Presidency rotating every six months.

At the bureaucratic level, the HR is supported by the European External Action Service (EEAS) – the so-called diplomatic service of the EU. The EEAS is composed of three bodies: diplomats seconded from Member States, officials previously working in DG Relex of the European Commission and officials previously working in the Council Secretariat. More specifically, following prolonged discussions, in 2010 the Council decided that the following administrative entities from the Council Secretariat would be transferred to the EEAS: Policy Unit; ESDP and crisis management structures (for example, EU Military Staff, EU Situation Centre) and Directorate-General E (External and Political-Military Affairs).

With regard to policy instruments, the Lisbon Treaty introduces more flexibility by defining the following formal possibilities for executing the CFSP: (a) the EU can define general guidelines and (b) the EU can adopt decisions defining actions and/or positions to be undertaken by the Union. In addition, the EU can use its diplomatic channels; it can offer and withdraw trade benefits, economic and financial assistance as well as other forms of cooperation; it can also utilise its limited capability of deploying civilian, police and military missions.

How likely are these reforms to provide the EU with greater coherence and thus enhance its 'actorness' in international security policy? They certainly offer an opportunity to bring a higher degree of cooperation and consistency across different EU policies and instruments, but this convergence is unlikely to happen automatically. Some scholars even suggest that inter-institutional cooperation within the EU tends to be better than intra-institutional cooperation – within a single institution. For example, Christiansen (2001) argues that structurally determined tensions between the Council General Secretariat and the Commission have led to the low level of expectations for close cooperation between them. Yet, against this low level of expectations, officials from both institutions have developed collegial approaches in the areas of shared responsibility. On the other hand, significant tensions could be identified within the Commission and the Council General Secretariat: 'the differing organizational logics of distinct administrative tasks constitute internal tensions which then require substantive institutional resources for their resolution' (Christiansen, 2001: 766). This argument would call for a degree of caution when assuming that bringing officials, instruments and resources into one institution will in itself assure consistency and close cooperation.

Furthermore, future research will also be necessary to examine potential tensions over competences at the higher level, between the High Representative and the President of the European Council. The latter was entrusted by the Lisbon Treaty with ensuring 'the external representation of the Union on issues concerning its common foreign and security policy (...)'. This ambiguity leaves room for manoeuvre for the two personalities elected for these posts; however, it can also be expected that over time and with longer practice, the competences of each post holder will become better defined. As to the position of the European Commission, on the one hand, its role in international security policy is hampered by the removal of DG Relex from this institution. On the other hand, as Nugent (2010: 392) argues, its role is strengthened by the merged post of the High Representative, which chairs the Foreign Affairs Council, and thus, in principle, is the key foreign policy planner.

From this analysis it is rather clear that the Lisbon Treaty introduces potentially significant institutional changes which can, eventually, enhance the EU's role as an international security actor. However, whether this goal is achieved will depend on a number of factors, such as the leadership role of the High Representative, and – ultimately – the willingness of Member States to cede more competence to the High Representative and the EEAS. At the same time, this analysis also demonstrates that there is nothing in the Lisbon Treaty reforms which suggests that the CFSP will become more 'supranational' in the foreseeable future. The principle of unanimity in the Council still applies, but the nature and role of the EEAS, as a partly supranational and partly intergovernmental body, require further research. The following section discusses the Lisbon Treaty changes to the AFSJ, demonstrating that Member States have moved much further in deepening the scope of integration in this policy area than they did in the CFSP.

The AFSJ after the Lisbon Treaty

This section examines the changes of the Lisbon Treaty in the AFSJ in order to provide a comprehensive picture of the legal competences of the EU since 1 December 2009, the date the treaty entered into force. With its entry into force, the AFSJ policy area has a prospect of becoming one of exponential future growth and development of EU action (Carrera and Geyer, 2008). Thus, Monar (2005) might have correctly identified that future historians are likely to regard the EU's creation of the AFSJ as one of the most significant developments in the European integration process. The Lisbon Treaty amended two separate bodies of treaties: (1) the TEU and (2) the Treaty on the Functioning of the European Union (TFEU). Article 3(2) TEU elevates the 'Area of Freedom, Security and Justice' to become an objective with the same status as the Internal Market (Article 3 (3) TEU). 'The Union shall offer its citizens an area of freedom, security and justice without internal frontiers, in which the free movement of persons is ensured in conjunction with appropriate measures with respect to external border controls, asylum, immigration, and the prevention and combating of crime.' The EU legal competences in the AFSJ are now also clarified. Article 4 (2j) TFEU defines the area as one of shared competences.

Furthermore, the Lisbon Treaty creates a simplified decision-making procedure. First, the pillar structure is formally abolished, which results in the advanced, but incomplete, communitarisation of the areas of criminal justice, policing and terrorism, albeit with drawbacks in the form of 'emergency brakes' and 'accelerators'. Second, the standard decision-making procedure in the AFSJ is co-decision according to article 294 TFEU (formerly article 251 of the Treaty establishing the European Community) and QMV in the Council. This gives the European Parliament joint decision-making power. The Commission is given the exclusive power to propose legislation. In criminal justice and policing legislation, the latter power is shared with a quarter of the Member States. Third, the disappearance of the pillar structure leads to a commonality of legal instruments between titles that were formerly pillar one and pillar three. In the Lisbon Treaty, this is achieved under the name 'ordinary legislative procedure'. It is important to note that for the first time the Union can use the 'ordinary legislative procedure' in principle for the whole area. Nonetheless, the Lisbon Treaty retains the traditional community instruments, that is regulations, directives, decisions and so on. The previous legal instruments in the AFSJ, that is framework decisions, common positions, conventions and so on, disappear. Judicial control is expanded by applying the normal court rules on the ECJ's jurisdiction to all AFSJ matters in all Member States (including the possibility for all national courts or tribunals to send questions to the ECJ).

Fourth, the legal status of the Charter of Fundamental Rights of the Union is clarified for the majority of Member States. By virtue of the first subparagraph of Article 6(1) TEU, the Charter has the same legal value as the treaties. This article provides a cross-reference to the Charter on Fundamental Rights which renders the Charter directly legally binding for the European institutions, Union bodies, offices and agencies as well as Member States when they implement Union law (except those that have exceptions to various degrees, such as the United Kingdom, Ireland, Poland and, in principle, the Czech Republic). This has the following significant implications: (1) EU institutions and other EU agencies and bodies can be held to account on the basis of the fundamental rights contained in the Charter and (2) Member States can be held to account on the basis of the same rights, generally when implementing EU legislation but possibly also when adopting national legislation with an EU dimension (depending on the ECJ interpretation). This will place EU actors and Member States under a clear legal obligation to ensure that fundamental rights are respected and will thus strengthen the freedom dimension of the AFSJ.

Fifth, these institutional changes may have very strong implications for the role of EU institutions in the AFSJ. The Lisbon Treaty provides for a very clear potential reshaping of the inter-institutional balance in the area. In general, the supranational institutions have been greatly strengthened. This implies an even stronger role for the European Commission, as its role as an initiator of legislations has been clearly reinforced. However, even more importantly, the European Parliament has been given the generalised role as a co-legislator in the area, which has the potential to influence greatly the future balance of power between the different EU institutions. Nonetheless, while this supranational dimension in the EU institutional structure has been strengthened, the role of the European Council as a strategic decision-making institution in the AFSJ has also been reinforced and strengthened. Overall, this might very well lead to a diminished influence for EU interior ministers, who had been widely seen as driving forces in the AFSJ before the entry into force of the Lisbon Treaty.

Finally, the introduction of an explicit principle of solidarity, that is a solidarity clause modelled on NATO article 5 (mutual defence clause), within the AFSJ is one of the most significant innovations of the Lisbon Treaty. The clause stipulates that in the case of a terrorist attack or a natural or man-made disaster, the Union shall act jointly to mobilise all instruments at their disposal. First, the procedure would require a European decision by the Council on a proposal from the Commission and the High Representative for Foreign Affairs for cases with military implications. In addition, the European Council acquires the legal responsibility to assess regularly the threats facing the Union. In conclusion, the normative question has now been conclusively answered as a political consensus of decision-makers – the EU should be legislating in the AFSJ. The AFSJ is the 'big winner' of the Lisbon Treaty arrangements.

3
The EU and Climate Security

> The dangers that small islands and their populations face [as a result of climate change] are no less serious than those faced by nations and peoples threatened by guns and bombs. The effects on our populations are as likely to cause massive dislocations of people as past and present wars. The impacts on social cohesion and identity are as likely to cause resentment, hatred and alienation as any current refugee crisis.
>
> Mr Aisi (Papua New Guinea), on behalf of the Pacific Islands Forum Small Island Developing States – Fiji, Nauru, Micronesia, Marshall Islands, Palau, Samoa, Solomon Islands, Tonga, Tuvalu, Vanuatu and Papua New Guinea, at the UN Security Council meeting concerned with climate change.
>
> (UNSC, 2007a)

This chapter assesses the role of the European Union (EU) as a security actor in the area of climate change, representing the so-called 'non-traditional' security problems, which nonetheless may have traditional security consequences. These consequences, as indicated by Mr Aisi during the unprecedented United Nations Security Council (UNSC) meeting concerned with climate change, may have significant bearing on the security of societies in vulnerable regions. The rise of temperatures may also further exacerbate problems such as the shortages of water, leading to radicalisation and conflicts in Africa, the Middle East and Central Asia. The EU has been playing an active role in introducing the climate security agenda to the international community, utilising global, regional and bilateral channels in this respect.

Notably, in 2003, climate change as a security issue was acknowledged for the first time at the highest EU level in the European Security Strategy

(Council, 2003a). Global warming was mentioned in the document, albeit only twice and very briefly. This has changed significantly five years later when the European Council, in December 2008, approved the Report on the Implementation of the European Security Strategy (Implementation Report) (European Council, 2008). This document addresses climate change as one of the 'Global Challenges and Key Threats', together with the proliferation of weapons of mass destruction (WMDs), terrorism, organised crime and energy security. The Implementation Report recognises climate change as a 'threat multiplier' and calls for further improvements of analysis and early warning capabilities.

However, the moves in the EU towards developing the security dimension of climate change do not alleviate the conceptual difficulties surrounding the debate on climate security. 'Security' itself is a highly contested concept, as the theoretical chapter indicated. Furthermore, '[l]inking it to environment complicates matters even further, and there is no commonly agreed understanding of how these terms might be linked or even whether they should be' (Dalby, 2009: 46). Nonetheless, there is a long tradition of linking the environment with the questions of security both in academia and, more recently, in the practice of national and international actors.

In academia, the discussion on environmental and climate security has been developing rapidly; in fact, this discussion itself became the subject of analysis (Hough, 2004; Floyd, 2008; Dalby, 2009; Trombetta, 2009). Most scholars recognise that, even though Cold War strategic debates were focusing mainly on military capabilities of the superpowers, some attempts to link the environment and security took place already in the 1970s (Falk, 1971; Brown, 1977) and 1980s (Buzan, 1983; Ullman, 1983; WCED, 1987; Westing, 1989). However, as Dannreuther (2007: 59) notes, 'these views remained marginal until the bipolar militarized structure of the Cold War finally disintegrated'. With the broadening and deepening of the security concept in the 1990s (Buzan and Hansen, 2009), it became conceptually easier to talk about the environment in the context of security.

Since the 1990s, there has been a scholarly divide on environmental security between those examining the links between the environment and security primarily through its impact on conflicts (traditional security) and those more recently investigating through the concept of human security (Barnett, 2007). The former approach is represented most adequately by the so-called 'Toronto Group' led by Thomas Homer-Dixon (1994). While his argument suggests that there is no straightforward connection between environmental change and war,

Homer-Dixon argues nonetheless that conflict may occur when a number of conditions are in place, such as scarcity of renewable resources and a bad economic situation. The latter is appropriately represented by the 1994 Human Development Report, which redefined security by concentrating on people and their 'safety from such chronic threats as hunger, disease and repression' as well as on the 'protection from sudden and hurtful disruptions in the patterns of daily life' (UNDP, 1994: 23). It actually criticised a narrow interpretation of security which focuses merely on territory and external aggression.

The September 2001 terrorist attacks eclipsed the debate on environmental security, but not for long. A few years later, this debate re-emerged, but this time it focused mainly on one aspect: climate change (Trombetta, 2009). A number of scientific publications provided impetus for the debate on climate security; some of the most important include the Stern Review (Stern, 2007), the 'Fourth Assessment Report of the Intergovernmental Panel on Climate Change' (IPCC, 2007), the report 'Climate Change as a Security Risk' (WBGU, 2007) and 'The Geopolitics of Climate Change' (Haldén, 2007). Interestingly, Floyd (2008: 61) notes that global warming does not have a unifying effect and ' "climate security" has simply become integrated into the various approaches of environmental security'. Some of these approaches focus more on the correlation between climate change and conflict (Brown et al., 2007; Lee, 2009), while others underline the 'human security' dimension (UNDP, 2007).

With the onset of scholarly debates on climate security, increasingly, scholars also started to analyse domestic and international policies to respond to this problem. At the domestic level, US policy has attracted most of the attention (Kimble, 2005; Busby, 2008; Campbell and Parthemore, 2008; Dabelko, 2009). The discussion in the United States was boosted in 2009 with a report called 'Global Climate Change Impacts in the United States' (Karl et al., 2009), commissioned by the US government. At the international level, scholars (Francesco, 2007; Penny, 2007; Sindico, 2007; Scott, 2009) have been focusing mostly on the first-ever debate on climate change held by the UNSC in 2007. Other early instances of environmental security analysis are discussed by De Wilde (2008).

Vogler (2002) examined the early efforts by the EU to securitise the environment. In order to 'understand how the EU (and indeed NATO) have approached the question of environmental security' (Vogler, 2002: 183), he referred in his analysis to the Copenhagen School of Security and particularly to the concept of securitisation. At the time of writing his contribution, environmental security only started to modestly appear on the EU agenda. Thus, the analysis focused primarily on examining the input by the European Commission to the Seventh Organisation for Security and Cooperation in Europe (OSCE) Economic Forum in 1999. At that time, the Commission attempted to define environmental security for the EU context. Yet, only after eight years, the EU started to approach environmental security in a more comprehensive manner, shifting the focus from environmental degradation to climate change.

As already indicated, the European Security Strategy (ESS) from 2003 briefly refers to global warming. First, the phenomenon is identified as an aggravator of the competition for natural resources and the potential cause of increased migration. Second, it is mentioned along with terrorism and the proliferation of WMDs as a kind of development which international law must take into account to preserve the 'rule-based international order' (Council, 2003a: 9). In 2008, the European Council revised the implementation of the ESS and reconsidered international security priorities for Europe (European Council, 2008). In the part concerning climate security, the Implementation Report refers to the most comprehensive official EU document on the consequences of climate change for international security, that is the Joint Report of the Commission and High Representative (HR) entitled 'Climate Change and International Security' (HR and European Commission, 2008).

This document lists potential security problems which may be induced by climate change in the near future. For example, it envisages that the altering of rainfall patterns will reduce freshwater availability by 20–30 per cent in vulnerable regions. Furthermore, food productivity may decrease in least developing countries. Another issue pointed out by the Joint Report is the so-called eco-migration, which is migration triggered by the shortages of food and water. Furthermore, the competition over energy resources could be the most profound result of climate change. The document concludes with a number of recommendations, such as the need for strengthening the analysis, research and monitoring capacities as well as reinforcing the EU's leadership role in multilateral climate change negotiations.

The EU policy developments in the area of climate security have taken place in parallel with its general climate change policy, such as the negotiations within the framework of the United Nations Framework Convention on Climate Change (UNFCCC). The EU climate security policy is driven forward primarily by a small group of officials working in the major EU institutions as well as a number of EU Member States.

In addition to evaluating the EU's role as an international security actor in climate change more broadly, this chapter also discusses the role of this group of 'norm entrepreneurs' in diffusing climate security norms within the EU and at the UN level. More specifically, the analysis in this chapter unfolds in the following manner. In the first section, the question of the EU's scope of integration in climate security is discussed, looking particularly at the role of supranational institutions and the legal framework in this policy area. Subsequently, the chapter assesses the capabilities of the EU to undertake actions addressing the security consequences of climate change. Finally, it is important to examine the extent to which the EU is recognised as an actor in climate security policy.

The EU and climate security: scope of integration

Just like how the EU's policy on the environment and climate change remains a shared competence of the EU and Member States, the security dimension of climate change has also been developed jointly by central EU bureaucracies and a few active Member States. The leadership in this regard has been undertaken by the so-called Steering Group on Climate Change and International Security (the Steering Group), initiated in 2008 to develop the security dimension of climate change policy within the EU (Zwolski and Kaunert, 2011). The Steering Group has been coordinated by the Commission and the Council Secretariat and involves a number of Member States who are particularly interested in the EU climate security agenda, including Germany, the Netherlands and Sweden. In fact, this group can be conceptualised as an epistemic community. According to Haas (1992), there are four main variables which can help to establish whether certain groups display the characteristics of an epistemic community. These include the following: (1) a common causal belief; (2) a common principled belief; (3) a common notion of validity; and (4) a common policy enterprise. Elsewhere, the authors demonstrate that the Steering Group fulfils these criteria (Zwolski and Kaunert, 2011).

The European Commission has been active in contributing to the EU's role as an international security actor in climate change. In addition to its extensive expertise in leading the EU's efforts on climate change more generally, the institution also got involved in developing the security dimension of this phenomenon. In particular, the climate security agenda was developed in Directorate General for External Relations (DG Relex), before this part of the Commission was integrated into the European External Action Service (EEAS). DG Relex's involvement in climate security complemented the Commission's role in environmental and climate change policy more broadly, which are primarily the competences of DG Environment. Consequently, DG Relex has traditionally had very limited representation at the annual summits of the UNFCCC. As one Commission official explains, 'you really need technical background to participate in these negotiations. We, in DG Relex, are concerned with international security and therefore we cannot add value in the area of the science of climate change' (COM-A, 2009). Consequently, DG Relex was concerned with advancing the EU's climate security agenda. In particular, DG Relex considered itself a contributor to the debate on climate change, emphasising that, if unchecked, it will have profound consequences to security and stability in the most vulnerable regions. The Commission emphasises that because there is a strong link between development and security, the EU's response must be comprehensive. To this end, one interviewee explains that the EU climate security approach must be integrated into other areas of the EU policy: 'It is not about some people holding climate change portfolio, but rather it is about networks where we can lobby to implement appropriate policies; we work in networks, not in solos' (COM-A, 2009). Thus, the contribution of DG Relex to addressing the problem of climate security could be conceptualised as follows (COM-A, 2009):

(a) DG Relex worked closely with other Commission DGs, disseminating their ideas and policies;
(b) DG Relex supported integrating climate change agenda into the external relations of the EU, most notably into its development policy;
(c) DG Relex supported the networks which it was a part of.

The Council General Secretariat, before it was rearranged following the establishment of the EEAS, was divided into functional DGs, a horizontal Legal Service and a number of units subordinate directly to the Secretary General. One of them was the Policy Unit (initially Policy Planning and Early Warning Unit), established under the provisions of the Amsterdam Treaty in 1999. In order to understand the role of the Policy Unit in developing the EU climate security agenda, it is important to note that its role (as well as the role of the DG E – External and Political-Military Affairs) in European foreign policy used to go beyond purely administrative tasks. In fact, both institutions have played 'an important conceptual and operational role in preparing, steering and ensuring follow-up of decisions in working groups, the PSC, COREPER and the Council' (Keukeleire and MacNaughtan, 2008: 83). The Policy Unit was divided into several Task Forces. Most of them were geographical, but there was also one on the CSDP and one called the Horizontal Security Affairs, Conflict Prevention and Human Rights Task Force. This Task Force used to be concerned with challenges that were transnational in nature, such as cyber-terrorism, energy, food security and climate change. The officials of this Task Force used to meet regularly at plenary sessions with representatives of EU Member States and an official from the Commission. This is how one official from the Council Secretariat described the early stages of developing the EU climate security agenda: 'Sometimes in the Policy Unit we meet to have brainstorming and this is when we look at new subjects raising on the international agenda. In 2007, we started looking at the correlation between water and security. Very soon we realised that we cannot limit our research to water, but that we have to go one step further and look at the challenge of climate change' (CON-C, 2009).

These new developments within the Council Secretariat were in line with the agenda of the German Presidency during the first half of 2007, which prioritised climate protection and energy. Since then, the Council Secretariat was regularly involved in promoting the climate security agenda within the EU and externally. In December 2008, it co-organised one of the side events at the UNFCCC summit in Poznan, called 'Climate Change & Security – The Next steps'. It brought together officials and experts from the EU as well as representatives of regions potentially endangered by climate change, such as Micronesia. On a bigger scale, in April 2008, the Council Secretariat co-organised a workshop on conflict prevention and climate change, which took place in the Justus Lipsius building of the Council. The former Council's Secretary General and the EU's High Representative for the CFSP, Javier Solana, also insisted that the security consequences of climate change must be taken into serious consideration at the global level (Solana, 2009).

In addition to the Commission and Council General Secretariat, the European Parliament (EP) has also been active in initiating and facilitating debate on climate security. It is interesting to note that the EP became involved in this area much earlier than the Commission and the Council. However, it does not necessarily entail that the EP is more progressive in its understanding of security compared to the other EU institutions. The reason why the EP initiated the debate on climate security already in 1999 is the fact that Mr Tom Spencer was chairing the EP's Foreign Affairs Committee (FAC) at the time. Spencer was interested in this particular topic as, prior to assuming this new role, he was the President of GLOBE International (Global Legislators Organisation for a Balanced Environment). Currently he is the Vice-Chairman of the Institute for Environmental Security (IES). In 1999, as Chairman of the EP's FAC, Spencer was allowed to propose an 'Own Initiative Report'. He recalls that, when he suggested preparing the paper on environmental security, there was a lot of scepticism and disregard towards this topic (Spencer, 2006). However, eventually his own ideas were combined with another report on the 'Role of the Military in Cleaning Up the Environment' prepared by Maj Britt Theorin. The final product went beyond an exclusive focus on the military and provided a broader outlook on climate change security (European Parliament, 1999).

The institutional reforms stemming from the provisions of the Lisbon Treaty prompt two questions necessitating further empirical investigation. First, to what extent is the European Council going to undertake leadership on climate security policy? Second, how will the bureaucratic rearrangements of the EU's external action impact the position of climate security agenda in the EU? The European Council has been both an engine and an obstacle in developing the EU's climate security policy. First, the European Council requested the Joint Report in June 2007, indicating a growing interest of Member States in this topic (Council, 2007a). However, in the subsequent year, the French Presidency referred the climate security agenda to the Agriculture and Fisheries Council, which in its December 2008 meeting merely 'took note of a report containing recommendations from the EU High Representative for the Foreign and Security Policy concerning climate change and international security' (Council, 2008b). The Lisbon Treaty provided for the establishment of the permanent President of the European Council, elected for two and a half years, in place of the rotating Presidency. This can, potentially, introduce more continuity to the EU's international security agenda, but the prominence of climate security in the EU will inevitably be affected by the economic crisis in the euro-zone.

The Lisbon Treaty has also rearranged central bureaucracies, bringing DG Relex and part of the Council General Secretariat into the EEAS, where EU officials are further joined by national representatives. The core of the EEAS structure constitutes geographical and thematic Directorates, including the one on Global and Multilateral Issues. It is further divided into four units, including the following: (a) multilateral relations and global governance; (b) human rights and democracy; (c) conflict prevention and security policy; and (d) non-proliferation and disarmament. Climate security agenda could be potentially incorporated into any of the first three units, but its prominence vis-à-vis other policy priorities will primarily depend on the leadership role of the High Representative.

The scope of European integration in climate security remains ambiguous. Following the adoption of the Joint Report on Climate Change and International Security and subsequent establishment of the Steering Group, it appeared that the role of EU institutions would continue to grow in this policy area. Notably, the European Commission and the Council General Secretariat provided leadership and their efforts were further strengthened by the involvement of a number of Member States. Following the implementation of the Lisbon Treaty reforms, the institutional units responsible for developing the security dimension of climate change have been largely incorporated into the EEAS, and it is unclear what the position of climate security on the EEAS agenda is going to be. Early conclusions are even more problematic, considering that at this early stage, it is still difficult to assess the role and position of the EEAS in contributing to the EU's international security role.

What remains unchanged is the continuous interest among some of the Member States in pursuing climate security agenda at the international level. For example, in July 2011, Germany re-introduced climate change to the UNSC, following the first debate on this topic which was organised by the British Presidency of the UNSC in 2007. Germany was supported in this debate by other EU Member States as well as by the Head of the EU Delegation to the United Nations, speaking on behalf of the EU. These intergovernmental efforts at the international level help to promote the recognition of climate security as one of the modern challenges, but the international position of the EU on climate security can be significantly strengthened if climate security is firmly identified as one of the core security agendas within the new institutional structure of the EU.

The EU and climate security: capabilities

When assessing the capabilities of the EU in the area of climate security, a broad approach is in order to capture material resources, such as those related to intelligence gathering capacity, but also some of the underlying enabling conditions which enhance the EU's 'actorness' in the area of climate security policy. Consequently, the analysis commences with a brief overview of ideological capabilities, most importantly a particular approach to the question of international security in the EU, followed by key capabilities understood in a more traditional sense, such as research policy and intelligence gathering. This indicates that positive integration instruments play the key role in enabling the EU to develop its 'actorness' in climate security policy. It was established in the previous chapter that the EU can pursue its security objectives by the utilisation of negative and positive instruments. Negative integration instruments entail mutual recognition among Member States in a given policy issue and are more appropriate for internal security objectives. Positive integration instruments are more relevant for international security policy; they include regulation and/or capacity-building measures.

Notably, non-traditional security problems require, in particular, the utilisation of longer-term preventive, capacity-building measures, due to the very nature of these problems. Intervention, which is another positive integration instrument, is typically not appropriate for tackling the so-called new security issues. This does not preclude that, in the medium- to long-term, intervention will not be appropriate to address the possible violent consequences of climate change in vulnerable regions. According to the German Advisory Council on Global Change, there are four possible conflict constellations related to climate change: (a) climate-induced degradation of freshwater resources can lead to violent conflicts; (b) climate-induced decline in food production can also lead to violent conflicts; (c) climate-induced increase in storm and flood disasters can trigger public disorder and in consequence lead to violent conflicts; and (d) notable rise in environmentally induced migration can also trigger violent conflicts (WBGU, 2007). Naturally, capacity-building instruments deployed to understand the problem and prevent violence typically necessitate significant financial commitments on the part of the main stakeholders. Research and assistance to less developed countries are all important in understanding climate change and addressing some of its consequences, but they also bring the expectation that richer EU countries will share more burden.

As already emphasised in the theoretical chapter, the EU follows a broad, pro-active approach to international security, which emphasises the complexity of security challenges and the necessity for a comprehensive response to some of the threats. In this chapter, the broad approach to security is considered a non-material asset because it provides fundamental, enabling conditions for the EU to develop other policies on climate security. In this approach to international security, reacting to international threats, such as terrorism, represents only one type of a necessary action. Equally important is to pro-actively contribute to the development of conditions preventing the emergence of security problems in the first place.

With regard to climate change, it is widely understood in Europe that even though this phenomenon may have implications for international security, there is no 'hard security' response to this problem. As the UK Foreign Secretary's Special Representative for Climate Change John Ashton points out, 'you cannot force your neighbour to change its carbon emissions at the barrel of a gun' (quoted in Vogel, 2007). This means that a different kind of response is necessary. Importantly for the EU, this is where its added value is considerable, taking into account the variety of resources at its disposal. In order to better understand the kinds of responses necessary, according to one European Commission official, the subject of climate security now needs to be broken down, in order to identify its impact on migration, state failure, radicalisation, rising of the sea levels and the availability of food. The official also admits that 'at some point we may even lose the phrase "climate change" and that's fine, as long as appropriate policies to respond to this problem are integrated into other policy areas' (COM-A, 2009).

Whereas this broad, pro-active approach to security in the EU provides enabling conditions for conceptualising climate change as a 'threat multiplier', the EU's research policy contributes to the provision of scientific data, thus helping to develop regional scenarios of climate change impact. In its research policy, the EU relies on a multitude of external actors. As one Council official notes:

> We, in the EU, know nothing about climate change. Of course, we have some scientists of our own. Yet, when we prepare a specialised report, we draw a lot on external resources. We ask different scientific institutions in different countries, such as Canada, to tell us what is going on' (CON-E, 2009). A Commission representative seconds these remarks, explaining that 'most of EU Member States are well developed countries, so we can use their think tanks, consultancy, etc.
>
> (COM-B, 2009)

The EU's research policy on climate change has different dimensions, focusing on issues such as low carbon technologies as well as challenges of mitigation and adaptation. In the first category, in 2007, the European Commission published a Communication entitled 'A European Strategic Energy Technology Plan (SET-Plan): Towards a Low Carbon Future' (European Commission, 2007b). The main goal of this plan is to accelerate the development of low carbon technologies in the EU, in order to help it reach some ambitious objectives regarding greenhouse gas-emission reductions. To this end, apart from urging additional funding for research in non-carbon technologies, the SET-Plan also aims to foster international research and development (R&D) cooperation. The Communication notes that traditional methods of cooperation between research institutes in different countries, such as joint projects, tend not to deliver satisfactory results. With an objective to help to overcome the fragmentation and duplication of resources in national research on climate change and green technologies, the Commission has proposed the creation of the European Energy Research Alliance (EERA). The EERA was launched in October 2008 by 12 European leading research institutes with the aim 'to strengthen, expand and optimise EU energy research capabilities through the sharing of world-class national facilities in Europe and the joint realisation of pan-European research programmes' (EERA website). Within this framework, national institutes have combined their annual R&D budgets in order to boost their energy research at the EU level.

Furthermore, DG Research of the European Commission funds research on the environment, including climate change, natural hazards and correlation between the environment and health. The key climate change research project funded by the Commission has been 'Adaptation and Mitigation Strategies: Supporting European Climate Policy' (ADAM). The project was initiated in 2006 and finalised in 2009. DG Research funded it with almost €13 million. ADAM was conducted jointly by 26 research institutions in Europe and overseas (Hulme et al., 2009). The ability of the EU to pull resources on climate research constitutes an important asset in itself. Although funding for energy and climate research in the Commission's Seventh Research Framework Programme or DG Research budget may be insufficient, EU-based and EU-funded research constitutes an important input to the development of international research on climate change and the EU's policy on climate change, including the climate security dimension.

The broad approach to security in the EU and its active research policy enhance other capacities contributing to the international 'actorness' of the EU on climate security. One of these capacities is the ability of the EU to mainstream climate change into its other policies, including international security policy. For the EU's external relations, one Commission official explains how this mainstreaming can work: 'In Bolivia we spend money on fighting poverty, drug trafficking and on creating a friendly environment for business development. If I go there and tell them to shift the money to combat climate change, they will tell me that, first, they need to make sure that people do not die of poverty. But what I can do is to emphasise how important climate change is, and, to suggest how this challenge can be integrated into other programmes' (COM-A, 2009). Similarly, for the UN level, the EU proposed to mainstream climate change into 'national, foreign, development, environmental, trade and security policies' (European Union, 2009). Importantly, the EU's size and its range of bilateral contacts constitute a significant capability in its own right, particularly when undertaking streamlining efforts at the international level. By the end of 2009, the EU raised the issue of climate security with more than 40 countries, including Australia, the United States, Brazil, China, Egypt, India, Indonesia, Israel and Russia (Council, 2009). Thus, the EU's weight helps to internationalise the norm of climate security in international politics, which in turn contributes to the recognition of the EU in this policy field.

Finally, reacting effectively to the consequences of climate change requires early warning capabilities. If the EU aspires to address potential security problems multiplied by climate change, it needs to be able to know as far in advance as possible what is about to happen in which region of the world. This is why the EU needs to further develop early warning capabilities and to adjust those already in existence to take into account the potential consequences of climate change. To achieve this objective, the EU aims to employ a wide array of institutions that it has at its disposal, such as the EU Satellite Centre and the Joint Research Centre of the European Commission (Council, 2008a). Towards the end of 2009, some early progress in this area was already achieved, such as the improved satellite monitoring of the Arctic ice-fields to assess the probability of the emergence of new Arctic routes or the monitoring of coastline changes (Council, 2009).

Capabilities constitute one of the key prerequisites of a political unit to become an international actor in a given policy area. However, climate change as a security problem poses significant challenges in this respect. For example, in contrast to more traditional security problems, the phenomenon of climate change as such remains discussed or even disputed, undermining the ability of actors to mobilise necessary resources. Furthermore, the link between climate change and security is ambiguous. Different international and non-governmental institutions have produced a wealth of possible medium- to long-term scenarios of how climate change may impact international security. However, to fully take them into account, the understanding of security itself would have to change, which proves difficult particularly beyond the Western world, as witnessed in UN Security Council debates. This entails not only incorporating the 'human' dimension into security considerations but also approaching security as a cooperative effort, rather than one focused on alliances and enmity.

The EU and climate security: recognition

The review of scholarly research on the EU and climate change allows to conclude that, in general, the EU is recognised as an important actor in this policy area (for example, Bretherton and Vogler, 2006; Cameron, 2007a; Schreurs and Tiberghien, 2007; Keukeleire and MacNaughtan, 2008; Kiliam and Elgström, 2010). Bretherton and Vogler (2006: 89) note that the role of the EU 'extends beyond participation in particular negotiations to encompass the propagation of environmental norms, the pursuit of sustainable development and, perhaps the most important of all, leadership of attempts to curb the menace of climate change'. A representative of the Brussels-based environmental NGO similarly concludes that 'we can debate whether the EU is a leader by default or because of a certain plan, but the EU is a leader. It is the only organisation in the world with clear numerical targets and such an ambitious policy' (NGO-A, 2009). Although at the climate change summit in Copenhagen in 2009, the EU was widely considered to remain in the back seat (Washington Post, 2009), it nonetheless remains one of the most important international actors in this policy area. How does this recognition translate into a narrower field of climate security policy?

As already mentioned, the EU attempts to establish climate security as an accepted norm of international relations (IR). In other words, it has undertaken an effort to promote the view that in addition to significant environmental and developmental consequences, climate change will also impact international security. Finnemore and Sikkink (1998) have particularly advanced the constructivist understanding of how norms emerge and diffuse in the international system. The authors suggest a three-stage model of a norm 'life cycle'. According to this model, the first stage involves 'norm emergence', the second stage involves 'norm acceptance', which the authors term 'norm cascade', and the third stage involves 'internalisation'. The second stage of the norm life cycle is of particular interest; it is characterised by a socialisation process – norm leaders are imitated by followers. After a certain 'tipping point', more actors adopt the norm. In order to achieve this socialisation, norm followers are praised while those who deviate are ridiculed. Norm entrepreneurs use mechanisms of persuasion in order to convince a critical mass of actors to embrace a norm. These entrepreneurs have strong notions of appropriate behaviour, and they are absolutely critical for success. Norms never enter a normative vacuum but instead access a highly contested space in which they need to compete with other norms. One condition for entrepreneurs at the international level is some kind of organisational platform from which to promote their norm.

One of the key institutional forums for debating the security consequences of climate change is the UNSC, which up to date held two debates on this topic – both introduced by EU Member States. In 2007, the initiative was put forward by the British Presidency and in 2011 the discussion was introduced by the German Presidency. Both debates were supported by the EU: in 2007, the EU was represented at the Security Council table by the German Minister for Economic Integration and Development, and in 2011 the block was represented by the Head of Delegation of the EU to the United Nations. The EU as a block only has an observer status within the United Nations, which means that it does not have the right to vote. Yet, it can participate in UNSC discussions on the basis of Rule 39 of the Security Council's Provisional Rules of Procedure, which states: 'The Security Council may invite members of the Secretariat or other persons, whom it considers competent for the purpose, to supply it with information or to give other assistance in examining matters within its competence.'

The climate security debates in 2007 and 2011 proved controversial, exposing often diverging understandings of security. Most importantly, many countries did not recognise the Security Council as an appropriate body to discuss climate change. For example, China pointed out that the institution 'has neither the professional competence in handling climate change – nor is it the right decision-making place for extensive participation leading up to widely acceptable proposals' (UNSC, 2007a). Furthermore, Pakistan, speaking on behalf of the 'Group of 77' and China, underlined that other bodies, such as the Economic and Social Council and the General Assembly, are more appropriate to address climate change (UNSC, 2007a).

Following the first Security Council debate on climate change, the EU, in cooperation with small island states, continued to work on the possible consequences of climate change for international security. They have found the UN General Assembly to be a more 'friendly' body to discuss the issue. In its 63rd plenary meeting in May 2009, the UN General Assembly requested the UN Secretary General to prepare a 'comprehensive report' on the possible security implications of climate change and to present it in September 2009 (UNGA, 2009). The EU continued to play an important role in this process; Ban Ki-moon even asked the EU to deliver its point of view on the issue (COM-E, 2009; CON-G, 2010). The document which the EU submitted to the UN Secretary General constitutes a direct attempt to diffuse EU climate security norms at the UN level (European Union, 2009). It was drafted by the very same officials from the European Commission and the Council Secretariat, who coordinate the activities of the aforementioned Steering Group, plus the Swedish EU Presidency of the time. The document, in its recommendations, outlines the policies which were undertaken at the EU level, noting that these policies 'may also be relevant for the UN-system' (European Union, 2009). One specific mechanism which the EU suggested to introduce at the UN level, as already indicated, is the mainstreaming of climate security into other UN policies. This fact suggests that even though the existence of climate change on the international security agenda is a relatively recent development, the EU has already established itself, at the UN level, as a recognised actor in this area.

Further preliminary conclusions can be drawn from the analysis of the EU documents. Most importantly, after the Joint Report was published in 2008, the Council Secretariat and the Commission, in cooperation with a number of Member States, have initiated the aforementioned Steering Group. This Steering Group has adopted the so-called Road Map for its activities in the area of climate security in 2008 and 2009, in the run-up to the summit in Copenhagen (COM-E, 2009). Three broad categories of planned actions have been identified:

(a) developing dialogue with third countries and international organisations (most notably the United Nations) in the form of bilateral discussions as well as conferences and workshops on the security consequences of climate change;
(b) launching new studies and scenarios on regional risks; and
(c) building capabilities at the EU level.

To advance the recognition of climate change as a legitimate concern of international security, the EU aims to become a leading actor promoting the norm of climate security at the international level. In fact, the 'global leadership' ambition has been expressed in a number of EU official documents. For example, the Joint Report from March 2008 contains a section about 'EU multilateral leadership to promote global climate security' (HR and European Commission, 2008: 10). Furthermore, the document from December 2009, formally reporting on the activities of the Steering Group to the Council, mentions 'the EU as a global leader on CCIS [climate change and international security] and its added value as partner and facilitator' (Council, 2009: 5). In the run-up to the Copenhagen summit in 2009, the following activities have been undertaken at the international level by the Steering Group (Council, 2009). The list is not exhaustive. All of these activities contribute to the recognition of the EU as an actor in the area of climate security:

(a) In the context of bilateral relations, the EU raised the issue of climate security with more than 40 countries, including Australia, the United States, Brazil, China, Egypt, India, Indonesia, Israel and Russia.
(b) South-East Asia: The EU, together with the ASEAN Regional Forum, organised a seminar 'International security implications of climate-related events and trends'.
(c) Mediterranean and Middle East: The EU continues to raise the issue of climate security at all levels.
(d) Central Asia: The EU, particularly under the EU Water Initiative (an initiative through which the EU aims to achieve water-related Millennium Development Goals), conducts numerous projects in the region. Water and environment constitute the priorities of the EU–Central Asia Strategy.
(e) Latin America: The May 2010 EU–Latin America Summit put sustainable development and social inclusion on top of the agenda.

These early examples indicate that, through a variety of initiatives, the EU has been able to start introducing climate security agenda into relations with other countries and organisations. This also suggests that the EU begins to be recognised as an actor who is legitimate and has capabilities to address the challenge of the security consequences of climate change. One of the key forums for the EU in this regard has been the United Nations. One official from the Council Secretariat indicates that the EU has had a strong influence over discussions on climate security in the UN General Assembly in 2009. To this end, he notes that the EU has helped to 'push the debate ahead' through the activities of EU Member States (CON-G, 2010).

When assessing the recognition of the EU as a security actor in climate change, it is important to recognise the role of the European Commission as a norm and policy entrepreneur and an important actor in its own right. The Commission has been particularly strongly recognised within the framework of the UNFCCC negotiations, due to factors such as the following: (a) the fact that the environment and climate change are the areas of shared competence between the EU and Member States;

(b) as a result of this provision, the Commission has a considerable representation in international climate change talks; (c) Commission officials do not rotate as frequently as the representatives of Member States in the Council, thus external actors get to know individuals from the Commission, working on specific issue areas; and (d) the complex nature of issues discussed during the UNFCCC negotiations enables the Commission to develop a high level of expertise, thus further enhancing its recognition among other partners and among EU Member States.

In the context of developing the security dimension of climate change, the Commission (and the EU more broadly) managed to develop a close relationship with the community of NGOs. The element of continuity plays an important role in this respect and recognition is mutual. In this context, Sherrington (2000) indicates that the political system of the EU, with the formal and informal policy processes, offers 'windows' for policy entrepreneurs such as think-tanks, allowing them to influence EU policy-making. One official from the European Commission working on climate security policy admits that the role of NGOs is fundamental: 'The participation of civil society is crucial for the work of the Commission and it is a "black and white" requirement on our part to do this. There is a lot of added value to our work in this process' (COM-E, 2009).

Conclusion

The EU's 'actorness' in climate security is a complex phenomenon, with some distinctive features not present to such a degree in the case of more traditional security threats discussed in this book. Most importantly, developing and internalising the norm of climate security at the global level by the EU is a 'work in progress'. In contrast to other security problems, such as terrorism and WMDs, climate change has only partially been accepted by the international community as a security threat or 'threat multiplier'. Thus, a significant portion of the EU's 'actorness' in this area consists of promoting the view that climate change requires an urgent and robust international response, partly because it will impact the international security and stability.

This chapter has indicated that there is an epistemic community in the EU, which promotes the norm of climate security. This epistemic community believes that climate change already has, or will have in the near future, consequences for international security and stability; therefore, urgent action is necessary. This group consists of a number of officials from the EU institutions (who are facilitating and driving the

EU climate security agenda), a few Member States and think-tanks (all of which are active in Brussels). Within the structure of the EU, the activities of this epistemic community used to be advanced by an informal Steering Group, coordinated by a few officials from the European Commission and the Council Secretariat. Since its creation in March 2008, the Steering Group has been active in promoting climate security. This task is easier at the EU level, where all Member States, in principle, do not object to the creation of this new norm anymore, and in fact have already accepted it. However, it is somewhat more difficult at the level of the United Nations, where more traditional notions of security still prevail among the UN Member States.

This chapter has also contributed to academic debates about the correlation between climate change and international security. It does not make assumptions about such a correlation; instead, it adds a new element to the literature on climate security policies of different international actors. Unsurprisingly, given their importance for international security, so far the literature has focused primarily on US climate security policy as well as on debates in the UN Security Council. This chapter has contributed to this literature by analysing the EU as a relatively recent security actor aspiring to raise its profile in IR. In particular, this 'actorness' has been assessed against three criteria of 'actorness', including the scope of integration, capabilities and recognition.

It has been empirically demonstrated that the EU enjoys a relatively high scope of integration in climate change. The policy entrepreneurship of central EU institutions has been of crucial importance in this respect, supported by a number of Member States. This reflects the fact that environmental policy more broadly remains a shared competence of the EU and Member States. Although the Lisbon Treaty does not introduce any changes to this arrangement, it nonetheless has provided for a significant rearrangement of the EU's foreign and security policy apparatus. Parts of the European Commission and the Council Secretariat have been moved to the newly established EEAS, and this raises questions about the future policy leadership on climate security. A strong incentive in this regard will have to come from the High Representative, who now is also the Vice-President of the Commission, thus having sufficient mandate to further develop the EU's 'actorness' in this policy area.

The case of capabilities is peculiar, because a non-traditional security problem of climate change requires non-traditional capabilities. Among these, the most important is a particular approach to security policy, which allows for including problems such as climate change on the security agenda. The EU's Security Strategies from 2003 and 2008 demonstrate that this broadened approach to security has been accepted in the EU. However, material capacities are also important. Among those, as the annual UNFCCC summits have amply demonstrated, is funding for adaptation to climate change in developing countries. The EU not only is an active player within the global multilateral framework but also attempts to commit relevant resources internally. Within the EU, research was identified as one of the key priorities to advance the EU's 'actorness' in climate change policy more broadly, but also specifically with regard to climate security.

This chapter has established that the EU is relatively well recognised as a global leader on climate security, although its global role in climate change may have decreased following the UNFCCC Copenhagen summit in December 2009, when the EU did not manage to secure its preferred outcomes. Notwithstanding the EU's role as a climate change policy leader, the Union has quickly advanced its position in a narrower policy area of climate security. This recognition is partially facilitated by the fact that the correlation between security and climate change remains ambiguous and many states are reluctant to incorporate environmental considerations into their security policies. This offers the EU a leverage and an opportunity to act as a 'norm entrepreneur' at the global level, attempting to establish climate security as an accepted norm relevant for the UNSC to debate. However, the future of the EU's leadership even in this narrower policy field is uncertain, following Lisbon Treaty-induced institutional reforms and the economic crisis. The leadership of the High Representative and of the President of the European Council will play a crucial role in this respect.

4
The EU and Counter-Terrorism

This chapter examines the second empirical case: the European Union (EU) counter-terrorism. Empirical developments seem to point to an ever-increasing role of terrorism on the security agenda of the EU. On 7 July 2005, four young Islamist suicide-bombers attacked London's transport system, killing 52 members of the public and injuring several hundred more. The perpetrators were British, the children of Pakistani immigrants. The London bombings were the first attacks on UK soil to be carried out as part of the global jihad, which was, of course, preceded by the horrific attacks on the United States on 11 September 2001 and on Spain on 11 March 2004 (Kaunert et al., 2012). Despite setbacks, militants continue to plan attacks, as evidenced by the 2007 suicide attack on Glasgow airport. On 14 May 2010, a young girl, Roshonara Choudhry, radicalised by Al Qaeda and antagonised by the War in Iraq, stabbed the British MP Timms almost fatally. In October 2010, warnings against terrorist attacks were issued in France, Germany and other European countries, and, subsequently, bomb packages sent from Yemen, designed to go off on a US-bound aircraft, were intercepted. This confirms the sentiments of the EU Terrorism Situation and Trend Report (Europol, 2011), published by Europol in 2010. In this, Islamist terrorism is still underlined as the biggest threat to most EU Member States, which many analysts still hold to be true despite the killing of Osama bin Laden in May 2011. The report suggests that the threat emanating from Islamist terrorism is driven by developments in countries such as Afghanistan, the Afghanistan–Pakistan border area, Iraq, Somalia and Yemen.

In this context, it is worthwhile to specify the understanding of terrorism underpinning this analysis (Kaunert, 2010a, 2010b, 2010c). Whilst recognising that there is no globally agreed definition of terrorism

(Wilkinson, 2006), this chapter will use the following working definition: 'the calculated use of violence or the threat of violence to inculcate fear, intended to coerce or intimidate governments or societies as to the pursuit of goals that are generally political, religious or ideological' (Wilkinson, 2006). This operational definition notwithstanding, it is recognised that an understanding of terrorism is an inherently political and calculated process (Hoffman, 2006). Forms of terrorism are often categorised according to the political motivations of the perpetrators (Hoffman, 2006; Wilkinson, 2006):

(1) Ethno-nationalist groups: these are secular terrorist groups aiming to achieve an ethno-nationalist ambition, such as the creation of a new state. Examples in this category are the groups such as Euskadi Ta Askatasuna (ETA) in Spain, the Irish Republican Army (IRA) in Britain or the Palestine Liberation Organization (PLO) in Israel-/Palestinian-Occupied Territories.
(2) Ideological groups: these are secular terrorist groups motivated by different ideologies, such as Marxism, Maoism, Anarchism and so on. Examples of such groups are the former Red Brigades in Italy, the Red Army Fraction (RAF) or Baader-Meinhof Gang in Germany, the FARC in Colombia or the Shining Path in Peru.
(3) Religio-political groups: these are non-secular, religiously motivated terrorist groups, such as Hamas with the objective of an Islamic Republic of Palestine, or Al Qaeda with the objective of a Pan-Islamic Caliphate in the Middle East.

With the terrorist attacks on the United States (11 September 2001), Madrid (11 March 2004) and London (07 July 2005) as well as the failed attempts on 21 July 2005, Al Qaeda increasingly emerged as the most dangerous terrorist organisation to EU member States, despite the killing of Osama bin Laden in 2011. According to terrorism scholars (Hoffman, 2006; Wilkinson, 2006), Al Qaeda mainly aims to (1) establish the Shari'a religious law across Muslim lands in order to facilitate the arrival of the 'Messiah'; (2) expel the United States and 'infidels' from Middle East and Muslim lands; (3) topple Muslim regimes that 'betray' true Islam; (4) ultimately establish a Pan-Islamist 'Caliphate', reminiscent of the 'glorious days' of the Ottoman Empire; and (5) lead a Jihad ('holy war') against the United States and its allies (not only the United Kingdom and Spain but, increasingly, also other European countries such as Germany, France and Italy), and set up a 'World Islamic Front for Jihad'. For EU Member States, the danger that Al Qaeda represents mainly relates to its specific organisation and structure, which make European cooperation crucial in order to tackle it (Hoffman, 2006; Wilkinson, 2006). Its structure is that of a large transnational movement or network, rather than a traditional 'terrorist' organisation. This makes it more difficult to establish good intelligence in a mono-national setting. Al Qaeda's *modus operandi* requires a response based on strong transnational cooperation. Furthermore, Al Qaeda has a large presence in over 60 countries; making it the most widely dispersed terrorist movement in history. In contrast to this requirement of cooperation to effectively tackle the threat represented by Al Qaeda, the situation in the EU at the time of the terrorist attacks on 11 September 2001 was characterised by a general lack of cooperation in counter-terrorism.

Amongst scholars of EU counter-terrorism, there are diverging opinions as to which extent EU competences matter in the fight against the global terrorist threat (Reinares, 2000; den Boer and Monar, 2002; Dubois, 2002; Occhipinti, 2003; Friedrichs, 2005; Gregory, 2005; Kaunert, 2005, 2007, 2010a, 2010b, 2010c; Bures, 2006, 2011; Deflem, 2006; Zimmermann, 2006; Mitsilegas and Gilmore, 2007; Spence, 2007; Bossong, 2008; den Boer et al., 2008; Müller-Wille, 2008). On the one hand, the EU is characterised as a 'paper tiger' (Bures, 2006; 2011) and thus an ineffective counter-terrorism actor. On the other hand, scholars point out that the EU has taken great strides towards increasing integration and encouraging co-operation between member-states since 9/11 (Zimmermann, 2006; Kaunert, 2007, 2010c). Zimmermann (2006: 123) asserted that 'on 21 September 2001, the Union prioritised the fight against terrorism, and accelerated the development and implementation of measures deliberated on prior to the events of 9/11'. Yet, Zimmermann (2006: 126) makes an important caveat to all EU action in the field of counter-terrorism: '[...] the Union does not have a "normal" government at the supranational level with all the requisite powers, competences, and hence, capabilities of regular government; it is not a federal European state'. This means, *a priori*, one would not necessarily expect EU institutions to provide significant leadership in counter-terrorism. These examples underline the complexity of the security environment, shaped by the threat of terrorism, in which the EU functions. In order to deal with these, the EU has undertaken a number of coordinated actions, including, among others, the adoption of the EU Security Strategy in 2003, the Information Management Strategy of 2009 and the Internal Security Strategy of 2010. However, despite those efforts to provide a direction and achieve more concerted European action in the field of security, there are still many unanswered questions about the extent to which the European approach is really sufficiently strategic.

The EU counter-terrorism policy has also begun to receive significant scholarly attention (Spence, 2007). The Journal of Common Market Studies published a special issue on this topic in January 2008. The introductory article (Edwards and Meyer, 2008: 1) suggests that the entire 'governance of the European Union has been changed through its responses to international terrorism'. This is not a surprising claim when one considers that European security scholars frequently identify terrorism as one of the most salient security threats in the public perception across Europe. This leads Edwards and Meyer to present the surprising finding that 'the politics of counter-terrorism have contributed to the blurring of differences between the so-called three pillars established by the Maastricht Treaty' (ibid.: 11). However, counter-terrorism, while clearly one of the most crucial security policy fields within the EU, is also one of the most complicated areas in institutional terms. Counter-terrorism is, of course, a broad term which can encompass measures across all the former three pillars of the pre-Lisbon Treaty, from trade sanction of state sponsors of terrorism (in pillar 1 and 2), to the implementation of UN Security Council resolutions (pillar 2), to police and judicial cooperation (pillar 3). Therefore, it is important to keep in mind the cross-pillar character of the EU counter-terrorism policy when drawing conclusions on the role of EU institutions from the following analysis, as they can only be generalised to the pillar concerned.

With this caveat, it must be underlined that the analysis of the EU counter-terrorism policy, precisely because of its institutional specificity, yields results of particular interest to those interested in EU policymaking more generally and in the Area of Freedom, Security and Justice (AFSJ), particularly. Counter-terrorism in this book represents a security threat between non-traditional and traditional security threats. While it is a very old phenomenon in global politics, dating back to many centuries, it achieved particular political salience only after the 9/11 attacks on the United States. Contrary to their role in the adoption of EU asylum policy, which will be discussed in more detail in the subsequent chapter, the EU institutions have actively dealt with terrorism as a security threat, for the most part, in particular the European Commission when proposing the European Arrest Warrant (EAW) after 9/11. This chapter, offering an empirical analysis of the EU's role in addressing this issue, is structured as follows. Firstly, it investigates the institutional arrangements and legal competences of the EU to develop policies in the area of counter-terrorism. Secondly, it examines the EU resources with respect to developing the security dimension of counter-terrorism. Finally, it investigates the extent to which the EU has been recognised as an actor in this policy area, especially in the context of EU–US counter-terrorism relations.

The EU and counter-terrorism: scope of integration

The scope of integration, identified as the first criterion of 'actorness', is defined as 'the procedures according to which policy decisions are taken focusing on the involvement of supranational bodies and Council voting rules' (Börzel, 2005: 220), much of which was explained in Chapter 2 for the area of EU counter-terrorism. What requires further empirical investigation is the involvement of supranational institutions and agencies in the security challenges discussed in this chapter. The extent to which these are involved in a given security policy issue determines the scope of integration in this area. However, this chapter goes even beyond this definition. The scope of integration is determined not only by the EU institutional involvement and legislative rules, such as qualified majority voting (QMV) but also by the *strength of legal instruments* at the disposal of the EU. The area of extradition is a perfect case in point. One of the crucial elements of fighting transnational terrorism is extradition cooperation, which has been revolutionised after 9/11. Despite its importance, however, extradition between EU Member States before the introduction of the EAW was based on a set of different inefficient conventions (Peers, 2001). All EU Member States were bound by the 1957 Council of Europe European Convention on Extradition, seven were bound by a 1975 protocol to the convention and eleven were bound by a 1978 protocol. In addition, all Member States were bound by the 1977 Council of Europe European Convention on Terrorism. The Schengen Implementing Convention of 1990 also contained provisions in this regard. In 1995 and 1996, EU Member States agreed on two conventions, supplementing the aforementioned conventions with regard to extradition in cases where a fugitive consents to it. However, both of these were not ratified by all Member States at the time of the European Commission's proposal on the EAW. This means that, at the time of the EAW proposal, EU Member States were still relying on inefficient and ineffective international conventions in their extradition relationships. These, being constructed as international law, did not have a similar force in law as the EAW. This means, it is very clear how intergovernmental the area was designed at that point. It is difficult to find many other areas in which the institutional role of the Commission has been more restricted.

This chapter will argue that EU institutions have capitalised on the presence of terrorism as a 'security threat' in order to drive forward the process of European integration (Kaunert, 2010c). The adoption of the principle of mutual recognition of judiciary decisions is often seen as the major advance for European integration in criminal justice and counter-terrorism matters. Wagner (2003a) claims that this principle may play a role 'similar to the 1979 Cassis de Dijon judgment of the European Court of Justice [...] which paved the way for the internal market'. In fact, according to Wagner (2003b), the Spanish government and the Commission both worked successfully on establishing this principle at the EU level, which had already been included in a series of Spanish bilateral treaties with Italy, France, the United Kingdom and Belgium.

However, a closer look at the precise point regarding extradition in the Tampere Conclusions makes it clear how many options were still open on the road to the EAW: Point 35:

> With respect to criminal matters, the European Council urges Member States to speedily ratify the 1995 and 1996 EU Conventions on extradition. It considers that the formal extradition procedure should be abolished among the Member States as far as persons are concerned who are fleeing from justice after having been finally sentenced, and replaced by a simple transfer of such persons, in compliance with Article 6 TEU. Consideration should also be given to fast track extradition procedures, without prejudice to the principle of fair trial [...].
>
> (European Council, 1999a)

This demonstrates the fact that the Commission's eventual EAW proposal went much further than the plans based on the 1999 conclusions of the Tampere European Council (Peers, 2001: 2; Wagner, 2003b: 706). Formal extradition was only planned to be abolished for convicted criminals but not for crime suspects as covered by the EAW. The road from 'consideration of fast track extradition procedures' to the EAW is still very long.

After the events of 11 September 2001, the EU adopted a framework to fight more effectively against terrorism. Immediately after the attacks on Washington and New York, the EU process went into action. The Justice and Home Affairs (JHA) Council met on 20 September 2001, agreeing on a package of measures in the fight against terrorism. These were endorsed by an extraordinary European Council meeting on the next day. In the extraordinary Council Meeting on 21 September 2001, held a few days after the attacks in the United States, the European Council launched an ambitious 'Action Plan to Combat Terrorism'. Its cornerstones were 'close cooperation between all the Member States of the EU' and the adoption of a 'coordinated and interdisciplinary approach embracing all Union's policies' (European Council, 2001). The European Council called for the use of all the tools at the EU's disposal, amongst which are legislative and operational, repressive and preventive, internal and external measures. This made the European collective response as comprehensive as possible and essentially multidimensional.

Firstly, the adoption of a Framework Decision on Combating Terrorism is significant. The European Commission presented a proposal to that effect to the aforementioned special meeting of EU JHA ministers in Brussels on countries in September 2001. It intended to put in place a definition of terrorism, alongside penalties and sanctions that come on extradition procedures and mechanisms for exchanging information. Effectively, this is the first time such a definition has been agreed to on a supranational level, especially in the light that a number of Member States did not even have definitions of terrorism (Douglas-Scott, 2004). The EU's Framework Decision on Combating Terrorism, agreed politically in December 2001, firstly defines what is meant by terrorist acts in three parts: (1) the context of an action; (2) the aim of the action; and (3) the specific acts being committed.

> They must be intentional acts [...] which, given their nature or context, may serve to damage a country or an international organisation. These acts must be committed with the aim of either seriously intimidating a population or unduly compelling a Government or international organisation to act or fail to act, or seriously destabilizing or destroying the fundamental political, constitutional economic or social structures of a country or international organisation.
> (Bures, 2006: 68)

In addition, a list defines eight specific acts. The definition also covers behaviours which may contribute to terrorist acts in third countries. The Framework Decision on Combating Terrorism thus ensures that terrorist offences are punished by heavier sentences than common criminal offences in all EU Member States. Furthermore, it approximates the level of sanctions between Member States according to the principle that sentences have to be both proportional and dissuasive. Member states are legally responsible to act in cases of terrorist incidents that take place in their own territory or are committed against their own people. As pointed out by Dubois (2002: 326), this Framework Decision is also favourable for EU–US cooperation in the fight against terrorism as this offence is now recognised as a criminal offence on both sides of the Atlantic.

Secondly, the EAW is exemplary for the scope of integration achieved in EU counter-terrorism after 9/11 – it abolishes extradition amongst EU Member States. Vogel emphasises the importance of the introduction of the principle of mutual recognition in the EAW to be a 'revolution in extradition law' (Vogel, 2001: 937). Until the adoption of the EAW, extradition between EU Member States was depended on several different intergovernmental measures based on international law (Peers, 2001), for instance the 1957 Council of Europe European Convention on Extradition, the 1975 and 1978 protocols to the convention, the 1977 Council of Europe European Convention on Terrorism, the Schengen Implementing Convention of 1990, a convention in 1995 supplementing the aforementioned conventions, as well as a 1996 convention. Unsurprisingly, all of these measures regarding extradition are based on sovereign nations agreeing to create international law between them to govern their relations with regard to extradition matters. The EAW is of a completely different kind. It does not create international law, but rather transnational or 'European' law (Wagner, 2003b). It replaces all of the aforementioned measures based on international law between the different Member States with a legal instrument of the EU. In effect, this is a European extradition law.

The Commission's proposal went much further than the plans to simplify extradition law within the EU based on the 1999 conclusions of the Tampere European Council (Peers, 2001: 2; Wagner, 2003b: 706). Firstly, the EAW abolishes the term extradition and replaces it with the term 'surrender' (Douglas-Scott, 2004). The national judicial authorities will be responsible for its enforcement, thus virtually excluding political decisions by excluding the national executives from the decision-making process. As mentioned above, this seems to suggest a change from international to transnational law (Wagner, 2003b: 707). Secondly, the legal effect of this measure is subject to the jurisdiction of the European Court of Justice (ECJ) (Peers, 2001) if Member States sign a declaration approving of this. This may be limited, but is an improvement to the previous legal position. The Commission chose to create the arrest warrant by means of a framework decision, one of the third pillar instruments introduced by the Treaty of Amsterdam, which is binding on the Member States as to the result to be achieved, leaving national authorities the choice of form and method of transposition (Peers, 2001; Wagner, 2003b). Thirdly, the EAW abolishes the principle of double criminality for serious offences (Douglas-Scott, 2004). Thus, an arrest warrant may not be contested on the basis that it is for an activity not criminalised in the surrendering Member States. In addition, the arrest warrant is applicable to all offences in a list and not just terrorist offences. This applies to 32 different categories of crimes, thus, virtually all crimes apart from petty crimes. Examples of these categories of crime are as follows: participation in a criminal organisation, terrorism, human trafficking, sexual exploitation of children and child pornography, corruption, fraud, money laundering and making counterfeit money. In conclusion, all these arguments corroborate the view that the EAW 'is a revolution in European extradition law' (Vogel, 2001) and that European integration has reached the spheres of 'high politics'.

The EU and counter-terrorism: capabilities in its relation with the Unites States

As explained in Chapter 1, following the categorisation introduced by Hill (1998), the EU's capabilities in this book are considered to consist of three components: resources, instruments and cohesiveness. The case study of the EU's counter-terrorism policy suggests that the EU has mostly utilised negative integration measures in this policy area, together with positive measures other than military intervention. In fact, the deployment of military measures in the 'war on terror' has been at the core of controversy in 2002 and 2003 between the EU and the United States as well as within the EU. However, this did not prevent the EU from developing and utilising a range of non-military instruments. Among these, a very significant negative integration instrument is the EAW, based on the principle of mutual recognition. Among positive integration instruments, the EU has adopted and utilised numerous legal instruments, enhancing its role in the 'war on terror' vis-à-vis the United States; these instruments are also discussed below.

The purpose of this section is to examine the role of the EU in the counter-terrorism relations with the United States and the various capabilities, notably instruments adopted in a cohesive manner, in a capacity to reach a collective decision and stick to it. This section aims to give a good overview of the many instruments created since 9/11. Many traditional terrorism scholars, such as Bruce Hoffman, have argued that the differences in terrorism perception have had negative implications on

The EU and Counter-Terrorism 97

the US–European counter-terrorism relations. Yet, a survey conducted by the German Marshall Fund in 2004 seems to cast doubt on this analysis (Cameron, 2007b). Both Europeans (71 per cent) and Americans (76 per cent) are found to share concerns about international terrorism, and thus have a similar perception of this threat. However, they differ markedly in their views on response to terrorism; Americans prefer a military response (54 per cent), whereas Europeans agree with this option only to a more limited extent (28 per cent). The conclusion that can be drawn from such a study is that EU–US cooperation on terrorism matters is not impossible, but, given these differences, is more likely to be achieved with regard to non-military measures.

The attacks of 9/11 have led to a significant increase in EU–US counter-terrorism cooperation. Two specific forms of structured dialogue have played an essential role in that respect: the Justice Dialogue and the Policy Dialogue on Borders and Transport Security (PDBTS) (Cameron, 2007b). The former actually began in 1998, bringing together representatives of the US Department of Justice with EU colleagues from the DG JHA. While it was initially established to ensure information flows to the United States, it has increased in importance with the development of new EU competences in criminal judicial and police cooperation. Since 2002, this dialogue has also been held at ministerial level. The Justice Dialogue has been the central forum for negotiating the agreements on mutual legal assistance and extradition that will be examined below, as well as discussing the issue of liaison with Europol and Eurojust. As the agenda of this dialogue became increasingly dominated by questions concerning US borders, it began to considerably overlap with other attempts to improve customs cooperation (Ibid.: 136). The US Administration took several measures to increase the security of its borders, including the Container Security Initiative (CSI), the collection of Passenger Name Record (PNR) data and the use of biometric passports. By extending the American zone of security outwards of its borders, the US Homeland Security policies had very significant implications for the EU and, as a result, these provided strong incentives for reinforcing cooperation. The following section focuses on four major aspects of EU–US counter-terrorism cooperation relating, respectively, to intelligence, police and law enforcement, the financing of terrorism and justice.

Intelligence cooperation: the PNR agreement

In November 2001, the US Aviation and Transportation Security Act introduced the requirement that airline companies operating passenger flights to, from or through the United States provide the US authorities with electronic access to PNR data, including passengers' names and addresses, bank numbers, credit card details and information about meals ordered for the flights (de Hert and de Schutter, 2008). Such a requirement put EU-based airlines at risk of breaking the data protection legislation of their homeland. Consequently, the European Commission stepped in to open negotiations with the United States to resolve the matter for all EU countries (Hailbronner et al., 2008: 189). Whilst US airlines were forced to rapidly comply with these new measures, the European Commission managed to negotiate with the United States a delay for EU-based airlines, on the grounds that they were required to comply with the 1995 EU Directive on the protection of personal data. The US Department of Homeland Security agreed to give the EU an extension until 5 March 2003 to comply with the new rules. Therefore, while the PNR initiative clearly emanated from the United States, the European Commission managed to construct a significant role for itself in the implementation of the PNR Agreement in Europe. In practice, it negotiated with US officials on a series of requirements and adopted a decision on adequacy based on article 25 of the EC Directive on data protection (European Commission, 2004b). This decision laid down a requirement for the United States to ensure an adequate level of data protection for the data transferred from Europe. Following this, the Commission negotiated the Agreement on the transfer of data with the US government, assuming legal competence through the implicit legal power provided by Community law regarding transport and data protection. The PNR Agreement was approved by the Council on 17 May 2004 and subsequently signed on 28 May 2004 in Washington.

However, the European Parliament, which had felt marginalised during the negotiations of the agreement, decided to start proceedings before the ECJ to annul the agreement. Whilst it also objected to this agreement on the basis that the US authorities did not guarantee adequate levels of data protection, its complaint focused on the choice of legal basis, as it claimed that the agreement should not have been based on Article 95 TEU on approximation of laws. In May 2006, the ECJ did annul the agreement, but not on substantive grounds relating to issues of data protection. Instead, it ruled that the agreement was incorrectly based on EU transport policy (a first-pillar provision), as it mainly aimed to enhance security and to fight against terrorism. As a consequence, the concerned data transfers fell within the public security framework established by the public authorities (Guild and Brouwer, 2006: 3). Thus, despite achieving its aim of overturning the agreement, the European

Parliament gained very little from the ruling. The ECJ did not address the issue of data protection guarantees by the US authorities. Moreover, one of the consequences of the judgement was that any new agreement, prior to the Lisbon Treaty which abolished the third pillar, had to be negotiated in the framework of the third pillar, in which the European Parliament was largely excluded from the decision-making process (de Hert and de Schutter, 2008: 328).

As a result of the ECJ judgement, the 'First PNR Agreement' had to be replaced. The second PNR Agreement was to be based on third-pillar provisions, which meant that its negotiation had to be led by the Council Presidency with the assistance of the Commission (Ibid.: 330). Given the tight deadline imposed by the ECJ to solve the legal problem, an Interim PNR Agreement was adopted in the meantime, which ensured similar levels of data protection as before. After several further negotiations, a final deal was reached by the end of June 2007, before being approved by the Council of Ministers in July 2007. Under this second PNR agreement, the US government agreed to receive fewer fields of data – 19, instead of 34 compared to the first PNR Agreement – although some categories were actually combined. In exchange, the Council agreed that the US authorities would be able to share the data with an increased number of federal authorities and to store them for longer, namely 15 years, instead of three and a half years (Occhipinti, 2008: 19). Thus, with its PNR requirement – which meant that, in the absence of any reaction, European airlines would have to breach either the EU law or the US law – the United States forced the EU into a position where it had to negotiate. If not, European airlines could have lost access to the US market. In addition, the less stringent nature of the PNR agreements that the EU has also signed with Australia and Canada suggests that the US administration was able to exert some pressure on the EU to fulfil its aims (European Parliament, 2007). The European Parliament criticised the lack of democratic oversight in the PNR draft Agreement of 2007, which it described as having been 'prompted by US requirements'. It also regretted the fact that EU–US negotiations took no account of the PNR agreements with Canada and Australia, 'which ensure higher standards of protection of personal data' (Ibid.). In this sense, as already observed by Argomaniz (2009), it is evident that the US can exercise substantial power over the EU, notably because of the power disparities between these two actors.

However, this is not the only conclusion that can be drawn from this case. This section underlines the fact that the European Commission has even been inspired to propose legislation for an EU PNR system on the basis of this experience of EU–US cooperation. Since November 2007, as part of the Commission's new counter-terrorism initiatives, the establishment of an EU Passenger Name Record (EU PNR) system has been under discussion, following the presentation by the European Commission of a Framework Decision on the use of PNR data for law enforcement purposes (European Commission, 2007c). The Commission has presented this EU PNR system as a major tool in the fight against terrorism and organised crime (European Commission, 2008: 4). According to its Impact Assessment study, this system would be extremely useful by (1) allowing for the identification of known terrorists and criminals (by running the PNR data against alert systems), passengers connected to a known terrorist or criminal and 'high risk passengers' (according to specific characteristics and behavioural patterns or risk intelligence) and (2) by providing intelligence on travel pattern associations after a terrorist attack (Brouwer, 2009: 4).

Nevertheless, the original proposal by the Commission and its subsequent versions rewritten by the Council proved controversial as they raised many issues concerning data protection and human rights (Brouwer, 2009). Compared to the Advanced Passenger Information (API) covered by Directive 2004/82/EC on the obligation of carriers to communicate passenger data, the PNR data would have been more extensive. Another major difference between the two instruments was that the 2004 Directive concerning the API only requires the transmission of data in response to a prior request, whereas the proposed PNR Framework Decision included the obligation of systematically transmitting the required data for each flight concerned. However, upon the entry into force of the Lisbon Treaty on 1 December 2009, the Commission proposal, which had not been adopted by the Council yet, became obsolete. The Commission tabled a new proposal to replace it in February 2011, which is based on the provisions of the Lisbon Treaty (European Commission, 2011). This new proposal takes into account the recommendations of the European Parliament, which has become a much more important player in the post-Lisbon institutional framework, as well as incorporates the demands of the European Council that were expressed in the Stockholm Programme of December 2009. This Framework Decision is still under negotiation at the time of writing.

In conclusion, the analysis of the PNR case has demonstrated that, while the United States may have initially irritated the European Commission by making demanding requests and also approaching some EU

Member States on a bilateral basis, the United States ultimately dealt with 'Europe' at the EU level and saw significant merit in dealing with the European Commission. The United States has thereby continued to show its willingness to recognise the EU as a counter-terrorism actor and work with the Commission as a matter of preference. In turn, such a position has made the United States a welcome partner for the EU. As a consequence, the European Commission has pushed very hard to ensure the conclusion of various EU–US agreements in the field of counter-terrorism and has also used US pressure to advance European integration on these policy issues (Kaunert 2010a, 2010c). It is noteworthy that the European Commission proposal for an EU PNR system of 2011 makes repeated references to the usefulness of PNR systems in the United States, Canada and Australia as well as the value of EU cooperation with these partners.

Agreements for the transfer of PNR data in the context of the fight against serious transnational crime and terrorism, limited to travel by air, have been signed between the EU and the United States, Canada and Australia. These require air carriers, collecting PNR data of passengers for their own commercial purposes, to transmit these data to the competent authorities of the United States, Canada and Australia. Other countries, notably South Korea and Japan, have also requested to negotiate such agreements (European Commission, 2011: 7).

Police and law enforcement cooperation

EU–US cooperation in police and law enforcement has mainly developed through agreements between the United States and the European Police Office (Europol). Before analysing how the cooperation between Europol and the United States has developed, it is necessary to briefly explain the functions of Europol and the legal framework that allows this organisation to cooperate with third states. Europol is a European Law Enforcement Organisation that aims to support cooperation amongst EU Member States with regard to terrorism, drug trafficking and other serious forms of international organised crime. It was set up on the basis of an international Convention that came into effect in 1999. Europol, prior to the Lisbon Treaty and the change of legal basis under the Council Decision of 2009, used to have legal personality and was therefore able to enter into binding agreements under international law. It now derives its legal personality from the EU's legal personality more generally, but does not possess a legal personality *per se* anymore. A significant proportion of Europol staff comprises Europol liaison officers, which represent the national law enforcement agencies from all EU Member States. The main control mechanism for Europol is its Management Board, which brings together high-level representatives of the Member States from the Ministries of Interior or Justice and from operational law enforcement organisations. While the Council of Ministers is responsible for the main control of Europol, the Management Board has some important functions such as approving Europol's work programme. According to Article 42 of the former Europol Convention, Europol was able to establish relations with third states and bodies. Consequently, in 1998, the Council adopted three regulations concerning, respectively, the receipt of information by Europol from third parties, the governance of Europol's external relations with third states and the transmission of personal data by Europol to third states and non-EU-related bodies.

Having established these legal foundations, which enabled and at the same time constrained Europol's actions, it is now possible to examine the development of police cooperation between the EU and the United States in the wake of 9/11. As early as 20 September 2001, the JHA Council, which was eager to demonstrate the EU's solidarity with the United States, invited the Director of Europol to establish informal cooperation with the United States – pending the conclusion of a formal agreement – and 'to finalise the formal agreement with the United States as quickly as possible so that the Council may authorise its conclusion at its meeting on 16 November 2001' (Council, 2001). The Council also indicated that the agreement was to provide, *inter alia*, for the exchange of liaison officers between Europol and US agencies concerned with policing. Moreover, the Council invited the Director of Europol to open negotiations with the United States on an agreement covering the transmission of personal data. The first of the two agreements was indeed promptly adopted on 6 December 2001. It mainly focuses on the exchange of strategic and technical information concerning 'serious forms of international crime', which include 'crimes committed or likely to be committed in the course of terrorist activities against life, limb, personal freedom or property' (Article 3). The agreement provides for the identification of points of contact, information exchange, mutual consultation, exchange of expertise as well as the exchange of liaison officers.

The second agreement between Europol and the United States, called the 'Supplemental Agreement on the exchange of personal data and related information', took longer to negotiate. This was mainly due to the differences in the approach to personal data issues between Europe and the United States. As explained by Rees (2006: 92), in Europe, a significant amount of legislation on data protection has been adopted, as states have tended to hold rather large amounts of information on their citizens. In contrast, in the United States, the approach towards data protection has been more *ad hoc* and relaxed, as relatively little data on citizens are held by the authorities. Despite this complex situation, the agreement was eventually signed on 20 December 2002 (Mitsilegas, 2003: 319). Although it was criticised by civil liberties campaigners, this Europol–US agreement actually contains a significant number of data protection safeguards that had not previously been conceded by US authorities, including the important principle of 'purpose limitation', according to which information obtained for a specific purpose can only be used for that purpose. In addition, Article 7 stipulates that all federal authorities which receive information are bound by this principle and only those US agencies that agree to it can be provided with information under the terms of the agreement. This Europol–US agreement was the first international agreement in which US authorities agreed to apply such specific data protection provisions. Thus, this analysis has demonstrated that EU–US cooperation on police and law enforcement to combat terrorism has considerably developed in the aftermath of 9/11.

Cooperation on combating the financing of terrorism

Since 9/11, targeting the financing of terrorism has become an increasingly important dimension of the fight against terrorism. Before examining the evolution of the EU's financial sanctions regime, it is necessary to briefly elaborate on its legal complexity. The entry into force of the Lisbon Treaty on 1 December 2009 has brought about some changes in that respect, including the introduction of new legal bases (see Cremona, 2009: 590–92; Eckes, 2009: 121–24). However, their full impact still remains to be seen. As the measures discussed in this section were adopted prior to the entry into force of the Lisbon Treaty, it is necessary to focus on the institutional arrangements that were in place at that time. In the pre-Lisbon era, the EU's financial sanctions regime involved various measures across the three pillars of the EU. First of all, a Common Position was adopted under (pre-Lisbon) Articles 15 and 34 of the Treaty on European Union (TEU) to set the EU's general approach on the matter. It contained measures relating to foreign policy – such as the 'strategic decision' to adopt individual sanctions (Eckes, 2009) – and police and judicial criminal matters – such as assistance in preventing and combating terrorist acts – that is, measures in the now former second and third pillars. Subsequently, a regulation instructing the European Community (EC) to implement the necessary operational measures was adopted in the then first (that is EC) pillar.

The EU's financial sanctions regime contains two main components. The first comprises the measures that have been adopted to freeze the assets of the Taliban, Osama bin Laden and his associates (for example, Al-Qaeda) in particular. The second relates to broader measures that provide for the freezing of the assets of terrorist individuals and entities in general. The first asset-freezing measures adopted by the EU were of the first type; they targeted the Taliban (Council Common Position 1999/727/CFSP of 15 November 1999) and Osama bin Laden and the persons and entities associated with him (Council Common Position 2001/154/CFSP of 26 February 2001, repealed by Council Common Position 2002/402/CFSP of 27 May 2002) (see Tappeiner, 2005). As explained earlier, these EU asset-freezing measures were two-tiered, as the common positions were supplemented by regulations. After adopting measures targeting the Taliban, bin Laden and his associates in particular, the EU later adopted broader financial sanctions targeting suspected terrorists in general.

In December 2001, the Council adopted a major package of four acts, comprising two common positions, a regulation and a decision. Council Common Position on combating terrorism (2001/930/CFSP) outlined a series of actions to be taken by the EU to combat terrorism, including the freezing of the funds and other financial assets and economic resources of individuals and groups facilitating, attempting to commit or committing terrorist acts on the territory of the EU. Council Common Position 2001/931/CFSP contained more specific measures to combat terrorism. More precisely, it provided that, pursuant to Community law, the EC should order the freezing of the funds and other financial assets or economic resources of 'international' (that is, non-EU) terrorists and ensure that those would not have access to alternative funds, financial assets, economic resources or financial or related services. This instrument also contained a definition of 'persons, groups and entities involved in terrorist acts', which was identical to that outlined in the Council Framework Decision of 13 June 2002 on combating terrorism.

In addition, Council Common Position 2001/931/CFSP required Member States to strengthen judicial and police cooperation with respect to both 'international' and 'domestic' (that is, the EU) terrorists. Finally, there was an annex to the Common Position, which listed the persons, groups and entities 'involved in terrorist acts' that were targeted by the instrument. In this first version, it contained 29 persons and 13 groups and entities. The Common Position indicated that the list would be reviewed regularly and at least once every six months. As for the connected regulation (Council Regulation EC 2580/2001), it defined the 'funds' and assets to be frozen and laid down a detailed freezing procedure, whilst the decision connected to this regulation (Council Decision 2001/927/EC of 27 December 2001) listed the persons, groups and entities to which the aforementioned regulation applied. This first version of the list contained ten entries, but it has been amended several times since then. Its most recent publicly available version at the time of writing contained 25 individuals and 29 groups and entities.

The components of the EU's asset-freezing regime have been developed to enable the EU to align itself on the financial sanctions against suspected terrorists that have been adopted by the United Nations. With regard to the measures specifically targeting the Taliban, bin Laden and Al-Qaeda, Common Position 2001/154/CFSP, which provides for the freezing of the funds and financial assets of bin Laden and his associates, has been mainly adopted by the EU in order to ensure the implementation of UNSCR 1333, which notably decided that all UN Member States should freeze the funds of Osama bin Laden and individuals and entities associated with him and should ensure that no other funds or financial resources should be made available to them. This Resolution was adopted under Chapter VII of the UN Charter, which means that, according to Article 25 of the UN Charter, its provisions are binding on all UN Member States. Council Common Position 2001/154/CFSP contains numerous references to UNSCR 1333 as well as to the 'UN Sanctions Committee'. Article 4 states that:

> [funds] and other financial assets of Usama Bin Laden and individuals and entities associated with him as designated by the UN Sanctions Committee will be frozen, and funds or other financial resources will not be made available to Usama Bin Laden and individuals or entities associated with him as designated by the UN Sanctions Committee, under the conditions set out in UNSCR 1333 (2000).

Thus, it is remarkable that the EU's asset-freezing measures concerning bin Laden and his associates have been directly and entirely based on a list drawn up by the UN Sanctions Committee, which has been accepted by the EU without any amendment. Any subsequent changes to the 1267 Committee list of terrorist suspects have been faithfully transcribed into Community law. This is particularly striking given the harsh criticisms that have been levelled at the work of this UN Sanctions Committee – also known as the '1267 Committee' – in particular the lack of transparency in its listing and de-listing of suspected terrorists, especially in the first years of its work (Rosand, 2004; Draghici, 2009; Mendelsohn, 2009). Thus, although the EU's position can be criticised from a human rights standpoint, it demonstrates a strong commitment on its part to cooperating with the United Nations in the implementation of the financial sanctions targeting bin Laden and his associates.

The other component of the EU's financial sanctions regime – namely the measures that provide for the freezing of the assets of terrorist individuals and entities in general – also finds its origins in the EU's willingness to align itself on the United Nation's financial sanctions regime. Council Common Position 2001/931/CFSP of 27 December 2001 was adopted by the EU with the specific aim of implementing UNSCR 1373, which had been passed on 28 September 2001. This Resolution, described by Rosand (2003: 333) as the 'cornerstone of the United Nations' counterterrorism effort' (see also Talmon, 2005), requires all UN Member States to strengthen various aspects of their counter-terrorism policies, although it actually does not define 'terrorism' (Stromseth, 2003). As it has been adopted under Chapter VII of the UN Charter, the counter-terrorism measures that it contains, including measures against the financing of terrorism, are binding on all the UN Member States. This Resolution notably lays down that all states should prevent and suppress the financing of terrorist acts, criminalise activities aiming to fund terrorism, freeze the resources of terrorists and prevent funds being made available to them. It also decides that all Member States should assist each other in criminal investigations and criminal proceedings relating to the financing of terrorism. Thus, this Resolution comprises various measures that were hitherto only part of international conventions and protocols, such as the Terrorism Financing Convention, which thereby became binding on all UN members – rather than just on those that had chosen to become parties to these international instruments (Alvarez, 2003; Rosand, 2003).

As shown by Eling (2007: 105), the EU rapidly decided to tackle this issue of terrorist financing very seriously, which was positively seen by the US authorities. The EU–US cooperation on the financing of terrorism has significantly grown. The EU experts have been invited to participate in US terrorist financing assessment missions and to send trainers to support the delivery of US training programmes for financial regulators (Council, 2006a, 2007b). The EU and the United States have also held a series of joint workshops on financial sanctions to combat terrorism (Ibid.). In April 2007, the EU and the United States also adopted a joint

Public Outreach Paper, which aims to outline an efficient, fair and clear procedure for targeted sanctions to combat terrorist financing. These examples demonstrate that the EU and the United States have developed close relations in the fight against the financing of terrorism.

Judicial cooperation

In addition to the policy areas already examined, the events of 9/11 have also led to an increase in EU–US cooperation in justice matters. As early as the 20 September 2001, 'in a spirit of great transatlantic solidarity following the tragic events of 11 September 2001' (Stessens, 2008: 342), the JHA Council 'agreed on the principle of proposing to the United States that an agreement be negotiated between the European Union and the United States, on the basis of Article 38 of the TEU, in the field of penal cooperation on terrorism' (Council, 2001). Following a positive response from the United States, negotiations led by the Presidency of the Council – assisted by the Commission and the Council Secretariat – started and led to the signing of the Extradition Agreement and the Mutual Legal Assistance Agreement in June 2003 (Stessens, 2008). These were the first agreements between the EU and a third country concerning criminal justice cooperation. Nevertheless, the negotiation of these agreements proved to be challenging at times, as there are some significant philosophical differences between Europe and America on judicial and extradition matters. In particular, Europeans tend to be very critical of the existence and execution of death penalty in several US states, whereas Americans tend to perceive European penal codes as unjustifiably too lenient, especially concerning sentencing in relation to murder (Rees, 2006: 86).

In terms of content, the EU–US Extradition Agreement aims to facilitate the extradition of persons having committed any offence punishable by deprivation of liberty of one year or more (Mitsilegas, 2003: 526). As far as the Mutual Legal Assistance Agreement is concerned, it foresees cooperation between the EU and the United States on a wide range of issues, including evidence sharing for criminal investigations and prosecutions, the streamlining of extradition arrangements, the establishment of central points of contact between judicial authorities and the sharing of sensitive data (Rees, 2006: 89). The adoption of both agreements was controversial (Gregory, 2005: 116) because their negotiation was conducted in secret, and their text remained confidential for a long time, making parliamentary scrutiny very difficult (Mitsilegas, 2003: 525). In addition, concerns relating to human rights and data protection were also raised, notably by the European Parliament's Committee on Citizen's Freedoms and Rights, JHA, in its report adopted in May 2003. In addition, an agreement between Eurojust and the United States was signed in November 2006. Eurojust is an EU body whose main task is 'to enhance the efficiency of the national investigating and prosecuting authorities, when dealing with serious cross-border crime' (Helmberg, 2007: 246). The Council Decision setting up Eurojust authorises it to negotiate cooperation agreements with third states, which require the approval of the Council before their final adoption (Council, 2002). The main aim of the agreement between Eurojust and the United States is to improve cooperation between the competent authorities to facilitate the coordination of investigations and prosecutions involving the United States and one or more Member State. Amongst the different measures foreseen by the Agreement, one can note the following: the secondment of a Liaison Prosecutor from the United States to Eurojust, the appointment of at least one contact point to Eurojust within the Office of the competent authority in the United States and the exchange of information in compliance with the existing data protection rules. Thus, the EU has also developed the judicial dimension of its cooperation with the United States, in particular through the adoption of three important agreements.

The EU and counter-terrorism: recognition by the United States

The criteria of recognition provide an important social constructivist element to the set of behavioural criteria for analysing the EU's 'actorness' in international relations. It implies that in order to be an international security actor, the EU must be recognised by other states and non-state actors. Jupille and Caporaso (1998: 215) specify that '[t]his criterion should be seen as a minimum condition that adds little substantive understanding of any given entity, but simply registers it on the analytical radar. Recognition by others allows for presence in global politics, which, not surprisingly is the sine qua non of global actorhood.' This section aims to explain and examine the link between the adoption of internal EU counter-terrorism measures and the relations between the EU and the United States – which provided the EU with the most important recognition it could have possibly achieved – that of the most important superpower in the world. The establishment of direct competences for the EU, as outlined in the beginning of this chapter, was vital for acquiring the political consensus to conclude an agreement with third countries and thus for becoming an interesting partner for the United States in its counter-terrorism relations through increased efficiency gains. Internal counter-terrorism instruments, such as the EAW, were crucial in the establishment of similar extradition agreements between the EU and the United States, such as the Mutual Legal Assistance Treaty (MLAT). The same is true regarding the establishment of information exchanges between Europol and the Federal Bureau of Investigation (FBI). But how was this achieved? Put simply, social and legal norms up until the Tampere Council Summit had evolved on two axes (Kaunert, 2005): (1) whether the EU should be legislating at all in the AFSJ; where the normative debate had been structured between those wishing to preserve national sovereignty and those wishing to pool sovereignty at the EU level Figure 4.1, and (2) what the aims and purposes of such a legislation are. This book suggests that regarding extradition matters, it is precisely this second dimension that was at the heart of the debate.

The attack of 11 September 2001 had a significant impact on the norms of decision-makers in Europe. In simple terms, there were four general choices of direction available to the EU. The first option for EU Member States may well have been not to join the 'war on terror' and continue to operate as before, adhering to the traditional principle of national sovereignty. This is represented by the first quadrant in the matrix. However, given the still positive state of transatlantic relations between Europe and America, this would have necessitated a clear rupture in relations. Hence, it was always unlikely to occur. The second option for EU Member States would have been to build a counterweight

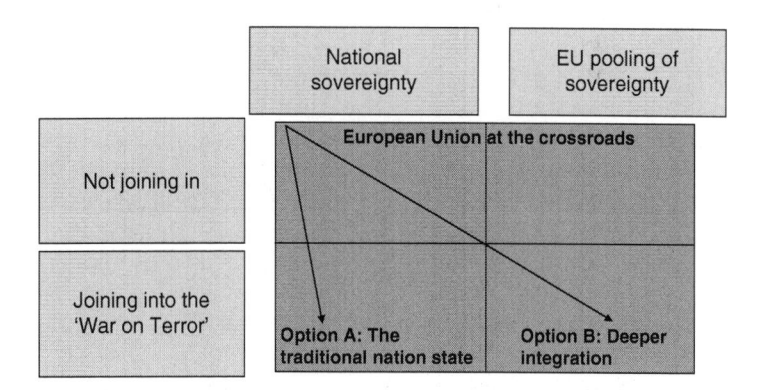

Figure 4.1 September 11 – The EU at a normative crossroad

against America's war and therefore not to join in. Yet, in order to realise being a counter-weight to the United States, the EU would have had to integrate more politically. For the same reason as the first option, this was also unlikely to happen. This means that the norm to join the 'war on terror', which emerged after 9/11, would make it difficult not to support the United States (Kaunert 2007, 2010c). The only realistic options at this point in time were Option A and Option B. Option A represents what nation states in Europe have traditionally practised for a very long time. This implies supporting the United States, while at the same time maintaining national sovereignty in the AFSJ. A good example here would be the provision of intelligence to the US government without any change of structures in intelligence relations. Option B represents the new option for European nation states. It implies full support to the United States and its 'war on terror', while restructuring the foundations of internal security relations in the EU. In essence, as argued in this book, the latter option was the one that was pursued by the European Commission and approved by the Council.

The political norm that the international community needed to join the war against terrorism emerged with the attacks on the United States on 11 September 2001. A close examination of the war discourse shows how the norm emerged and ultimately made it difficult to do anything other than joining it. This demonstrates the fact that, ultimately, the EU had to support the United States – even if more in appearance than substance. In fact, the appearance of support would increase peer pressure for EU Member States to adopt the EAW in the end. The platform for the emerging norm to join the 'war on terrorism' was first established with Bush's 'act of war speech' (BBC News, 2001a). In this, he declared: 'The deliberate and deadly attacks, which were carried out yesterday against our country, were more than acts of terror. They were acts of war.' [...] 'This enemy attacked not just our people but all freedom-loving people everywhere in the world.' [...] 'We will rally the world.' [...] 'This will be a monumental struggle of good versus evil, but good will prevail.' One should note the significant pressure for countries to adopt the norm to fight the 'war on terror'. Bush defined appropriate action in terms of fighting in the 'war against terrorism' and made an even stronger case by distinguishing between 'good and evil'. Later, Bush (BBC News, 2001a) enforced this emerging norm by stating that 'you are either for us or against us'. Thus, the political pressure is such that the appropriate course of action became defined in its support of the United States.

The rest of Europe rallied behind the United States. For example, Germany's Chancellor Gerhard Schroeder called on European nations to band together within the framework of the EU to fight global terrorism (BBC News, 2001b): 'Only if we put in place common policing and judicial resources can we ensure that there will be no hideouts for terrorists and other criminals in the European Union' 'We are ready to make Europe into an international player with global influence.' It was now quite clear that the EU would take part in the 'war on terror'. The question now was in which way the EU was going to take part. In speaking to the European Parliament, the Commissioner responsible for the AFSJ (formerly better known as JHA), Antonio Vitorino, remarked (Norman, 2001):

> Terrorist acts are committed by international groups with bases in several countries, exploiting loopholes in the law created by the geographical limits on investigators and often enjoying substantial financial and logistical resources. Terrorists take advantage of differences in legal treatment between States, in particular where the offence is not treated as such by national law, and that is where we have to begin.

Vitorino made the link that was established very clearly earlier. In order to combat terrorism, these measures – the EAW – were vital (Ibid.). Therefore, in Vitorino's view, anyone opposing these measures behaved out of line, inappropriately, and effectively supported terrorism indirectly by not closing the legal loopholes. The Commission moved extremely fast to make this link.

In the case of the EAW, the Commission followed this rhetoric up politically with a very timely proposal. This proposal for the policy had already been under preparation for about two years before it was launched. Vitorino initially intended to launch it under the Spanish Presidency in the first half of 2002 due to Spain's strong support of the issue in order to solve its own problems with the ETA terrorists. Yet, with the emerging norm of the 'war on terror', it became apparent that fast action was required. Ministers in the AFSJ would be under intense pressure to behave appropriately and settle their differences. Vitorino remarked: 'If we do not get agreement, and it should be a substantial agreement to cope with the global threat, it will be difficult to explain to the public why we failed' (Norman, 2001). Therefore, the Commission's strategy was for the arrest warrant to be presented as an anti-terrorist measure and to be amalgamated with other such measures, such as the Framework Decision on the Definition on Terrorism (Kaunert, 2007, 2010c).

On 17 September 2001, the Commission drafted an internal strategy paper to amalgamate the EAW and the framework decision on a common definition of terrorism with several measures. This document was timed just ahead of the crucial extraordinary JHA on 20 September as well as the European Council on 21 September. The document is highly indicative of the Commission's strategy at the time. It stated that the EAW and the framework decision on terrorism only addressed the internal dimension of the EU and were, thus, insufficient as a response to 9/11. Following the high-level political discourse of European leaders in the first days after the attacks, the EU needed to come up 'rapidly with a comprehensive and coherent response, internally and in cooperation with the US and other key partners, and moving beyond the narrow confines of a legal and political/security perspective' (Ibid.). The Commission proposed that 'some areas' the 'EU [could] make a real contribution' and the United States would welcome to deal with the Union as 'one interlocutor'. This argument could then be levelled against integration-sceptic Member States (Ibid.).

The first attempt to link the construction of internal EU counter-terrorism competences to the construction of an international role for the EU occurred shortly after 9/11 when the Director General of the Commission, Sir Adrian Fortescue (European Voice, 2001), attended a meeting with Colin Powell, the US Secretary of State, on 21 September. In a personal interview, the late Sir Fortescue confirmed that the Commission's strategy to work closely with the United States also partly aimed to enhance internal competences for the EU in the field of counter-terrorism. However, the European Commission had to use a 'carrot and stick' approach in its relations with the United States. Thomas Ridge, the former US Homeland Security Secretary, stated in his farewell speech that his greatest regret was not to have worked more closely with the EU from the start (Lebl, 2006: 125). Initially, the US officials were rather cautious to engage with the EU institutions in order not to damage their bilateral relationships with EU Member States. They also worried that dealing with the EU would be less efficient, or even counter-productive, compared to working with national and local officials.

This is where the Commission used the 'stick approach', in particular regarding the container security agreements. In 2002, the US negotiated bilateral agreements with several Member States on container security, culminating in the decision to admit Belgium, France, Germany and the Netherlands to the United States' CSI by June 2002, and the United Kingdom, Italy, Spain and Sweden by January 2003. Holding the view that this would infringe upon EC exclusive legislative competence, the European Commission began legal infringement proceedings against these Member States before the ECJ. Threatened with this stick, the United States and the EU expanded their own 1997 co-operation agreement to include transport security and, in particular, elements of the US CSI. Consequently, the Commission withdrew its legal infringement procedures, having amply made its point. The Commission was ready to help the United States to increase its legal competences in the AFSJ for as long as the United States respected the role and competences of the EU (Lebl, 2006) – which the United States did after this episode.

The Commission also invited the United States to provide information as to how the EU could help and support its counter-terrorism efforts after 9/11 – the 'carrot approach'. President George Bush listed 47 demands in a letter to the EU, covering judicial and diplomatic co-operation, data protection, the proliferation of biological weapons and other issues, and hence strengthening cooperation with the EU in fighting terrorism. It also mentioned that extradition processes from the EU to America should be streamlined, in addition to asking the EU to facilitate extradition procedures internally. The fact that the EU agreed on the EU-wide extradition policy from December 2001 onwards, with the EAW analysed previously, enabled the EU to start negotiations on extradition with the United States. Without the EAW, the political consensus to conclude an international extradition agreement between the EU and the United States would not have existed. For the EU, this would have meant that it might have become sidelined in future counter-terrorism agreements. In conclusion, the norms changed demonstrably in the few weeks after 11 September 2001, and the Commission was very important in this process. It played the role of a strategic 'first mover' in order to shape the debate in a way that placed the EU at the centre of Europe's 'war on terror'. It also assessed very well politically how the norm environment would produce political pressure on Member States to act. Consequently, the European Commission and its Commissioner Vitorino proposed action which clearly demonstrated its support for the United States and its 'war on terror'. The ensuing EU–US counter-terrorism cooperation has significantly grown since then.

Conclusion

The EU's 'actorness' in counter-terrorism has a number of distinctive features: it has achieved very significant scope of integration, very significant capabilities as well as the recognition of the most important actor in global politics – the United States. It presents an exemplary case study of how much the EU has become an actor in world politics, in counter-terrorism probably more than in other areas. The scope of integration has been mainly informed by the energetic roles of the European Commission and the Council Secretariat. Both institutions have acted in an alliance to push the area of counter-terrorism, as evidenced by the cases of the EAW and the EU–US counter-terrorism cooperation (Kaunert 2007, 2010c). In particular, the Commission has become to play a key role in European counter-terrorism integration after the terrorist attacks on 11 September 2001. It is fair to say that these attacks became a normative defining point for the EU and its scope of integration on internal security matters.

Reflecting its central role in the EU, the Commission quickly emerged as a leader in the EU's 'war on terror'. In particular, the Commission managed to construct an important role for the EU in counter-terrorism by serving as a 'strategic first mover' in order to shape the debate. It also allied with the United States to put pressure on reluctant Member States – the EAW was the result of a complex process and the political actions of the Commission. The transatlantic cooperation wasn't easy, though. The former US Homeland Security Secretary Thomas Ridge stated that his greatest regret was not to have worked more closely with the EU from the start (Lebl, 2006: 125). As a result of the Commission's policy entrepreneurship, the central EU bureaucracy boosted the supranational nature of the EU's counter-terrorism response. This achievement, in turn, tightened the European integration in this policy area.

With regard to counter-terrorism capabilities, the EU is primarily relying on legal instruments developed after 9/11, mainly as a result of its bumpy cooperation with the United States and the leading role of the Commission. Among the most important instruments of the EU are the international agreements on the exchange of passengers' data, law enforcement cooperation involving Europol and various measures tackling the financial side of terrorist threat. As this chapter has demonstrated, the EU counter-terrorism capabilities can be closely linked to the recognition of the EU as an international security actor. In terms of the EU–US cooperation in this policy area, there were advantages stemming from this cooperation for both sides, with the EU being recognised as an important international actor in counter-terrorism by the only remaining world superpower. Yet, it also demonstrated the importance and political significance of three actors. Firstly, the United States put significant pressure on the EU to strengthen cooperation. In the war on terror, it was a case of 'for us or against us'. The EU chose to support the United States as much as possible, without offering military means. Further, the EU bodies and institutions have had a significant impact on the ways in which the EU has provided its support, including Europol and Eurojust. Significantly, for the European Commission in particular, support for the United States became equated with advancing European integration. This included internal action as well as EU external action on counter-terrorism with the United States. The larger global agenda of the 'war on terror' was seized as a promising opportunity to advance European integration in the counter-terrorism field. However, the EU had to establish internal counter-terrorist instruments, first in order to be able to establish fully functioning counter-terrorism relations with the United States, which had traditionally always relied on bilateral counter-terrorism relations with Europe (Wyn Rees, 2006). This chapter outlined the major shift in the scope of integration with the EAW as well as the significant increase in capabilities, and, finally, the tremendous recognition the EU has acquired by the world's only remaining superpower, the United States.

5
The EU and Refugees

Policy developments after 9/11 have prompted a number of scholars (Bigo, 1996, 1998a, 1998b, 1998c, 2001, 2002; Guild, 1999, 2002, 2003a, 2003b, 2004, 2006; Guiraudon, 2000, 2003; Huysmans, 2000, 2004; Kostakopolou, 2000; Ceyhan and Tsoukala, 2002; Karyotis, 2003; Faist, 2004) to argue that migration has been constructed as a security threat in Europe. These scholars often draw upon the Copenhagen School's securitisation theory and argue that migration issues have been securitised in the European Union (EU). Levy (2005: 35) comments that 'the trend towards liberalisation seemed to be stopped dead in its tracks by the events of 9/11', whereas Boswell (2007) remarks that while EU migration policies were not securitised since 9/11, this does not hold for asylum policies.

However, this fear should be counter-intuitive. Especially the European Commission is well known for its legalistic approach to policy problems, always following the letter of the law; in fact, the Commission is often derided for being technocratic. It seems thus counter-intuitive that the Commission would 'securitise' the EU asylum policy. According to the Copenhagen School, who argue that an issue is transformed into a security problem (that is, securitised) after a securitising actor presents it as an existential threat, and this 'securitising move' is accepted by the audience, this would mean that EU institutions, such as the Commission, deliberately construct refugees as a security threat in order to be able to use 'emergency measures' (Buzan, 1991; Wæver et al., 1993; Wæver, 1995; Buzan et al., 1998). Buzan, Wæver and de Wilde (1998: 25) note that 'the existential threat has to be argued and just gain enough resonance for a platform to be made from which it is possible to legitimize emergency measures or other steps that would not have been possible (...)' (Ibid.). This means that the same EU institutions that want to give the impression of following the letter of the law want to construct a situation in which the letter of the law can be disregarded ('emergency measures'). The way in which the EU institutions would aim to achieve this would be through a discursive construction of threats, thereby lifting the issues 'outside the normal realms of politics' (Buzan, 1991; Wæver et al., 1993, Wæver, 1995; Buzan et al., 1998). On the face of it, this seems plausible for right-wing politicians at the national level but rather unlikely for EU bureaucrats who loathe nothing more than the 'political limelight'.

Moreover, this goes against several academic arguments that were often made about asylum cooperation in Europe. Amongst academic scholars in the field of immigration and asylum, the argument has been advanced that EU governments decided to 'venue shop'; they decided to circumvent domestic pressures and obstacles and therefore 'escaped' to legislate at the EU level, where they were protected from these issues (Freeman, 1998; Joppke, 1998, 2001; Lavenex, 1998, 1999, 2001a, 2001b, 2004, 2006; Geddes, 2000, 2001; Guiraudon, 2000, 2003; Stetter, 2000, 2007; Guiraudon and Joppke, 2001; Thielemann, 2001a, 2001b, 2004, 2005, 2006; Boswell, 2003a, 2003b, 2007, 2008; Occhipinti, 2003; Thielemann and Dewan, 2006; Ellermann, 2008). EU Member States, in this argument, have thus decided to enhance their cooperation in the field of asylum and migration in a process driven by national bureaucracies. These state-centred accounts (esp. Freeman, 1998; Joppke, 1998) stress the resilience of nation states, their ability to control 'unwanted immigration' and the use of the EU by its Member States as a device for attaining immigration and asylum (see Thielemann, 2001a, 2001b) policy objectives that are unlikely to be achieved at the domestic level alone. If indeed, national policy-makers are perfectly able to circumvent national pressures in order to restrict immigration and asylum at the EU level, why should they then 'securitise' the issues in order to achieve what they are already achieving? Why should national policy-makers go to a forum where technocracy is valued in order to securitise, which would be far easier in a national context? What are the constraints for political actors to securitise at the EU level?

Refugees in this book represent another category of the so-called non-traditional security risks, with similarities to climate security, albeit a strong difference; most notably the fact that the construction of refugees as a security threat has, for the most part, been resisted by EU institutions, such as the European Commission. This chapter, offering an empirical analysis of the EU's role in addressing this issue, is structured as follows. Firstly, it investigates the institutional arrangements and legal competences of the EU to develop policies in the area of global migration and refugees. Of particular importance here is the question of whether the EU used its competences to depict refugees and migrants as a security threat at all. Secondly, this chapter examines EU resources with respect to developing the security dimension of global migration, which remains notoriously difficult to develop. Finally, this chapter investigates the extent to which the EU has been recognised as an actor in this policy area, despite the fact that security constructions of refugees do not remain shared.

The EU and refugees: scope of integration

The scope of integration, identified as the first criterion of 'actorness', is defined as 'the procedures according to which policy decisions are taken focusing on the involvement of supranational bodies and Council voting rules' (Börzel, 2005: 220), much of which was explained in Chapter 2 for the area of EU asylum policy. What requires further empirical investigation is the involvement of supranational institutions and agencies in the security challenges discussed in this chapter. The extent to which these are involved in a given security policy issue determines the scope of integration in this area. However, this chapter goes even beyond this definition. The scope of integration is determined by EU institutional involvement and legislative rules, such as QMV, but is also determined by the strength of legal instruments at the disposal of the EU. The area of EU asylum policy is a perfect case in point, which is embedded in a variety of international legal regimes as well as various treaty obligations for the EU. The Common European Asylum System (CEAS) is embedded in a long-standing international regime of refugee protection (Marrus, 1985, 1988; Loescher, 1989, 1992, 1993, 1995, 2004; Noll, 2000; Peers, 2002, 2004, 2006; Peers and Rogers, 2006), which aims to keep the balance between security and liberty firmly towards liberty and the rights of victims of persecution. The international regime was established on 14 December 1949, when a Resolution of the United Nations General Assembly created the office of the United Nations High Commissioner for Refugees (UNHCR). The first instrument was created in 1951, when the Geneva Convention Relating to the Status of Refugees was adopted for Western Europe. Ever since, it has been the cornerstone of contemporary international refugee law, only supplemented by the 1967 New York Protocol, which extended the Geneva provisions to the rest of the world.

Signatories to the convention, which include all EU Member States, are required (according to Art. 1A (1) of the Geneva Convention) to offer refuge to a person:

- who has a well-founded fear of being persecuted
- for reasons of race, religion, nationality, membership of a particular social group or political opinion
- who is outside the country of his nationality
- who is unable or (due to such fear) is unwilling to avail himself of the protection of that country or
- who, not having a nationality and being outside the country of his former habitual residence, is unable or unwilling to return to it due to such fear.

Despite being the cornerstone of international refugee protection, not all Member States interpret and apply the Geneva Convention in the same way. Differing definitions of 'refugee' create different levels of protection and an uneven sharing of the responsibility. Most Member States have a range of statuses to confer on refugees, with varying socio-economic and judicial rights. They differ sharply on whether to award refugee status (which confers full legal protection and access to social security and the labour market) in cases of persecution by non-state agents, such as war lords, paramilitary groups or mafia organisations. This gap in interpretation provides clear opportunities for an EU asylum policy.

Schengen and beyond

When it was established by the Treaty of Rome in 1958, the European Community (EC) did not receive any formal competence on asylum matters. Though the preamble of the treaty stated that its signatories were 'determined to lay the foundations of an ever closer union among the peoples of Europe', the EC started as an essentially economic enterprise, the main purpose of which was to set up a common market. At the time, asylum matters seemed to fall beyond the scope of this project and the EC was thus not granted any competence in this area. This was also in line with the attitude of most, if not all, governments who considered asylum a matter of national sovereignty. Therefore, the EC institutions did not play any noticeable role in the field of asylum for almost three decades, with some minor exceptions.

The main political impetus in the 1980s for asylum cooperation derives from the so-called 'Schengen zone', which originated in the Saarbrücken Agreement of 13 July 1984, in which Chancellor Kohl and President Mitterrand agreed on the gradual abolition of controls at the Franco-German borders. Shortly afterwards, the Benelux countries joined France and Germany on this initiative and the five countries signed the Schengen Agreement on 14 June 1985. Five years of negotiations were then necessary to adopt the Convention applying the Schengen Agreement on the Gradual Abolition of Checks at the Common Borders. This document, drafted mostly by representatives of the national Interior ministries, widely focused on compensatory measures necessary to safeguard internal security after the lifting of checks at the internal borders. Of the 142-artticle Convention 128 articles were dedicated to those compensatory measures (Berthelet, 2003: 220). Thus, the Schengen Convention comprised a substantial number of provisions relating to the entry, movement and expulsion of non-EC citizens, notably asylum seekers. Firstly, the Schengen Convention contained several measures aimed at strengthening the controls at the external borders. They notably included using mobile units to patrol the borders between crossing points, increasing cooperation to make checks and surveillance more effective, exchanging relevant information and establishing liaison officers (Title II, Chapter 2).

Secondly, Title II, Chapter 7 of the Convention laid down provisions concerning the responsibility for processing applications for asylum. The members of the Schengen group decided that only one state should be responsible for examining an asylum claim, namely the state 'which had played the main role in authorising entry either by issuing a visa, or having issued the visa of longest duration, or by not requiring any visa'. In the case of illegal entry, the first border reached would determine 'which state was responsible' (Joly, 1996). The main purpose of those rules was to curb the growing phenomenon of 'asylum shopping', that is multiple applications for asylum in several states simultaneously or successively. It is noteworthy that, regarding the procedures for the handling of applications, the members of the Schengen Group did not develop any common approach. They decided that each state would process asylum claims in accordance with its national law (article 32). While the Schengen Convention was initially outside the framework of the EU, it became of vital importance with the Treaty of Amsterdam 1997, when it was integrated into the framework of the EU. Despite the fact that EU institutions had not been very influential in its conceptions until then, the Tampere programme, which started with the entry into force of the Treaty of Amsterdam in 1999, created significant new opportunities for EU level actors, such as the European Commission.

European Union competences from Maastricht to Lisbon

There have been significant changes gradually affecting the EU institutional framework in recent years and some of those have had an important impact on the EU asylum policy (see notably Niemann,

2008). The asylum policy institutional structure had been strongly intergovernmental initially. Indeed, the Maastricht Treaty had established two new 'intergovernmental pillars', one for the Common Foreign and Security Policy (CFSP) and the other for Justice and Home Affairs (JHA) matters, which included asylum issues. With regard to asylum matters (see Article K of the Maastricht Treaty), Member States were largely dominant in the policy-making process. The European Commission was only 'fully associated with the work' in the area of asylum, whilst the role of the European Parliament was limited to being informed and consulted on the initiatives of the Member States. As for the European Court of Justice (ECJ), it was not given any role with respect to EU asylum provisions.

This institutional architecture was significantly changed by the Amsterdam Treaty, which entered into force in 1999. Several of these institutional changes had an important impact on the EU asylum venue, leading to an increased 'communitarisation' of asylum. The role of the European Commission was reinforced as it received the competence to draft proposals on various aspects of the EU asylum policy, as has been illustrated in the previous section. However, during a transitional period of five years, the European Commission was to share its right of initiative with the Member States, before acquiring the sole right of initiative (Article 73o of the Amsterdam Treaty). Although this institutional arrangement was aimed as a 'brake' on the powers of the Commission in the legislative process, in practice, the European Commission managed to push for its more inclusive asylum agenda. It was successful in significantly influencing the EU asylum provisions adopted during the transitional period by playing the normative role of 'supranational policy entrepreneur', as demonstrated by Kaunert (2009a, 2010c). This was notably shown by the way it managed to largely remain in control of the asylum policy agenda in the medium term in the face of the British government's (unsuccessful) attempt at setting the agenda with its proposal on the extra-territorial processing of asylum claims. During the transitional five-year period, the Council took decisions unanimously after consulting the European Parliament. The Amsterdam Treaty also contained a provision granting the Council the possibility to decide, after the five-year transition period, that the co-decision procedure was to apply to various policy issues, including asylum. The Amsterdam Treaty also gave the ECJ a more prominent role in the EU asylum policy venue. With regard to asylum matters, the ECJ was granted the competence to rule, when asked by a national court or tribunal, on two types of questions: those on the interpretation of the Treaty provisions on asylum and those on the validity or interpretation of acts of the institutions of the Community based on the Treaty provisions on asylum, but only in cases 'pending before a court or tribunal of a Member State against whose decisions there is no judicial remedy under national law' (Article 73(p) of the Amsterdam Treaty). Although the limitations to the role of the ECJ have often been criticised (Peers, 2005), this was nevertheless a significant change, since it led to several cases on asylum being brought before the Court.

The Lisbon Treaty, which entered into force on 1 December 2009, has further strengthened the role of the ECJ and the European Parliament, respectively. This has in turn reinforced the liberal character of the EU asylum policy structure. The Lisbon Treaty has amended and reorganised existing treaties into two separate treaties, namely the Treaty on European Union (TEU) and the Treaty on the Functioning of the European Union (TFEU). The EU legal competences in the Area of Freedom, Security and Justice (AFSJ), which comprises asylum matters, have been clarified, as Article 4 (2j) TFEU has categorised this policy area as one of shared competences. The Treaty of Lisbon has also significantly altered the institutional arrangements presiding over the development of the EU asylum policy. Indeed, it foresees that all asylum legal instruments should be adopted in accordance with the ordinary legislative procedure, which is laid down in Article 294 TFEU. This means that the European Parliament has now acquired joint decision-making powers on asylum, which represents a significant increase in power for this institution compared to previous institutional arrangements, whilst the Council takes decisions by qualified majority voting. In addition, judicial control has been expanded, as the Court's role has been strengthened with respect to the AFSJ, including the EU asylum policy. In particular, the Court's preliminary jurisdiction, which used to be limited, has been expanded and generalised to all AFSJ matters by the Treaty of Lisbon, with respect to both primary and secondary law. This reform already resulted in the first preliminary ruling request from a lower court, in Luxembourg, to the Court in March 2010 (Garlick, 2010: 60). Thus, the role of the EU institutions has been greatly strengthened in the asylum policy area, with growing roles for the European Commission, the European Parliament and the ECJ.

In the areas of asylum, migration and external border controls (Art. 77–80 TFEU), significant new competences are transferred to the EU level under the Lisbon Treaty. Legally, according to the previous treaties, it was only possible to legislate on minimum standards for asylum measures. The Lisbon Treaty provides the competence to adopt, acting in accordance with the ordinary legislative procedure, laws for a *uniform* status of asylum valid throughout the Union, a uniform status of subsidiary protection, a common system of temporary protection, common procedures for the subsidiary protection, standards for reception conditions (formerly only minimum standards) and partnership and cooperation with third countries for the purpose of managing inflows of people. The areas of migration and illegal migration bring similar new competences for the EU. In addition, according to the Lisbon Treaty (LT), incentives for integration measures for third-country nationals can now be legislated by the EU. Both treaties also provide for a burden-sharing mechanism within the EU Member States.

The EU and refugees: capabilities

As explained in Chapter 1, following the categorisation introduced by Hill (1998), the EU's capabilities in this book are considered to consist of three components: resources, instruments and cohesiveness. Resources include the use and threat of force, diplomacy, economic carrots and sticks. Instruments are established based on the provisions of the treaties to enhance the EU's effectiveness as an international security actor. Of course, what matters in each case study representing a security policy challenge is not merely the existence of these instruments, but the ability by the EU to deploy them effectively. This requires cohesiveness, which is defined as 'the capacity to reach a collective decision and to stick to it' (Hill, 1998: 23). The purpose of this section is to examine the role of the EU in asylum policy and the various capabilities, notably instruments adopted in a cohesive manner, in a capacity to reach a collective decision and stick to it, created by the EU.

All the legal instruments considered here were adopted after 1999, once the EU was allowed the use of more effective instruments than the 'soft law' measures and conventions of the Maastricht era, which, overall, had only a limited impact (Geddes, 2008). To date, the EU's main achievements in the area of asylum comprise the adoption of four key directives – the so-called Temporary Protection, Qualification, Procedures and Reception Conditions Directives – and the 'Dublin II Regulation' as well as the decision to establish a European Asylum Support Office (EASO) in 2010. These four directives establish common minimum standards with regard to various aspects of national asylum systems, whilst the 'Dublin II Regulation' establishes the criteria and mechanisms for determining the Member State responsible for examining a given asylum application lodged in one of the Member States by a third-country national (see Kaunert and Léonard, 2011a). This overview indicates that, in the area of asylum and migration, positive integration instruments are of key importance. These primarily include harmonisation efforts among EU Member States.

The Temporary Protection Directive (Council Directive 2001/55/EC of 20 July 2001) lays down provisions on temporary protection for displaced persons in the context of a mass influx of persons seeking protection. The existence of such a situation of 'mass influx' is to be established by the Council voting according to the qualified majority voting procedure and on the basis of a proposal from the Commission. The Council decision is binding on all Member States, although none of them is obliged to admit a specific number of persons in need of international protection. Every Member State is to ascertain its own reception capacity in a spirit of 'Community solidarity' (Hailbronner, 2004: 41). Thus, this represents an attempt at establishing an EU system of 'burden-sharing' in cases of mass influx of displaced persons from third countries. However, it is a rather modest attempt, as the directive, for example, does not foresee any mechanism of financial solidarity amongst Member States.

The Reception Conditions Directive (Council Directive 2003/9/EC of 27 January 2003) lays down minimum standards for various aspects of the reception of asylum seekers in the EU Member States, including information, residence and freedom of movement, employment, education and vocational training, material reception conditions and health care. Although some have criticised that these minimum standards on reception conditions do not apply to the recipients of temporary protection (Guild, 2004: 213), the efforts to ensure the provision of minimum reception conditions across the EU have been generally welcome, notably with a view to reducing secondary movements of asylum seekers (Hailbronner, 2004).

The Dublin II Regulation (Council Regulation (EC) 343/2003 of 18 February 2003) establishes the criteria and mechanisms for determining the Member State responsible for examining an asylum application lodged in one of the Member States by a third-country national. The main goal of this regulation is to ensure that an asylum seeker has access to an asylum procedure in one of the EU Member States on the basis of responsibility criteria. Thus, the regulation aims to tackle the problems of 'asylum shopping' (that is, multiple applications for asylum across the EU by the same person) and 'refugees in orbit' (that is, asylum seekers unable to find a state accepting to examine their application in the EU). The Dublin II Regulation replaces and addresses some deficiencies of the

Dublin Convention, which was adopted in 1990. Although the directive establishes a hierarchy of criteria, the main principle underpinning the system is that the state responsible for processing an application is the state responsible for the asylum seeker's presence in the EU, that is the state through which an asylum seeker has entered the EU (Da Lomba, 2004: 119; Hailbronner, 2004). However, there is no provision in the regulation preventing a given Member State from examining an asylum application, even if it is not formally responsible for its processing. The implementation of this so-called 'Dublin system', which entails transfers of asylum seekers amongst Member States for the processing of their application, relies on a large database of fingerprints called EURODAC to a significant extent. This instrument is a database containing the fingerprints of asylum seekers, which is used to ascertain whether (and in which EU Member State) a given asylum seeker has already applied for asylum in the EU. It has been operational since January 2003 (Hailbronner, 2004).

The Asylum Qualification Directive (Council Directive 2004/83/EC of 29 April 2004) lays down minimum standards for 'the qualification of third country nationals or stateless persons as refugees or as persons who otherwise need international protection and the content of the protection granted' (Article 1). It outlines the criteria that a person needs to fulfil in order to qualify for subsidiary protection and for being a refugee, respectively, as well as elaborates on the status associated with each of these categories. Whilst the definition of 'refugee' is that of the Geneva Convention, 'a person eligible for subsidiary protection' is defined as a person who does not qualify for refugee status but is nevertheless at risk of suffering serious harm in his (or her) country of origin. The directive is particularly innovative in two respects. Firstly, whereas, traditionally, most Member States only recognised state actors as actors of persecution or serious harm, the directive foresees that non-state actors can also be considered actors of persecution or serious harm in certain circumstances. Secondly, the directive outlines various examples of 'acts of persecution', which indicate that this concept is to be interpreted more broadly than is generally the case in existing national legislations. As also emphasised by El-Enany and Thielemann (2011), these important provisions have had a profound impact on the legislation and practices in several EU Member States, including France and Germany (Storey, 2008: 1). As a consequence, this directive has generally been received positively by pro-migrant non-governmental organisations and asylum experts such as Storey (2008: 1), who has called the Refugee Qualification Directive 'a remarkable development'. Others have been more circumspect. For example, McAdam (2005: 461) has welcomed the codification of *ad hoc* practices of complementary protection into a 'subsidiary protection' regime but has deplored the entrenchment of the differentiation made between refugees and recipients of subsidiary protection.

The Asylum Procedures Directive (Council Directive 2005/85/EC of 1 December 2005) provides for several minimum procedural standards, regarding issues such as access to the asylum procedure, the right to remain in the Member State pending the examination of the application, guarantees and obligations for asylum seekers, personal interviews, legal assistance and representation, detention and appeals. In addition, the directive also codifies some important concepts (Hailbronner, 2004), such as 'safe country of origin' and 'safe third country'. Some have criticised the contents of this directive, in particular the lack of suspensive effect for appeals (Byrne, 2005: 71) and the concepts of 'safe country of origin' and 'safe third country'. However, it is important to note that these minimum procedural standards have actually required several EU Member States to raise their standards from the point of view of the protection of asylum seekers (Ackers, 2005). For example, Portugal and Spain have had to significantly restrict the grounds on which asylum applications can be declared inadmissible (Fullerton, 2005). Finally, it was decided in 2010 to establish the EASO, which aims to provide further expertise and technical assistance to the EU Member States in the field of asylum (Comte, 2010). Once it is fully operational, its main objectives will be to facilitate practical cooperation on asylum amongst Member States (on matters such as access to information on countries of origin and dissemination of good practice), to coordinate support teams comprising national experts in Member States faced with a mass influx of asylum seekers, and to support the implementation of the CEAS.

First of all, it is important to emphasise that the four asylum directives only lay down minimum standards, which can be exceeded by individual Member States. They do not oblige Member States to decrease more generous standards in any way. However, they do curtail any potential 'race to the bottom' amongst Member States to a significant extent by setting minimum standards from which they cannot derogate. Second, contrary to some predictions, there has not been any evidence that Member States have generally used the adoption of the four directives as an opportunity to lower their asylum standards to the level of the minimum standards. Some observers had initially expressed the concern that Member States having more generous provisions would naturally feel compelled to make them more restrictive in order to render themselves 'less attractive' to asylum seekers (see, for example, Garlick, 2006: 47). However, there is no conclusive evidence that this predicted degradation of the asylum standards has taken place in practice (Hailbronner, 2008; El-Enany and Thielemann, 2011). This prediction appears to have assumed that Member States with more generous provisions were only waiting for a 'good excuse' to decrease their protection standards. However, different national asylum standards reflect 'different experiences, traditions and social and geographical conditions' (Hailbronner, 2009: 2).

It is therefore unlikely that those EU Member States that have over time adopted relatively more generous asylum provisions for various reasons would necessarily be driven to drastically alter them by the EU's setting of common minimum standards. Far from using the EU instruments as an excuse to decrease their asylum standards, the EU Member States have generally proved reluctant to alter their domestic asylum provisions, in line with the aforementioned argument by Börzel (2003) that Member States tend to favour the adoption of the EU provisions that are most akin to those already in place at the national level. This has been particularly evident in the case of the negotiations of the Procedures Directive, where most Member States 'attempted to make the text reflect what they were doing at the time' (Ackers, 2005: 32) and did not display any intention of changing and downgrading their own standards to the level of the common minimum standards. Hailbronner (2009: 4) has also observed a 'frequently partial or total non-transposition of directive provisions of the first generation by Member States arguing that by maintaining more favourite national laws no transposition is needed'.

Third, the EU asylum provisions have not only caused an overall drop in legal protection standards across the EU but have also actually raised legal standards in several respects (Kaunert, 2009a, 2010c; Levy, 2010). In particular, the Qualification Directive has significantly increased protection standards in the EU (Sidorenko, 2007: 217; Storey, 2008). It has codified a 'subsidiary protection' status, which is an improvement on the often *ad hoc* and discretionary character of complementary protection measures that were in existence in several EU Member States (McAdam, 2005), in addition to extending the scope of 'actors of persecution or serious harm' to non-state actors. These important provisions have had a profound impact on the legislation and practices in several EU Member States, including France and Germany, which have been required to introduce these new grounds for protection in their national legislation (El-Enany and Thielemann, 2011: 106–7). The Temporary

Protection Directive has also been seen as facilitating the provision of international protection to persons requiring it in situations of 'mass influx' (Garlick, 2006). It is true that the other EU asylum instruments have not been so favourably received (Guild, 2004, 2006). The Asylum Procedures Directive has been particularly criticised (Costello, 2005). However, it is important to note that its minimum procedural standards have actually required several EU Member States to raise their protection standards (Ackers, 2005: 32; Fullerton, 2005), whilst some of its most controversial provisions were annulled by the ECJ in 2008 (Kaunert and Léonard, 2011a: 87). Thus, as emphasised by Boswell and Geddes (2011: 151), 'while the EU has contributed to the rolling out of restrictive approaches in some areas, in many instances it has influenced countries to adopt more liberal approaches'. This assessment is also shared by El-Enany (2008: 334) who argues that '[in] a number of ways, the European refugee is better treated than ever before; guaranteed broader and more equitable protection in each Member State'.

Fourth, it is important to emphasise that these higher asylum standards do not 'only exist on paper' but have had a significant impact in reality. Although it is true that some Member States, notably Greece, have had difficulties so far to meet the EU's new asylum minimum standards, those are increasingly being implemented in practice as a result of both assistance and pressure from the EU. Since 2000, the efforts of EU Member States to develop and improve their asylum systems have been supported by a financial solidarity mechanism, the European Refugee Fund (ERF). Although some may still find it too modest, this has steadily grown to reach €628 million in its third phase (2008–2013). In addition, it was decided in 2010 to establish the EASO, which aims to provide further expertise and technical assistance to EU Member States in the field of asylum (Comte, 2010). Pressure on non-compliant Member States has also been exercised by the European Commission, which, since 2004, has launched infringement proceedings against several states for not fully implementing the various EU asylum directives and regulations (Peers, 2007: 91). As a result, those have had to amend their national asylum policies in order to comply with the EU's standards. Thus, the analysis of the main legal instruments adopted by the EU in the asylum venue has shown that, overall, the EU policy has led to more generous, legal standards for asylum seekers and refugees.

The EU and refugees: recognition

This section will analyse the external dimension of asylum and migration – an area which was used, particularly by the Commission, in order to prevent the construction of refugees as a security threat in the EU. As a side effect, the Commission managed to block the recognition of the EU as a security actor, most notably because it aimed to preserve the image of the EU as a humanitarian actor in refugee policy, or even a normative power, on the global stage. While the criteria of recognition is a vital element of the behavioural criteria for the EU to become a global actor, given the fact that the EU must be recognised by other states and non-state actors in order to really become an actor, this section demonstrates that the Commission perceived it is preferable to be seen as a humanitarian actor than a security actor in this field. Recognition by others allows for its presence in global politics, but this case demonstrates that the kind of presence it can acquire matters to the EU. While Member States may have attempted to securitise refugees as security issues at the national level, at the EU level the Commission has resisted this. Therefore, it has successfully managed to prevent a potential recognition as a securitising actor of refugees – and thus has managed to preserve the EU's image as a humanitarian actor in asylum policy.

The so-called 'external dimension' or 'internationalisation' of the EU immigration and asylum policy has become increasingly important in recent years from both policy and scholarly points of view (van Selm, 2002; Boswell, 2003a, 2003b; Lavenex, 2006). There is no precise definition of this concept, which broadly refers to the external relations in the area of border, asylum and migration. As migration issues, by definition, concern the crossing of borders and involve different states, the definition of the 'external dimension' of the EU asylum and migration policy could cover a very large number of issues, if not the policy as a whole. This would decrease its usefulness as a concept. In this section, therefore, it is decided to analyse how the European Commission skilfully exploited the problems encountered by a radical British proposal on asylum and migration to externalise asylum processing, that is to push the processing of asylum claims outside the territory of the EU. It will show how the British government failed to wait for the right moment and did not manage to convince enough of its fellow governments to support its proposal. In doing so, it opened the policy window for the Commission. This managed to successfully divert the attention away from the British proposal towards its own proposal, which itself drew upon previous work. While the aim of the Commission in this case was not to push through a particular proposal but rather to stop the British proposal, it also fits in with the Commission's general approach to the area of EU asylum discussed in the preceding section, that is anchoring this policy in international refugee norms. In contrast, the British proposal aimed to push the EU in the opposite direction and ultimately failed.

This case can also be seen as a form of policy entrepreneurship of the Commission aiming to protect its other achievements in the field of asylum. The British proposal, if successful, would have had the capacity to considerably undo these achievements.

The EU debates the British proposal on the extraterritorial processing of asylum claims

As the EU was about to enter the final year of the 'Tampere programme' and Member States were engaged in the long and complicated negotiations of several directives in the area of asylum as seen in the previous section, the British government made a proposal on asylum that dominated the EU debates in this policy area for a few months in 2003. It suggested processing the claims of asylum seekers having reached the EU – or on their way to the EU – outside the territory of its Member States, a policy known as the 'extra-territorial processing of asylum claims'.

This idea proved to be highly contentious (interviews NGO 1 to 10, IGO1, COM2, COM7, COM12 and COM16) and gave rise to intense debates amongst the Member States of the EU, the European Commission, the UNHCR and the NGOs active in the field of asylum and migration. The proposal, described by some as aiming to 'radically change European Union asylum policy' (BBC News, 2003a), was harshly criticised on legal, moral, economic and practical grounds (interviews NGO 1–10). Amnesty International (2003) branded it 'unlawful' and 'unworkable'. This section opens with a chronological presentation of the debates in the EU on the British proposal in 2003. It outlines the evolution of the EU debates on the British proposal with regard to the extraterritorial processing of asylum claims. It also presents in detail the British proposal as well as the two other proposals on the same topic that were considered at the same time, which had been tabled by the UNHCR and the Commission, respectively. In effect, there was a competition between these three proposals as to which one would shape the future development of the external dimension of the EU asylum policy.

The British proposal 'New International Approaches to Asylum Processing and Protection' (March 2003)

On 10 March 2003, Tony Blair sent a letter to Greek Prime Minister Costas Simitis – the then President of the Council of the EU – asking for a discussion at the upcoming Brussels European Council on an idea developed 'to help deal with the problems of refuges and migration'.

Attached to the letter was a six-page document bearing the title 'New International Approaches to Asylum Processing and Protection' (UK Government, 2003). This document started by highlighting the premise underpinning the British proposal, namely that the 'current global [asylum] system [was] failing' for various reasons (UK Government, 2003: 1). Firstly, financial support for refugees was inequitably distributed, as Western states devoted a lot of money to processing asylum applications, whereas little money was spent in the regions of origin of the refugees. Secondly, the current system required asylum seekers to enter the West illegally, often with the help of criminal organisations. Thirdly, between half and three quarters of those claiming asylum in Europe did not meet the criteria of 'full refugees', whereas 12 million 'genuine refugees' remained in their region of origin to find protection. Finally, there were high costs and difficulties involved in returning the asylum seekers whose application had been rejected, which, in turn, undermined the confidence of the public in the asylum system. Especially the fact that the UK government attempted to link the refugees to organised crime in this proposal can be seen to establish asylum seekers as a potential security threat.

Based on the aforementioned assessment, the British proposal aimed to develop a 'better management of the asylum process globally' (UK Government, 2003: 1) through a reduction in the number of unfounded applications and the improvement of the protection granted to genuine refugees. For this purpose, it proposed the establishment of a new asylum system, whereby asylum seekers would no longer arrive illegally in Europe in order to claim asylum but would rather arrive through legal channels, including refugee resettlement. In what can be interpreted as an attempt to increase the legitimacy of its proposal, the British government claimed that it drew on the 'Convention Plus' initiative of the UNHCR (UK Government, 2003: 2). The 'Convention Plus' is an initiative that was launched by the UNHCR in 2002. It aimed to build on the Geneva Convention, by creating special agreements on the secondary movements of asylum seekers (that is, movements of asylum seekers from a first country of refuge to another country) and ensuring lasting solutions for refugees in regions of origin. This proposal would have had very clear consequences, not only regarding the number of refugees potentially accepted in the EU, but also for the image of the EU globally. The EU would have clearly become to be seen as a securitising actor in the area of global refugee flows.

The British proposal had two complementary components, namely (1) the adoption of measures to improve the regional management of migration flows, including the establishment of 'protected areas' for asylum processing and (2) the establishment of processing centres on transit routes to Europe. The British government emphasised in the document that its ultimate objective was 'to deal more successfully with illegal migrants within their region of origin' through the adoption of four types of measures (UK Government, 2003: 2). Those, respectively, aimed to tackle the root causes of migration and to improve the protection capacities in the source regions, establish better managed resettlement routes to Europe on a quota basis and raise the awareness and acceptance of the states of origin of their 'responsibility to accept returns' (UK Government, 2003: 4), possibly through the conclusion of new readmission agreements. However, the British government was aware that its proposal could only be implemented in the long term. It rested on the idea that countries of origin would have protection standards high enough to convince European domestic courts of the lawfulness of the transfer of asylum seekers over there. Given the currently low protection standards of many of these countries, this could only be considered a remote perspective. Therefore, the proposal of the British government also suggested medium-term action in order 'to deter those who enter the EU illegally and make unfounded claims' (UK Government, 2003: 4), whilst preserving the right to protection for those who are genuinely entitled to it.

More precisely, the suggestion put forward was the creation of the so-called 'Transit Processing Centres' (TPCs) for asylum seekers. Such centres would be established outside the EU, for example on migration transit routes to the EU. They could be managed by the International Organisation for Migration (IOM) and financed by the participating states, with perhaps – at least this is what the British government seemed to hope – some financial support from the EC budget. Asylum seekers arriving in the United Kingdom (or in another EU participating state) would be transferred to those TPCs where their application for asylum would be processed, 'with a screening system approved by the UNHCR' (UK Government, 2003: 5). Those persons granted refugee status would be resettled in the EU on a quota basis. The asylum seekers whose application had been rejected would normally be returned to their country of origin. Only in the case where they could not be returned safely to their country of origin might asylum seekers be given temporary refuge in the EU, until the situation in their country of origin improved. The British proposal also mentioned the idea of sending to the TPCs 'illegal migrants intercepted en route to the EU before they had lodged an asylum claim' (UK Government, 2003: 5), if they appeared to have a clear intention to do so.

This proposal had been developed over the previous months by a joint Cabinet Office/Home Office Committee. It had already been presented to Ruud Lubbers (interview IGO1), the UN High Commissioner for Refugees, at a meeting in London on 10 February 2003 as the British government hoped to get the UNHCR's endorsement and its agreement to participate in the implementation of the proposal. At the Brussels European Council on 20–21 March 2003, there was only a brief and preliminary discussion of the British proposal. The Heads of State and Government decided to invite the European Commission to 'explore these ideas further, in particular with UNHCR' (Council, 2003b: 30) and to report to the next European Council in June 2003.

The Veria Council: debates on the British proposal and the UNHCR's 'three-pronged' proposal

At the informal meeting of the EU JHA Council in Veria on 28 March 2003, it appeared that the EU Member States were divided on the British proposal (Financial Times, 2003a; Independent, 2003). Some Member States indicated their support for the proposal, in particular Italy, Denmark and the Netherlands and also, although to a lesser extent, Finland, Spain, Ireland, Austria and Belgium. Some of them made their approval conditional upon the approval of the plan by the UNHCR (Financial Times, 2003a). In contrast, German Interior Minister Otto Schily expressed his scepticism towards the plan and received the support of other Member States, notably Sweden and Portugal. European Commission officials also had reservations about the British proposal, which, in their view, was not fully thought through and raised numerous legal and budgetary questions (Financial Times, 2003a).

The media reported that Ruud Lubbers, the UN High Commissioner for Refugees, took part in the Veria meeting (Financial Times, 2003a). What the media did not explain at the time was that, at the Veria Council, Lubbers did not merely comment on the British proposal. He also tabled a rather comprehensive counter-proposal, the so-called 'three-pronged' proposal, the content of which suggested that the UNHCR largely shared the British government's appraisal of the state of the global asylum system. The documents in which it was exposed in detail were not made public by the UNHCR and only became accessible after they were leaked to Statewatch. The 'three-pronged proposal' was named after its three prongs or main dimensions: (1) improving the national asylum systems of the destination states, (2) improving access to solutions in the regions of origin and (3) processing the 'manifestly unfounded' cases in EU-operated closed reception centres within EU borders.

The first prong, the 'regional prong', aimed to improve access to protection and solutions in the regions of origin of refugees 'while addressing certain asylum dilemmas confronting host States' (UNHCR, 2003: 1). The purpose of the second prong, called the 'domestic prong', was to improve the national asylum systems of the destination states. The UNHCR argued that, after the wide array of asylum reforms adopted by many states, the time had come 'to refocus efforts to establish clearer and simpler procedures, which concentrate on well-resourced, and faster yet quality initial decision-making with appropriate safeguards' (UNHCR, 2003: 11). The third prong, called the 'EU prong', proved to be the most controversial. Its aim was to encourage EU Member States to address the issue of 'mixed movements', that is migratory flows of both asylum seekers and economic migrants, by processing jointly presumed 'manifestly unfounded asylum claims' from selected non-refugee-producing countries of origin. In other words, persons originating from designated countries of origin would be considered as economic migrants resorting to the asylum channel. Upon arrival anywhere in the EU, they would be immediately transferred to a joint EU centre for the processing of their claim, with the exceptions of persons medically unfit to travel or stay in a closed centre.

Such a centre would be a closed reception and EU-funded centre, where interpretation services and legal counselling would be available for asylum seekers. The processing of applications would be conducted in accordance with 'commonly agreed procedures respecting international standards' (UNHCR, 2003: 7). First instance decisions would be taken promptly and appeals could be limited to a simplified review. The UNHCR would monitor the determination process and could also be part of the review process. In contrast to the British proposal which foresaw centres located inside the EU, the UNHCR proposed to create centres 'initially in one or two EU Member States' (UNHCR, 2003: 7). Those found in need of protection would be distributed within the EU in accordance with pre-agreed criteria, as there would be expanded resettlements quotas in the EU. The asylum seekers whose claim was rejected would be returned through operations jointly organised by the EU Member States, in cooperation with the IOM. Thus, in addition to the British proposal, there was now a second proposal on the negotiation table – that of the UNHCR. In some respects, it was in broad agreement with that of the

The EU and Refugees 135

British government, notably with regard to the current problems of the global asylum system, the importance of strengthening protection in the regions of origin and the need to implement reforms. The UNHCR's proposal also contained the idea of establishing processing centres as had been suggested by the British government.

By the end of the Veria Council, Member States had not been able to reach a common position on these proposals for the extraterritorial processing of asylum claims. They decided that these matters should be discussed again at the Thessaloniki Council in June. It was expected that, by that time, the European Commission would have published a new Communication exploring these ideas further, as requested by the European Council in March.

The role of the EU institutions and the UNHCR

As explained earlier, the British proposal was received with interest by some EU governments, although some of them insisted on its endorsement by the UNHCR. The European Commission stated that the proposal gave rise to several legal and practical issues. This opinion may have been shared by several governments, but only two made their opposition to the British proposal publicly known, namely Germany and Sweden (Financial Times, 2003b; Guardian, 2003a). Consequently, it was the Commission that played a key role in the evolution of the discussions by tabling a proposal that would divert the attention away from the British proposal, thereby reducing its chances of success. In doing so, the Commission would manage to protect its own achievements in the asylum field, which have been analysed before, and more importantly, the Commission would preserve the recognition of the EU as a humanitarian actor in the area of global refugee flows.

The European Commission's counter-proposal

In the following weeks, as the Thessaloniki Council drew closer, the idea of the extra-territorial processing of asylum claims dominated the European asylum and migration debates. The media regularly reported on this topic, notably the Observer (2003), which claimed that the British proposal was already being implemented as a '[s]ecret Balkan camp [was being] built to hold UK asylum seekers' in Croatia. This turned out to be wrong, but other media outlets had already reproduced the story (BBC News, 2003b; EUobserver, 2003). According to several media reports, the British government continued to champion the idea of creating 'zones of protection' for asylum seekers near conflict areas, an idea which, it claimed, had the support of the UNHCR, the European

Commission and 'a number of [Britain's] EU partners' (Guardian, 2003b; see also Financial Times, 2003b). As a first step in that direction, it hoped to gain EU political support and funding for pilot projects, the first of which was expected to be carried out in the Horn of Africa (Financial Times, 2003b; Guardian, 2003a).

However, at the Thessaloniki Council on 19–20 June 2003, the idea of 'zones of protection' 'did not (...) make it past the first working session of the three-day summit' (BBC News, 2003a). After hearing the objections of the European Commission and several other EU Member States, notably Sweden and Germany, at the pre-summit dinner, the British government decided to withdraw its proposal (BBC News, 2003a). Nevertheless, it announced its intention to form a 'coalition of the willing' with other like-minded Member States, such as Denmark, Austria, the Netherlands and Ireland, in order to pilot some trial schemes of regional protection zones (BBC News, 2003a; Financial Times, 2003b; Guardian, 2003a). As the British proposal was being withdrawn from EU debates, the Commission capitalised on the policy dynamics of the time to push the policy in a different direction (interview COM16). At the Thessaloniki Council, Member States began to discuss a Communication on asylum that the European Commission had published on 3 June 2003 under the title 'Towards more accessible, equitable, and managed asylum systems' (European Commission, 2003a) (interviews PR 1, 4–8, 15). Although this document started by analysing the British proposal as well as UNHCR's contribution to the debates, it would be misleading to interpret it as a purely *ad hoc* reaction to these developments. It actually built on a series of Communications on asylum that the Commission had been releasing since 2000. Before examining this 2003 Communication in greater detail, it is necessary to present briefly the Communications that preceded it in order to understand its foundations.

In 2000, the Commission tabled a Communication entitled 'Towards a common asylum procedure and a uniform status, valid throughout the Union, for persons granted asylum' (COM(2000) 755). It notably argued that processing asylum claims in the region of origin of refugees and facilitating their arrival into the EU through the establishment of a resettlement scheme would allow them to access protection rapidly, without having to migrate illegally or use the services of criminal gangs. The Commission underlined that this option could only be complementary to the treatment of spontaneous applications for asylum on the territory of the EU Member States. Subsequently, it commissioned two feasibility studies on the processing of asylum claims outside the EU and on an EU-wide resettlement scheme, respectively. In 2001, the

Commission published another Communication on asylum, bearing the title 'On the common asylum policy, introducing an open coordination method' (COM(2001) 710). Again, it mentioned the idea of 'evaluating the merits of resettlement programmes [and] the possibility of processing asylum applications outside the Member States (...)'. In the same year, the Commission also published a Communication 'On a common policy on illegal immigration', in which it suggested that

> Member States should (...) explore possibilities of offering rapid access to protection so that refugees do not need to resort to illegal immigration or people smugglers. This could include greater use of Member States' discretion in allowing more asylum applications to be made from abroad or the processing of a request for protection in the region of origin and facilitating the arrival of refugees on the territory of the Member States by resettlement scheme. Such approaches could ensure sufficient refugee protection within and compatible with a system of efficient countermeasures against illegal migratory flows.
>
> (European Commission, 2001a: 8)

In its Communication of June 2003, the Commission drew on the results of the two feasibility studies commissioned earlier to develop these ideas further (European Commission/Danish Centre for Human Rights, 2003). It mentioned that it agreed with the assessment of the British government that asylum procedures were being abused in Europe and that 'new avenues' ought to be explored. However, it differed from the British proposal by emphasising again the 'need to fully respect international legal obligations of Member States' (European Commission, 2003a: 11) – a concern ignored in the British proposal. The Commission also emphasised that 'managed entry' proposals should be complementary to the traditional territorial processing of asylum claims. It criticised the British idea to replace, rather than complement, the existing asylum system by a 'new approach to the international protection regime'. More importantly, it radically dissociated itself from the British government's idea of 'transit processing centres' by not considering this policy alternative at all. The two main proposals that the European Commission put forward in this Communication were the introduction of Protected Entry Procedures (PEPs) and the creation of an EU-wide resettlement scheme. PEPs would allow a non-national approach to a potential host state outside its territory with a claim for asylum (or other form of international protection) and to be granted an entry permit in case of a positive response to that claim, be it preliminary or final. In a refugee resettlement scheme, refugees would be transferred from a first host country to a second host country where they would enjoy guarantees of protection, including residence, and prospects for integration and autonomy.

At the Thessaloniki Council, Member States asked the Commission to 'explore all parameters in order to ensure more orderly and managed entry in the EU of persons in need of international protection, and to examine ways and means to enhance the protection capacity of regions of origin' with a view to present a report to the Council before June 2004 'suggesting measures to be taken, including legal implications' (Council, 2003c: 8). A draft text of the Presidency Conclusions read differently as it called on the European Commission to 'examine ways and means to enhance the protection capacity of regions of origin and first countries of asylum, in particular on the basis of experience gained by pilot projects to be conducted in full partnership with countries concerned and in close cooperation with UNHCR' (Financial Times 2003b). However, several Member States rejected the mention of the pilot projects, which explains why only the broader and less committal reference to the 'protection capacity of regions of origin' remained in the final text (Guardian, 2003a). In sum, the Thessaloniki Council brought an end to the discussions of the British government's ideas of 'transit processing centres' and 'regional protection areas (or zones)', as the European Commission and several other EU Member States expressed their scepticism or, in some cases, strong opposition. Instead, it was the Commission's proposal, which notably suggested strengthening the protection capacity of regions of origin, which took centre stage in the development of the external dimension of the EU asylum policy.

The role of the Commission

On 1st October 2004, the European Commission announced at the informal JHA Council that it had decided to fund the €1,000,000 UNHCR project 'Towards a protection space in North Africa' in conjunction with the Netherlands (Bulletin Quotidien Europe, 2004). This project concerned Morocco, Libya, Tunisia, Mauritania and Algeria. Its objectives were to enhance knowledge of transit migration, to develop basic protection mechanisms in North Africa, to examine media and public attitudes, to support NGOs and to prepare a multilateral approach to protection on the high seas. In September 2005, the European Commission announced that it was to develop 'Regional Protection Programmes' (RPPs) in close cooperation with the UNHCR and the third countries involved (European Commission, 2005). RPPs would aim to deliver direct benefits to refugees and to contribute to improving the protection and human rights situation in third countries hosting large populations of refugees. Each RPP would focus on five or six actions, including the delivery of practical benefits such as training, infrastructure building, the provision of equipment and so on. The Commission announced that the first pilot RPP would be implemented in the Western Newly Independent States (WNIS) (Ukraine, Moldova and Belarus), as this region emerged as a clear priority in the discussions between the Commission and the Member States. This RPP would focus on strengthening already existing protection capacity, notably by giving practical support to the examination of asylum applications, the reinforcement of subsidiary protection, integration and registration. The identification of a second pilot RPP was also discussed in the Commission's Communication. It mainly discussed the suitability of the Great Lakes Region, in particular Tanzania, for this purpose, but also mentioned other possibilities such as North Africa, the Afghanistan region and the Horn of Africa (European Commission, 2007d).

Therefore, the development of the Commission's idea of RPP and its subsequent implementation demonstrate that, with regard to this crucial stage in the development of the external dimension of the EU asylum and border management policy, the Commission was able to push its own proposals forward to a considerable extent. Moreover, what is remarkable is that these proposals were significantly different from those made by the British government, which was the main rival of the Commission for agenda-setting in this policy area at the time. Thus, this section demonstrated how the European Commission skilfully exploited the problems encountered by the British proposal on asylum and migration to push through its own ideas. This underlines the need to wait for the right moment, which the British government had failed to do, and to convince enough of its fellow governments to support its proposal. Consequently, this case is a form of policy entrepreneurship of the Commission aiming to protect its other achievements in the field of asylum, while pushing further its own agenda. In the end, the Commission did not aim for external recognition by third actors as a securitising actor, but it aimed to maintain the achievements in its asylum instruments. The fact that it rejected the approach of dealing with refugees as a security threat meant that the EU would not be recognised as a security actor in this field – much to its delight. Thus, the Commission managed to maintain the image of the EU as a humanitarian actor in the field of global refugee flows.

Conclusion

The EU's 'actorness' in the EU asylum policy has a number of distinctive features: it has achieved an important scope of integration and quite significant capabilities. However, the Commission prevented the recognition of the EU as a securitising actor in asylum policy at the global level, against the wishes of Member States, such as the UK, in order to maintain its image as a humanitarian actor in asylum and refugee policy. This chapter has presented an exemplary case study of how much the EU has become an actor in asylum policy, but without presenting this policy area as a security threat and thus without achieving that type of recognition. It has been demonstrated that the Commission played a crucial role in this case study, which shows that the EU achieved a high scope of integration, and, furthermore, has acquired a high degree of capabilities, as the four asylum directives show. Yet, there were two differences in asylum policy as compared to the area of counter-terrorism. Firstly, the success of the four asylum directives, which achieved these very significant capabilities, was in fact a long and tedious process. It took almost five years to achieve the four directives, whereas the European Arrest Warrant (EAW), for example, took less than one year of negotiation and two years of preparation. This suggests that it is easier to acquire capabilities when policies are perceived as security threats than when granting refugee rights.

This should not be very surprising given that Member States were negotiating these legislative capabilities during the 'war on terror'. The bulk of the negotiations were conducted after the terrorist attacks of 11 September 2001 in New York and Washington. Madrid (11 March 2004) and London (7 July 2005) soon followed. Why would the Commission push for the rights of refugees in such a difficult political climate? It would have been far easier to link asylum to security and terrorism, as had been done in the case of the EAW. It worked very well as a strategy in that case – why change? Actually, the Commission did not pursue this strategy in the area of asylum and border management and actively resisted it in the external dimension. It continued to push for refugee rights under the Geneva Convention and opposed the perception of asylum seekers as security threats. It notably managed to divert the British proposal to externalise asylum claims outside the borders of the EU. This is in many ways an even more remarkable success for the Commission than the 'easier' success in counter-terrorism cooperation, which demonstrates the central role of EU bureaucracy in this case and – as a result – the high degree of capabilities. All four asylum directives actually increased the legal value of the Geneva Convention, as discussed above. The area was communitarised after the first-phase instruments of the Tampere programme, further reinforced with the Lisbon Treaty, which also strongly reinforced the very high degree in the scope of integration in the area.

However, the Commission actively resisted bringing recognition for the EU as a security actor in asylum and migration issues. As a consequence of this political strategy, the EU remains primarily a humanitarian actor in asylum policy, even when some member states, such as the United Kingdom, would have liked to change that approach. Why did the Commission not aim for the recognition as a security actor? Firstly, when the Commission started to construct a role for the EU in national asylum policy, it had decided to link it to both the single market – to push the project – and the internationally prevailing refugee protection norms – to gain legitimacy. The latter is particularly important as the Commission was frequently attacked for not being democratic, particularly during the 1990s, and even today to some extent. The essence of its legitimacy problem is that the 'unelected' Commission is widely perceived as detached from the concerns of EU citizens. Thus, its own legitimacy needed to be increased through the legitimacy of other actors in the field – the UNHCR, NGOs and the European Parliament. Secondly, the anchoring of the EU asylum policy within the international prevailing refugee rights norms became vital after 11 September 2001. At this point, norms could have easily shifted towards a securitisation of asylum – the construction of asylum as a security threat. Yet, from the documentary and interview evidence, it is clear that the Commission took the political decision at that time to not link the asylum issue to the 'war on terror' (interviews COM10 and COM16).

Van Selm (2003: 143) describes it as remarkable that the Commission's proposal for a Framework Decision on combating terrorism made no mention of refugees, asylum or the exclusion of any person seeking refugee status. In her view, this was particularly remarkable as the Geneva Convention did provide grounds for exclusion from refugee status for terrorists. Yet, the Commission decided not to link the issues of asylum and terrorism. In the end, the Commission managed to keep the policy anchored within international norms and thereby prevented a shift into security (COM (2001) 743 final). Consequently, in the working document entitled 'the relationship between safeguarding internal security and complying with international protection obligations', the Commission did not advocate any change in international refugee protection and based the Geneva Convention at the heart of any response.

There are two main premises of the Commission working document: (1) *bona fide* refugees and asylum seekers should not become victims of the then recent events and (2) no avenues should exist for the supporting of terrorist acts. The document made it clear that a scrupulous application of the exceptions to refugee protection available under the current laws was the appropriate response. It was therefore an outright rejection of placing security in contradiction to existing refugee protection instruments. Moreover, while the Commission acknowledged that terrorists might use asylum channels, it considered this as not likely, as other channels would be more discreet and more suitable for criminal practices. It was suggested for the Member States to use existing legal instruments (COM (2001) 743 final), based on the Geneva Convention. In essence, this document did not deviate from accepted international norms. In fact, it demonstrated the legal value of the Geneva Convention and thereby strengthened it. It resisted the temptation to move an issue into the security area when it was perceived as a human rights issue. In fact, the Commission rescued this political perception by trying to reconcile the demands for greater security with the international refugee protection norms. Thus, the Commission managed to maintain the EU's global image as a humanitarian actor in the field of global refugee flows – much truer to its form as 'normative power Europe'.

Thus, this chapter has contributed to academic debates about the correlation between asylum policy and international security, analysing the EU as a relatively recent actor intending to raise its profile in international relations. This 'actorness' was assessed against three criteria of 'actorness', including the scope of integration, capabilities and recognition. Empirically, the EU enjoys a significantly high scope of integration in asylum policy. The policy entrepreneurship of central EU institutions, notably the European Commission has been of crucial importance in this respect, even when it managed to obstruct some Member States such as the United Kingdom. Regarding the EU's capabilities, the EU has also achieved very strong advances; the four asylum directives can be considered as very significant legal capabilities for the area of asylum and migration. Furthermore, with the new competences provided by the Lisbon Treaty and thus the increased degree in the scope of integration in the area, there is a very strong likelihood for even more increased legal capabilities in the second phase of the four asylum directives negotiated during the Stockholm Programme. With its close links to the UNHCR, we can also observe the fact that the EU is an active player within the global multilateral framework and thus aims at achieving international recognition. Thus, this chapter has established that the EU is relatively well recognised as a global actor on asylum policy, although its global role does not extend into areas of security regarding this policy. While the EU has achieved recognition globally, it has aimed to achieve this as a humanitarian actor and not as a security actor, despite Member States such as the United Kingdom. Very clearly, the correlation between security and refugees remains somewhat ambiguous and very contested within the EU. Many states are reluctant to perceive asylum policy under the security label. This offers the EU an opportunity to act as a 'humanitarian actor' at the global level, attempting to distinguish refugees from security policy. However, the future of the EU's leadership in this area is uncertain, with different Member States pushing in different directions. The resolution of the 'Euro crisis' will play a crucial role in this respect; if growth returns, the EU could remain primarily a humanitarian actor, especially in this post-Bin Laden environment. However, equally, during this crisis, the temptation to reduce the costs for national budgets by reducing the number of refugees accepted in the EU could tempt some Member States to use security arguments to achieve increased cost reductions. A potential future security role for the EU in the asylum field is therefore not entirely inconceivable and only time will tell.

6
The EU and Non-proliferation: The Case of Russia

> With hundreds of tons of nuclear materials, an unwelcome holdover from the Soviet era, the Russian Federation is the most promising source of illicit fissile materials for Al Qaeda and kindred groups.
>
> (Busch and Holmes, 2009: 325)

This chapter assesses the European Union's (EU) international security 'actorness' with respect to preventing the proliferation of weapons of mass destruction (WMDs) from the territories of the former Soviet Union, most notably Russia (Zwolski, 2011a, 2011b). Although the threat of nuclear conflict between the West and the East has essentially disappeared together with the dissolution of the Warsaw Pact, the enormous stockpile of insufficiently protected chemical, biological, radiological and nuclear (CBRN) materials has emerged as a major security concern. This time it was not the state which was the source of threat, but rather unauthorised individuals and non-state actors acquiring access to poorly protected Russian CBRN materials, as indicated by Busch and Holmes (2009). As a result, the US Congress has launched an enormous programme of financial and technical assistance to Russia, aiming to prevent the spread of sensitive materials. The EU, as the only non-state actor, has undertaken its own efforts in this area. This chapter investigates the EU's contribution in preventing the proliferation of WMDs, primarily from the former Soviet Union, through a range of legal, technical and financial instruments.

For the EU, preventing the proliferation of WMDs appears to be increasingly important. Notably, the ESS (Council, 2003a) identifies WMD proliferation to be 'potentially the greatest threat'. In particular, three challenges associated with WMDs are recognised in this document, that is (a) the danger of arms race, particularly in the Middle East; (b) biological weapons may become more deadly as a result of technological advances; and (c) terrorist groups may acquire WMDs. Further, the Implementation Report (European Council, 2008) assigns even more urgency to the threat of the proliferation of WMDs. In particular, this document notes that the risk associated with WMD proliferation had increased between 2003 and 2008, pointing to Iran and North Korea in the context of their nuclear programmes. Furthermore, the Strategy against Proliferation of Weapons of Mass Destruction (WMD Strategy (European Council, 2003) underlines not only that the threat of proliferation is taken seriously in Europe but also that the EU aspires to develop a common policy in this area. To this end, the WMD Strategy states: 'WMD and missile proliferation puts at risk the security of our states, our peoples and our interests around the world. Meeting this challenge must be a central element in the EU's external action. The EU must act with resolve, using all instruments and policies at its disposal' (European Council, 2003: 2).

'Weapons of Mass Destruction' can be conceptualised in a narrower or a broader manner. In a narrower sense, WMDs refer exclusively to nuclear weapons. Some scholars advocate this narrow understanding on the basis that the inclusion of chemical and biological weapons into the category of WMDs weakens the 'nuclear taboo' (Pal Singh Sidhu, 2008: 363). This chapter follows a more conventional understanding of WMDs which encompasses all three kinds of weapons: nuclear, biological and chemical. This broader understanding has been, for the most part, embraced by the international Community; for example, the UN Security Council, in its Resolution 1540 adopted in 2004 (UNSC, 2004), committed 'to take appropriate and effective actions against any threat to international peace and security caused by the proliferation of nuclear, chemical and biological weapons and their means of delivery (...)'. In a similar vein, G8 leaders, through the 'Global Partnership against the Spread of Weapons and Materials of Mass Destruction' (Global Partnership), committed to 'prevent terrorists, or those that harbour them, from acquiring or developing nuclear, chemical, radiological and biological weapons (...)' (G8, 2002). Thus, this chapter uses terms such as WMDs and CBRN interchangeably.

Why is it important to focus on the threat of proliferation from Russia? With the collapse of the Soviet Union, Russia has emerged as the country with the largest stockpile of CBRN materials in the world, located in the world's largest number of buildings. This fact, in itself, does not have to be the source of the threat of proliferation. Yet, in the 1990s, 'Moscow's ability to exercise adequate command and control and to prevent unauthorised access into its WMD complex became frequently challenged' (Turpen and Finlay, 2009: 304). There were a few important sources of this concern. First, the change of the political system from the one which was closed and heavily infiltrated by the Committee for State Security (KGB), in which nuclear, chemical and biological programmes were developed in secrecy and were unlikely to be penetrated from the outside to the system relatively more open, with inadequate security measures, was the source of major concern in the Western world. Second, on top of this enormous political transformation, Russia and former Soviet Union countries faced difficult economic conditions throughout the 1990s. This, combined with the fact that CBRN knowledge, materials and weapons are highly marketable, also became an important source of concern, particularly in the context of potential theft coming from the inside, rather than the outside.

Third, about 130,000–150,000 scientists in former Soviet Union countries were considered to possess knowledge which could contribute to developing a nuclear device. Most of them lacked employment and thus the prospect of their migration to countries seeking to develop WMDs became another significant source of concern. In an unprecedented survey concluded in 2003, 20 per cent out of 602 Russian physicists, biologists and chemists responded that they would consider working in Iran, North Korea, Syria or Iraq (Ball and Gerber, 2004). Fourth, in addition to these concerns associated with nuclear weapons and technologies, Soviet extensive biological weapons programme has become the source of concern because '[o]ver the course of decades, the Soviet Union weaponised thousands of tons of viruses, toxins, and bacteria, including anthrax, smallpox, botulinum toxin and the plague' (Turpen and Finlay, 2009: 305). After the disintegration of the Soviet Union, the expertise associated with these weapons became more available. Moreover, over 60,000 scientists used to work for the Soviet biological complex over the course of the Cold War. Those scientists have become an important source of proliferation concern. Ken Alibek, a Soviet-era biological weapons scientist, admits that he and his former colleagues have been approached on numerous occasions to share their knowledge (Alibek, 2000).

Busch and Holmes (2009) point to an additional problem, which underpins all of these concerns, making them even more serious. Focusing on the human factor, they analyse Russian nuclear security culture. They argue that even the most sophisticated security measures, installed with the support of the United States, the EU and other stakeholders cannot be effective if workers managing these systems on a daily basis are not adequately prepared. For example, the authors note that 'numerous reports have documented guards shutting off security and monitoring systems out of annoyance at frequent false alarms or simply because they found the systems too burdensome for routine use' (Busch and Holmes, 2009: 332-33). This attitude results from, among other factors, decades of arbitrary rule and the habit of mistrusting written rules.

Preventing the threat of proliferation from Russia has gained new urgency after the 9/11 terrorist attacks. Already in 2000, the US Department of Energy convened a special Task Force which aimed to evaluate US non-proliferation programmes in Russia. The Task Force concluded: 'The most urgent unmet national security threat to the United States today is the danger that weapons of mass destruction or weapons-usable material in Russia could be stolen and sold to terrorists or hostile nation states and used against American troops abroad or citizens at home' (Baker and Cutler, 2000: 1). In response to the 9/11 attacks, G8 countries initiated the Global Partnership, initially focusing their efforts on Russia. The most recent assessments indicate that Russia has now '[s]ubstantial security and accounting measures in place for its nuclear weapons and materials' (Bunn, 2010: 31), but potential problems remain, such as an issue of the aforementioned security culture. This chapter aims to assess EU 'actorness' in preventing the proliferation of WMDs. It focuses mainly on Russia because the EU's efforts in this geographical region have been slightly overlooked in research terms. Denza (2005: 293) finds it surprising: 'Given the extensive and justified fears expressed in the early 1990s that the break-up of the Soviet Union would lead to a leap in the number of nuclear-weapon states, the international effort and the European Union's contribution to that particular exercise in containment deserves greater acknowledgement than it has received'.

Instead, the majority of scholarly literature focuses on negotiations with Iran over its nuclear programme (Denza, 2005; Kile, 2005; Leonard, 2005; Harnish, 2007; Overhaus, 2007). While important, these negotiations do not represent the whole image of the EU as a non-proliferation security actor. Moreover, it can be argued that the threat of the CBRN proliferation from Russia has represented a much greater security problem than the Iranian nuclear programme, because it potentially involves non-state, unaccountable actors (Alibek, 2000; Baker and Cutler, 2000; Ball and Gerber, 2004; Busch and Holmes, 2009; Turpen and Finlay, 2009).

The structure of this chapter is as follows. The first section assesses the scope of European integration in the non-proliferation area.

In this context, of particular importance is the fact that up until the establishment of the European External Action Service (EEAS), the EU's non-proliferation policy was developed in two central EU institutions, that is the Council General Secretariat and the European Commission. Thus, a degree of competition developed among these institutions, with the Lisbon Treaty aiming to bring more unity and consistency. Subsequently, the chapter assesses different kinds of instruments that the EU has developed in the non-proliferation area, ranging from purely technical assistance programmes to higher-profile, political and diplomatic assets. Finally, in the third section the chapter examines the reasons why the EU tends not to be recognised as an important actor in the non-proliferation area.

The EU and non-proliferation: scope of integration

Under the European Political Cooperation (EPC) framework (1970–1993), European cooperation on non-proliferation was informal and non-binding (Smith, 2002; Sauer, 2003). The work for ministers was prepared by the Political Committee, further divided into working groups. One of these working groups, established in 1981 at the British–Dutch initiative, concerned the policy on the non-proliferation of WMDs (Sauer, 2003). The purpose of this working group was defined as follows: 'Anxious to ensure that the civil use of nuclear energy does not contribute to the proliferation of nuclear arms and explosives, the Ten sought it necessary to have discussions, consultations and exchanges of information on questions involving aspects of non-proliferation which could be discussed in political co-operation' (quoted in Goens, 1987: 44). Its establishment resulted in adopting a number of common declarations within the framework of international non-proliferation regimes, but these efforts were of purely intergovernmental character, not embedded in any formal institutional framework.

The Treaty on the European Union (TEU) integrated the EPC as the second pillar of the newly established EU, developing it into the Common Foreign and Security Policy (CFSP). Consequently, two new legal instruments of the EU included common positions and joint actions. One of the first areas defined by Member States as a possible object of joint actions, agreed upon even before the Maastricht Treaty came into force, was policy on the non-proliferation of WMDs. Soon after joint actions became available, Member States started utilising these instruments to coordinate their position on non-proliferation, most notably at the Non-Proliferation Treaty (NPT) Review Conferences.

According to Schmitt (2005: 7–8), at the 1995 and 2000 Review Conferences, 'the Union played an active role, establishing itself as a recognized actor in this field'. For example, already in 1995, the EU prepared for the Conference through adopting a joint action opting for the indefinite extension of the NPT (Council, 1994). In 2000 and 2005, the EU adopted common positions supporting further strengthening of the NPT regime. In 2005, according to some observers, the EU played a more important role than ever before, but nobody actually noticed it (Müller, 2005).

Non-proliferation policy, as a matter of external security, naturally falls under the CFSP institutional and legal framework. Yet, as this chapter demonstrates, the European Community has started developing its profile and expertise in this policy area as early as at the beginning of the 1990s with regard to the external dimension, and already in the 1950s with the establishment of the European Atomic Energy Community. Within the Community framework, article 249 of the Treaty Establishing the European Community (TEEC) introduced legal instruments 'concerned with translating the general principles of the treaties into specific rules' (Nugent, 2003: 238). One of them, a regulation, has been utilised to enable the European Community to provide external assistance to the countries of the dissolved Soviet bloc. In this respect, the Technical Assistance to the Commonwealth of Independent States (TACIS) programme was the main instrument of the Commission for providing Russia with assistance and recovery funds in the area of nuclear safety and non-proliferation. Consecutive Council regulations enabled the Community to acquire important experience in developing non-proliferation projects.

However, as already mentioned, within the Cold War context, the institutional instruments of European Community Member States to conduct joint foreign and security policy were mainly confined to the informal EPC. This was problematic from the 'actorness' perspective, because 'an international organization, to be an actor, should have a distinctive institutional apparatus, even if it is grounded in, or intermingles with, domestic political institutions' (Jupille and Caporaso, 1998: 217). The TEU provided the EU with the institutional structure in the area of international security policy, but it was only in 2003 when permanent bureaucratic apparatus was established in the Council Secretariat dedicated to non-proliferation policy. Following the adoption of the WMD Strategy (European Council, 2003), the Council Secretariat has become home for the EU's non-proliferation office, headed by the Personal Representative on non-proliferation of WMD, Annalisa Giannella.

When Javier Solana appointed his WMD Personal Representative, the post-holder was entrusted with the following tasks: (a) contributing to the further development of the EU WMD Strategy; (b) further enhancing the profile of non-proliferation policy in EU's relations with third countries; (c) contributing to the implementation of the EU SALW (Small Arms and Light Weapons) Strategy (since 2005); (d) assisting EU Member States in their efforts to coordinate policies in the area of conventional arms exports controls; (e) assisting E3 (Germany, France and the United Kingdom) and the High Representative (HR) in negotiations with Iran over its nuclear programme (since Autumn 2004).

The adoption of the WMD Strategy and consequent establishment of permanent institutional structures in the Council Secretariat marks the most important step in developing the EU's external non-proliferation policy. Yet, it also contributed to the fragmentation of EU's efforts, with non-proliferation also being on the agenda of the European Commission through its external financial assistance programmes (Zwolski, 2011b). As one high-level Council official has put it, 'it is a disaster that we don't have a unified representation. Countries such as the US and Russia are fed up with this situation, it is annoying to them' (CON-A, 2009). Particularly controversial in this context was the 2004 Commission's proposal for a new 'external relations' financial instrument, namely the Instrument for Stability (IfS), which would identify non-proliferation as one of the key priority areas. This would significantly raise the profile of the Commission as a non-proliferation actor vis-à-vis the newly established non-proliferation office in the Council Secretariat, with relatively lower CFSP budget. In 2005, Annalisa Giannella expressed her concerns:

> As I have said, there are procedures which are different; there are prerogatives which are different in the two pillars; and there are financial resources which are very different. Despite the fact that I believe non-proliferation is mainly a foreign and security policy area, I think there is a tendency to try, through the budgetary procedures and instruments, putting it in a simplistic way, to 'communiterise' non-proliferation. If you look at the financial perspectives and at the stability instruments put forward by the Commission, stability instruments basically would work as a Community programme. There would be a sort of framework decision by the Council and then the programme would be managed and all the projects would be prepared and decided by the Commission with very little power in the hands of Member State.
>
> (Great Britain, 2005)

In the final version of the regulation, almost all references to non-proliferation policy were removed. Instead, the IfS is primarily intended (under article 3) to allow a prompt response to situations of crisis or emerging crisis. Around 77 per cent of the budget allocated for the IfS for the years 2007–2013 is designated for this purpose. The remaining 23 per cent is intended for providing assistance in the context of stable conditions for cooperation, including 'risk mitigation and preparedness relating to chemical, biological, radiological and nuclear materials or agents' (European Commission, 2004a: 4). Important institutional reforms introduced by the Lisbon Treaty offer an opportunity to alleviate the problem of institutional duality in the EU's non-proliferation policy. Formally, the quest for consistency in European external policy-making has a long history. For example, the Single European Act states that 'The external policies of the European Community and the policies agreed in European Political Co-operation must be consistent'. The Treaty of Maastricht further emphasises the need for consistency in the EU's external relations, security, economic and development policies. In this context, 'Council and the Commission shall be responsible for ensuring such consistency'.

Yet, following the formal 'pillarisation', ensuring institutional consistency in the EU's foreign and security policy was easier said than done, considering the duality of institutional cultures, competences and resources available within the Community and CFSP pillars. This duality, as this chapter suggests, turned into inter-institutional competition between the Council General Secretariat and the Commission in the area of policy on non-proliferation of WMDs, undermining the EU's performance on the world stage. Before the Lisbon Treaty came into force, the main attempt to ensure consistency and the flow of information between relevant EU actors involved in non-proliferation policy was the WMD Monitoring Centre. This initiative aimed particularly at 'enhancing effectiveness and consistency without any modification of institutional settings and prerogatives, by establishing a cooperative working method which allows the Council Secretariat/High Representative, the Commission services and Member States to work together, and ensure better synergy' (Council, 2006b).

This indicates that Member States recognised the challenge of ensuring institutional consistency in non-proliferation policy long before establishing the EEAS. In fact, the idea of creating the WMD Monitoring Centre was already expressed in the WMD Strategy, which called for '[s]etting up, as agreed in Thessaloniki, a unit which would function as a monitoring centre, entrusted with the monitoring of the consistent implementation of the EU Strategy and the collection of information and intelligence, in liaison with the Situation Centre. This monitoring centre would be set up at the Council Secretariat and fully associate the Commission' (European Council, 2003: 13). Yet, it was only in 2006, when the concept paper, providing for the establishment of this informal body, was drafted and adopted by the Council.[1] The Centre proved to be a valuable forum for various parties (including the Council General Secretariat and the Commission), not only to discuss more specific thematic issues, but also to have a more general exchange of information (de Jong et al., 2010).

Another outcome of the WMD Strategy, the organisation of a six-monthly debate on the implementation of the WMD Strategy, also contributed to bringing Council General Secretariat and the Commission closer together. To this end, the Personal Representative on non-proliferation of WMD, together with the Commission, drafted reports on the EU's non-proliferation activities every six months. These drafts would then go through the usual procedure in the Council, where they would be discussed by working groups, the Political and Security Committee, Committee of Permanent Representatives (COREPER) and ministers.

The Lisbon Treaty aims to bring a structural solution to the consistency problems in the EU's external policy, by bringing relevant bureaucracies and processes from the Council Secretariat and the Commission together into the EEAS. Following prolonged discussions, in 2010 the Council decided that the following administrative entities from the Council Secretariat would be transferred into the EEAS: Policy Unit; CSDP and crisis management structures (for example, EU Military Staff, EU Situation Centre); Directorate-General E (External and Political-Military Affairs). Further, the Council decided to also move into the EEAS almost the entire DG Relex of the European Commission (Council, 2010a). This means that the entire bureaucratic apparatus involved in conducting the non-proliferation policy of the EU has been moved into the EEAS. This rearrangement offers an opportunity to bring a higher degree of cooperation and consistency across different EU non-proliferation policies and instruments, but this convergence is unlikely to happen automatically.

Some scholars even suggest that inter-institutional cooperation within the EU tends to be better than intra-institutional cooperation – within a single institution. For example, Christiansen (2001) argues that, on the one hand, structurally determined tensions between the Council General Secretariat and the Commission have led to the low level of expectations for close cooperation between them. Yet, against this low level of expectations, officials from both institutions have developed collegial approaches in the areas of shared responsibility. On the other hand, significant tensions could be identified within the Commission and the Council General Secretariat: 'the differing organizational logics of distinct administrative tasks constitute internal tensions which then require substantive institutional resources for their resolution' (Christiansen, 2001: 766). This argument would call for a degree of caution when assuming that bringing officials, instruments and resources into one institution will in itself assure consistency and close cooperation on non-proliferation policy.

The EEAS is arranged in a way that roughly one-third of the unit dealing with non-proliferation in the EEAS consists of officials formerly working in DG Relex of the European Commission; another one-third is composed of officials who used to work in Ms Giannella's office in the Council General Secretariat; the remaining one-third consists of the representatives of Member States. This means that three bodies with distinctive diplomatic cultures and experiences are working together. They are involved in developing two dimensions of the EU's non-proliferation policy, formerly developed by separate bureaucracies.

Firstly, the diplomatic dimension of non-proliferation policy, including international negotiations, are conducted mainly by officials previously working in the Council General Secretariat. Secondly, the capacity-building dimension, including the development of strategies and multi-year planning for the IfS and the Instrument for Nuclear Safety Cooperation (INSC), are carried mainly by officials previously working in DG Relex of the European Commission. One of the indicators determining the degree of consistency achieved as a result of these institutional reforms will be the extent to which officials previously working in one institution will now be involved in developing policies which are historically the competence of another institution. Consequently, the EU has now an opportunity to overcome the duality in its non-proliferation policy and thus to enhance the profile of the EU as an international actor in international relations.

However, to achieve this result, a high degree of mutual trust and understanding will be necessary among all the bodies working together in the newly established EU's diplomatic service. In particular, it will be crucial for all parties to recognise their mutual added value. On the one hand, officials who used to work in the Council General Secretariat must recognise the value of activities formerly developed in the

Commission; most importantly, these include capacity building through utilising flagship thematic instruments, that is the IfS and INSC. One of the most important projects in this respect is the creation of the regional centres of excellence on CBRN, envisaged in the IfS Indicative Programme for the years 2009–2011. The centres will aim to bring regional actors together in order to pursue the objectives defined in article 4(2) of the regulation establishing the IfS, such as the promotion of civilian research activities, enhancing the safety of CBRN facilities, establishing and enforcing frameworks for controlling the export of dual-use items. Seven regional centres are envisaged: three in Africa, one in the Middle East, one in South-East Asia, one in Central Asia and one in Caucuses.

On the other hand, officials formerly working in the Commission must recognise the value of diplomatic efforts aiming to develop new and manage existing multilateral non-proliferation agreements and regimes. However, in the long term, in order to best utilise different types of non-proliferation resources at the EU's disposal (diplomatic, political and financial), it will be critical to merge not just institutions and processes, but also competences and policies. This means that (a) capacity-building instruments must be developed in a way that fully supports the political and diplomatic non-proliferation goals of the EU and (b) political goals and agreements at the international level must support building long-term capacities in regions of proliferation concern.

The EU and non-proliferation: capabilities

Before the EEAS merged EU's non-proliferation bureaucracies in January 2010, there was an inter-institutional controversy concerning which capabilities are the most important in developing the EU's non-proliferation policy. On the one hand, officials of the European Commission used to point to the instruments of the European Community, namely the IfS and the INSC. On the other hand, Council officials underline the importance of the political dimension of the EU's non-proliferation capacities. As one Council Secretariat official has pointed out (CON-D, 2011): 'Now, the EU's non-proliferation policy is not merely about having some funds and spending money on projects; instead, now the EU has a policy. Of course, budgetary elements play a role in our policy, but we have the political direction introduced by the WMD Strategy. Since 2003, the EU is a political actor, not just a funder.' As the reminder of this section suggests, mainly positive integration instruments are relevant for the EU's external security policy on non-proliferation of WMDs. These include, primarily, not only capacity-building instruments and resources but also instruments enhancing the EU's diplomatic leverage, that is the non-proliferation clause.

On the financial side, already at the beginning of the 1990s, the European Community initiated technical assistance (TACIS) (Sodupe and Benito, 1998) to the former Soviet Union, with the security and safety of nuclear installations constituting an important component of this assistance. TACIS was launched in 1991, but its implementation had to be delayed due to political turbulences in the Baltic States and Russia. The financing memoranda were signed only a few days before the Soviet Union ceased to exist. In 1992 it was agreed that the Community's assistance would be adapted to the new geopolitical environment (Sodupe and Benito, 1998). Already in 1991, nuclear safety was given a high profile in the EEC's relations with Russia, constituting the largest component of the Community's assistance in the area of energy. The focus at that time was on providing training and developing studies analysing Soviet nuclear installations (Commission, 1993). The nature of TACIS required the EU to cooperate primarily with non-military officials, mostly those working in civil nuclear infrastructure. The main focus of the US government, on the other hand, was on working with Russian military establishment. One expert observes that by complementing US efforts, the EU inevitably lowered its profile, because TACIS projects were implemented mainly through the Joint Research Centre; thus, they were not well publicised (WMDExp1, 2009).

A project of particular significance, which the European Community has been supporting right from the beginning, is the redirection of scientists through co-financing the International Science and Technology Centre (ISTC) in Russia, and later also the Science and Technology Centre in Ukraine (STCU). The idea behind these initiatives is to employ scientists possessing knowledge related to WMDs and missile delivery systems, so that they could use this knowledge and skills for peaceful purposes. The ISTC was created in 1992 by the United States, Japan, the European Commission and Russia. The STCU was created in 1994 by Ukraine, Canada, Sweden and the United States. The Commission joined in 1998 (European Commission, 2001b). Table 6.1 indicates how important these two institutions have been in preventing the proliferation of WMDs. It covers the period from 1994 to 2003.

This data indicate that more than 60,000 scientists have been supported through the centres in Russia and Ukraine. More than

Table 6.1 ISTC and STCU statistics covering the years 1994–2003

	ISTC	STCU
Total budget from all parties	$441 million	$64 million
Funding by the European Commission	€77 million	€12 million
Number of projects financed	1628	455
Number of scientists involved	51,000	11,000

Source: European Commission (2003b).

$500 million has been invested in their activities. Of this sum, the Commission has committed almost €90 million, which constitutes the second largest contribution after that of the United States. According to Höhl et al. (2003), it does not come as a surprise that the EU decided to support this particular initiative, considering the international nature of this programme and also the Joint Research Centre's expertise in the area of nuclear technologies. Höhl et al. (2003: 13) note that 'the Commission, with its technical expertise, financial flexibility and back-up from nuclear research centres (which can help evaluate incoming research proposals), was an ideal partner for this endeavour'. One of the problems with evaluating the importance of ISTC/STCU activities is that it is impossible to estimate how many proliferation acts they have prevented. Nonetheless, the Abdul Quadeer Khan network proved that there is always need for CBRN experts; thus the centres in Russia and Ukraine must be considered to be of crucial importance in international and EU non-proliferation policy.

TACIS expired in 2006. Subsequently, some of its tasks were assigned to two new instruments of the European Commission: the aforementioned IfS and the INSC. The IfS, through its long-term component (article 4), allowed the Commission to provide assistance in the context of stable conditions for cooperation (European Parliament and the Council, 2006). Importantly, the IfS continues to fund redirection of scientists, but it has broadened its geographical scope. Currently, it also contributes to non-proliferation initiatives in regions such as Africa, Middle East and South Asia (for example, the aforementioned CBRN Centres of Excellence). While the INSC focuses on financing nuclear safety projects, the IfS used to be (before moving it to the EEAS) 'the sole Community instrument that can directly address issues relating to the risks presented by the weaponisation of chemical, biological, radiological and nuclear agents' (European Commission, 2007a: 20).

Over the period of 1991–2006, the Commission allocated €1.3 billion from the TACIS budget for non-proliferation and nuclear safety projects in the former Soviet Union (European Commission, 2007e). Under the budgetary framework covering the years 2007–2013, the IfS and INSC have an average annual budget of €112 million for non-proliferation and nuclear safety. At the same time, the CFSP budget for non-proliferation has been much more modest, with over €22 million in 2010 (Council, 2011).

However, Council officials underline that funding constitutes only one (minor) component of the EU's non-proliferation policy. Importantly, the WMD Strategy equipped the EU non-proliferation efforts with a sense of strategic direction and a strong political dimension, in contrast to the de-politicised character of budgetary programmes. For example, the document envisaged the establishment of the aforementioned WMD Monitoring Centre and provided for the organisation of six-monthly debate on the implementation of the strategy. Furthermore, in order to 'mainstream' the non-proliferation policy into EU's relations with third countries, the EU introduced, also in 2003, the so-called non-proliferation clause (Council, 2003d); the clause has subsequently become an important diplomatic asset at the EU's disposal. Since 2003, it has been inserted into all so-called mixed agreements between the EU and third countries. The first section of the clause commits parties to fully comply with their existing obligations. Although these obligations are not explicitly mentioned, it is understood that they encompass the NPT including safeguards, the Chemical Weapons Convention, the Biological and Toxic Weapons Convention and the UN Security Council resolutions, most notably Resolution 1540. The second section encourages parties to join any other relevant international non-proliferation frameworks and also to establish an effective system of export control (Council, 2003d).

The question as to what kind of steps the EU can take if a country breaches the clause then arises. The former Personal Representative on non-proliferation of WMD Annalisa Giannella explains that the mechanism of the non-proliferation clause entails more than merely signing an agreement and then finding out at some point that other party has breached it. Instead, Ms Giannella argues that the EU needs to stay involved after an agreement is achieved. She notes: 'We have to work with this country and see what they need in order to comply with the clause' (Great Britain, 2005: 34). However, such monitoring is costly. Ms Giannella underlines in this respect that the CFSP budget is very limited and only a fraction of it is allocated to the EU non-proliferation policy. This, in turn, may affect the extent to which the non-proliferation clause can be effectively utilised in preventing the proliferation of WMDs.

Although the establishment of the permanent non-proliferation office in the Council Secretariat in 2003 aimed to enhance the political dimension of the EU's non-proliferation profile, Member States in the Council have also utilised the CFSP budget to develop some joint assistance programmes. Notably, the Council has been active in developing its profile in the area of non-proliferation since the TEU, through joint actions and common positions. In 1999, the Council adopted a Joint Action establishing the EU Cooperation Programme for Non-proliferation and Disarmament in the Russian Federation (Joint Action Programme) (Council, 1999). This programme has identified three objectives for the EU's non-proliferation assistance to Russia: (a) to help Russia dismantling and transforming its WMD-related equipment in a safe, secure and environmentally sound manner; (b) to enhance EU participation in Cooperative Threat Reduction (CTR) activities in Russia; and (c) to enhance the coordination of various EU programmes in Russia.

The reason why the Council adopted this Joint Action Programme in 1999 is that in the same year the European Council agreed on a Common Strategy of the EU on Russia (European Council, 1999b). It was the first time that this EU instrument was utilised by Member States working together in the European Council. The Common Strategy on Russia has underlined the 'critical importance to European security of EU-Russia co-operation and of Russia's development as a stable, democratic and prosperous country' (Marsh and Mackenstein, 2005: 195). Since the adoption of the Joint Action Programme, the Council has become active in contributing to various non-proliferation projects in Russia, further utilising joint actions as a primary instrument. For example, in 2004, the Council has agreed to contribute €8 million to projects enhancing the physical protection of Russian nuclear facilities (Council, 2004). Furthermore, in 2007, the Council has committed €3 million for the destruction of chemical weapons in Russia (Council, 2007c).

These figures are modest compared to the overall costs of projects towards which they have contributed, thus the primary focus of the Council is to contribute to already existing projects, developed bilaterally between EU Member States and Russia. For example, Germany has been active in providing assistance to Russia in the area of physical protection of nuclear facilities. Therefore, the Joint Action from 2004 entrusted Germany with the technical implementation of the EU's commitment 'in the framework of its bilateral programme in this area' (Council, 2004: 57). Similarly, the United Kingdom has been active in supporting the destruction of chemical weapons in Russia. Thus, this country was entrusted with the implementation of the aforementioned Joint Action from 2007 (Council, 2007c). A high-level Council Secretariat official confirms that the EU often contributes to existing bilateral projects: 'In the CFSP we have to be flexible. Sometimes within the EU, there is no idea on how to approach a certain non-proliferation task. In such a case, EU Member States get together and decide on resources to be deployed. Yet, sometimes there already is a country with scientific know-how or with a bilateral relationship with Russia and it asks the EU for support' (CON-A, 2009). According to Höhl et al. (2003), joint Member State–EU initiatives have a number of benefits such as the following: (a) bilateral projects supported by the EU gain greater visibility; (b) they tend to be more stable in the long term; (c) smaller Member States can also participate, which otherwise would be too costly for them; and d) some of the projects could not be undertaken by the European Commission, because they are military in nature. In such cases, they can be launched within the framework of the CFSP, implemented by a Member State and then the Commission could get involved with extra funding.

The EU and non-proliferation: recognition

The extent to which the EU is recognised as an important non-proliferation security actor depends on who is asked. The EU officials underline that the adoption of the WMD Strategy significantly enhanced the EU's recognition not only by external partners but also among EU Member States (CON-D, 2011). Yet, this view is not widely shared outside of the EU. In fact, external actors, such as non-proliferation experts, tend to disregard the role of the EU as an actor in non-proliferation policy; this section identifies the main reasons for this.

First, extensive EU bureaucracy is considered one of the key factors undermining EU recognition in non-proliferation policy. As one non-proliferation expert notes, 'if the UK runs a project worth €70 million and the Commission contributes €3 million, the paper-work for spending €70 million and €3 million is similar' (WMDExp1, 2009). Marc Deffrennes from the European Commission underlined these difficulties, pointing to the 'heavy procedures, heavy bureaucracy' and the fact that there is a long time span 'between a decision-making process to run a programme or a project, the start of implementation, and the end of implementation' (Great Britain, 2005: 55). Another expert, from Canada, confirms these observations, pointing out that the EU is not effective with short-term non-proliferation projects because it lacks flexibility. As a result, something which needs to be done 'now' is a problem for the EU (WMDExp5, 2009). This lack of flexibility and long-term focus undermine the EU's visibility as an actor, because 'with longer-term projects, it is more difficult to observe the outcomes; the outcomes are fuzzier. It is hard to say exactly what has been done or prevented in quantitative terms' (WMDExp5, 2009).

Second, in addition to internal EU problems, there are also significant external factors which negatively affect the recognition of the EU as a non-proliferation actor. For example, even though Russia has traditionally been the main recipient of the EU's non-proliferation technical and financial assistance, the EU has never been Moscow's favourite partner. In fact, Russia appears to have a hierarchy of preferred partners. These include the following:

(a) The United States: working with Washington on non-proliferation matters validates Russian position as an important actor on the world scene (WMDExp1, 2009). Furthermore, Washington is perceived to have the largest resources at its disposal.
(b) EU Member States: working with individual states is a preferred option for Moscow because the work tends to be more flexible, discussions take place at the working level and are not highly politicised (WMDExp1, 2009). For example, Germany has been the biggest European partner of Russia in the non-proliferation area since the end of the Cold War. This is how one expert explains this close relationship: 'Germany has excellent relations with Russia based on historical connections. Many German officials went to school with their Russian partners, they speak Russian, so it is easier for them to work together' (WMDExp4, 2009).
(c) The EU is only in the third position of preferred partners because it is considered less flexible than individual Member States and generally more complicated to work with. As one interviewee phrased it, 'for Russia, the best partners are those which can provide the biggest amount of money faster than others' (WMDExp5, 2009). Additionally, according to another American non-proliferation expert, Russia prefers to cooperate with actors possessing nuclear capabilities, because Russian military establishment does not trust that non-nuclear actors can fully appreciate all the aspects related to possessing such capabilities (WMDExp3, 2009).

Third, there are differences concerning priorities for the EU's involvement. Marc Deffrennes from the European Commission admits: 'Working with Russians is very hard (...) It is as difficult today as it was at that time [1992] because they have their own priorities' (Great Britain, 2005: 56). Other Commission officials specify that Moscow would like the EU to become more involved in chemical weapons destruction and in nuclear submarine dismantlement (COM-D, 2009). Yet, the Commission is reluctant to become more involved in these priorities. Not only are they very expensive, but the culture of secrecy surrounding all military activities in Russia prevents the Commission from scrutinising the implementation of projects. Instead, the Commission would prefer to focus on nuclear safety, where it has developed extensive expertise. It would also like to continue supporting projects contributing to the redirection of CBRN scientists, which give the EU first-hand knowledge about Russian programmes (COM-D, 2009). Former Commission officials admit that this exchange of information is particularly important in the area of bio-security and bio-safety, because officially the EU is not allowed to know anything about these programmes (COM-D, 2009). John Mattiussi (2006), a former Commission official working in the area of non-proliferation, admits: 'The Soviet Union maintained a large and sophisticated bio research programme – what happened to the materials/expertise? We do not know. Russia refuses to discuss past programmes' (Mattiussi, 2006: 2).

There is one more important factor undermining the recognition of the EU as a security policy actor in the area of non-proliferation. It concerns the number of other frameworks, through which states channel their non-proliferation policies. The G8 Global Partnership constitutes one significant example. It brings together countries, including EU Member States, to cooperate on non-proliferation projects, initially focused on Russia. One American non-proliferation expert admits in this context: 'The G8 has emerged as a primary way of dealing with non-proliferation and I consider this to be the primary forum. I am aware that the EU is also committing some funding, but the involvement of EU Member States is more significant in this regard' (WMDExp2. 2009). One interviewee observes that in the 1990s it was actually the European Community which was a more important contributor of non-proliferation assistance to Russia than individual EU Member States (WMDExp1, 2009). However, he does agree that later, especially since the G8 summit in Canada in 2002 launching the Global Partnership, the EU Member States have started initiating their own projects and the momentum had passed to individual Member States. This observation is also corroborated by an expert from Canada, who notes that whilst in the 1990s the EU had played an important role because it 'filled up a big hole', after 2002, the EU's involvement has become relatively smaller compared to the commitments of some of the EU Member States and other countries (WMDExp5, 2009).

Importantly, all of these factors affecting the recognition of the EU as an actor in non-proliferation policy concern the provision of non-proliferation assistance. They indicate that the EU has not been considered an important player in this respect both by external observers and by Russia, even if Moscow has largely benefited from the EU's funding. In this context, one Council official cautions that one should not exaggerate the extent to which Russia disregards the role of the EU in the area of non-proliferation. He has pointed out that Moscow needs EU funding, even though Russian leaders do not like to admit it; if Moscow did publicly admit that it needs the EU, according to this interviewee, that would be 'the first time ever that they openly say that they rely on EU assistance' (CON-F, 2009).

The possible causal relationship between Lisbon Treaty reforms and the political recognition of the EU as an actor in non-proliferation is a rather speculative exercise at this early stage. However, it is certain that this recognition will be closely linked to the recognition of the EU as a foreign and security actor more broadly. In the broader sense, the capability–expectation gap (Hill, 1993, 1998) has become prominent again recently, when the EU and the High Representative were criticised for failing to speak with one voice and to convey a strong message from the EU with regard to revolutions in Egypt and Libya. This criticism demonstrates a rather paradoxical situation, in which strengthening the institutional capacity of the EU's High Representative can actually lead to more disappointments among those who expect a stronger EU voice in international politics. This will inevitably affect the recognition of the EU as an actor in non-proliferation.

However, a few other factors will also play key roles. First, recognition will depend on whether the EU will be able to take advantage of its newly acquired legal personality, in order to seek full membership in international institutions and regimes concerned with non-proliferation. Second, the leadership role of the High Representative will be important, both at the international level and in developing the institutional ethos of the EEAS. Third, the EU will not be recognised as an important non-proliferation actor unless Member States decide to channel more of their policies and resources through the EU rather

The EU and Non-proliferation: The Case of Russia 163

than bilaterally or through other frameworks. In theory, this should not be as controversial as the coordination of EU actions in other areas of international security, because an important framework (and a strong commitment) for cooperation already exists in the form of the WMD Strategy, not to mention the European Security Strategy.

However, disagreements remain, particularly between nuclear weapon states (NWS) and non-nuclear weapon states (NNWS). According to the analysis by Friedrich Ebert Stiftung, '[t]hese differences result in various intra-EU cleavages and ultimately enable or encourage individual Member States to engage in various interest coalitions outside the EU' (Katsioulis and Mölling, 2010: 5). Further, none of these groups is homogenous. Diverging approaches exist between France and the United Kingdom with regard to disarmament and nuclear deterrence as well as among NNWS (NATO members versus countries like Ireland and Sweden) (Katsioulis and Mölling, 2010). Until these differences between NWS and NNWS as well as NATO and non-NATO EU Member States are resolved, the EU's role as a non-proliferation actor will be hampered.

Regardless of these disagreements and of the low level of the EU's recognition as a non-proliferation actor in general, the EU has been able to advance its position within international non-proliferation regimes. This has been achieved even though the position of the EU in international institutions remains often ambiguous. G8 forum is one example, with one Council official who used to work on non-proliferation admitting that 'in the G8 nobody knows what status we have. I don't know what status we have' (CON-A, 2009). Formally, the EU has been participating in G7 (and later G8) meetings since 1977. It has been represented by both the President of the European Commission and the rotating EU Presidency. Yet, the limitations imposed on the EU's membership are often the source of confusion. For example, the Commission cannot host or chair the summit; it also does not assume the role of G8 rotating Presidency. Even though the role of the EU in the G8 can sometimes be ambiguous, it is fully recognised as a contributor within the framework of the Global Partnership. G8 leaders pledged $20 billion for cooperation projects in Russia over the years 2002–2012 (G8, 2002), as a response to the threat of terrorist actors acquiring access to WMDs in Russia. Former President of the European Commission Romano Prodi announced in 2003 that the EU would contribute €1 billion (European Commission, 2007f). The Compliance Report covering the period July 2008/June 2009 noted that the EU was 'well on track to meet its financial commitment to the Global Partnership' (G8 Information Centre, 2009: 209).

Conclusion

The empirical evidence suggests that the EU now has all the necessary means to become an important actor in preventing the proliferation of WMDs. First, the Lisbon Treaty has reshaped the central institutions entrusted with the EU's external action, providing an opportunity for a more consistent and stronger role of the EU in non-proliferation. In fact, the aims of ensuring institutional consistency and overcoming inter-institutional competition in the EU's international security policy are at the core of creating the EEAS. The EU's policy on non-proliferation of WMDs has been in dire need of such a reform, considering that two different bureaucracies were entrusted with developing non-proliferation policies and projects for the EU. Consequently, the reforms potentially strengthen the scope of European integration in non-proliferation policy.

On the one hand, the European Commission was involved in non-proliferation and nuclear safety capacity-building projects in Russia and former Soviet Union countries, through a number of geographical (TACIS) and thematic (IfS, INSC) instruments. More recently, the Commission recognised the importance of moving beyond this geographical region, thus programming projects in places such as the Middle East, Africa and Asia. The most prominent amongst these new initiatives are the regional centres of excellence on CBRN, aiming to bring regional actors together, in order to further advance the culture of non-proliferation and nuclear safety. On the other hand, following the adoption by the EU of the WMD Strategy in 2003, former High Representative (HR) for the CFSP Javier Solana appointed his Personal Representative on WMDs. Consequently, a permanent bureaucratic structure was established in the Council General Secretariat, entrusted with implementing the WMD Strategy. Yet, rather paradoxically considering the solid legitimacy of this new body, the Council's Directorate for Non-Proliferation of WMDs was chronically underfunded, receiving only a small portion of the already limited CFSP budget. The Lisbon Treaty reforms therefore provide an opportunity to shrink the gap between the two types of non-proliferation policy-making, thus increasing the scope of European integration in this policy area.

Further, this chapter identified two categories of capabilities in the EU's non-proliferation policy. Concerning the financial instruments, the European Commission has played an important role particularly in the 1990s, when it was contributing to non-proliferation projects undertaken in the former Soviet Union. Currently, the EU (through the EEAS and the Commission) still commits resources to this geographical region (for example, it still supports the redirection of scientists), but at the same time it shifts its focus to the new regions of concern, particularly the Middle East, South and South-East Asia and parts of Arica. In addition to this financial dimension, the WMD Strategy contributed to the development of diplomatic and political profile of the EU, further strengthened by the non-proliferation clause.

This chapter has also indicated that the EU is, as yet, not recognised as an important actor in the area of non-proliferation. A number of factors affecting negatively the EU's recognition have been identified. These include issues such as extensive and complicated bureaucracy and diverging preferences of EU Member States, largely based on their status with regard to the possession of nuclear weapons. Yet, they also include factors such as Russian politics and preferences, particularly with regard to partners that Moscow perceives as the most valuable. Additionally, the number of international non-proliferation frameworks severely undermines the EU's recognition, because often EU Member States prefer to utilise these frameworks to pursue their non-proliferation objectives.

Further research is necessary to assess the extent to which the EEAS will indeed bring synergy into the EU's non-proliferation policy, thus enhancing the effectiveness and recognition of the EU as an actor in this field. This in turn will greatly depend on mutual trust and understanding among different entities working together in the newly established diplomatic service of the EU. However, it has also been suggested that, in a longer term, the merging of bureaucracies will have to be followed by developing a truly coherent policy, in which relatively low-key capacity-building projects in regions of proliferation concern are supported by high-level diplomatic efforts and vice versa. Catherine Ashton's leadership role will be crucial in this respect.

The EEAS, under the leading role of the HR of the Union for Foreign Affairs and Security Policy, may potentially help to overcome competition which used to take place between the Council Secretariat and the Commission. However, further research will also be necessary to examine the division of tasks at the higher level, between the HR and the President of the European Council. The latter was entrusted by the Lisbon Treaty with ensuring 'the external representation of the Union on issues concerning its common foreign and security policy (. . .)'.

To be sure, Herman Van Rompuy already started exercising this competence in the area of non-proliferation, for example by representing the EU at the April 2010 Nuclear Security Summit in Washington. In addition, the European Parliament is increasingly asserting its role on matters of foreign and security policy, 'trying to have an ever bigger say on expenditure, appointments, and policy guidelines'. Its ambitions in matters such as non-proliferation policy deserve close attention.

7
The EU and Somali Piracy

> You can't ignore the pirates anymore. They're getting more and more muscle. They used to invest their money in just boats and going out to sea, but now they're building up their military side.
> (Mohamed Aden, a clan leader in Central Somalia, quoted in Gettleman, 2010)

Maritime pirates have often been romanticised in popular culture. Steven Spielberg's *Hook*, based on early 20th-century novels by J.M. Barrie, features Peter Pan and his main antagonist, pirate Captain Hook, who is the widely feared lord of the pirate village Neverland. He wears a big iron hook where his right hand should have been. Unfortunately, it was cut off by Peter Pan and subsequently eaten by a salt-water crocodile. Portrayed as a dangerous character, Hook is also frustrated and tragic, at some point even contemplating suicide. In the end, however, good wins against evil when Hook is defeated by Peter Pan during the final battle. In the movie *Pirates of the Caribbean*, pirate Captain Jack Sparrow is a romantic and intelligent pirate, who prefers to achieve his goals using wit and intellect, rather than resorting to violence. In contrast, the 17th-century book *The Buccaneers of America*, by a French writer Alexandre Exquemelin, offered an eyewitness story filled with violence, torture and murder. While entertaining, the piratical fictional characters played by Dustin Hoffman and Johnny Depp, respectively, do not represent an entirely accurate image of modern-day maritime pirates. Instead of wearing colourful clothes and travelling on three-mast vessels, modern organised-crime groups use skiffs and can be more accurately portrayed as 'carrying rocket launchers, demanding multimillion dollar ransoms and hijacking 1080-foot oil tankers' (MSNBC, 2008). In recent years, the Horn of Africa witnessed the outburst of violence at sea, with most of the piratical attacks and almost all cases of hijacking occurring in this region.

There is no single definition of piracy. This means that 'the classification of violent maritime incidents can become a matter of dispute and confusion' (Great Britain, 2006: 11). One of the most recognised experts on contemporary piracy, Martin Murphy, defines the problem as 'unlawful depredation at sea involving the use or threat of violence possibly, but not necessarily, involving robbery' (Murphy, 2009: 7). Maritime piracy has also been addressed extensively by the international law, which is discussed later in this chapter. In terms of geography, modern piracy is not limited to the coast of Somalia. In particular, South-East Asia has traditionally been a favourable ground for piratical activities, where 'pirate traditions go back virtually uninterrupted to the fifth century' (Murphy, 2009: 72). The 2008 EU's Implementation Report defines piracy as a 'new dimension of organised crime', noting that '[p]iracy in the Indian Ocean and the Gulf of Aden has made this issue more pressing in recent months' (European Council, 2008: 8).

Somali pirates have traditionally been associated with organised crime, thriving within the environment of lawless Somalia. In this context, Lehr and Lehmann (2007: 3) note: '[T]he magnitude of Somalia's pirate problem now seems to be comparable with that in South-East Asian waters: in both regions, we are basically confronted by a flourishing organised crime or a veritable "piracy industry", as compared with mere "maritime mugging" elsewhere'. This observation provides an accurate image, except that in the last few years Somali piracy seemingly has become an even more serious problem than piracy in South-East Asia. A distinctive characteristic of Somali pirates is that they do not merely steal commercial vessels or their cargo. Instead, they exploit the lack of law enforcement in their home country by kidnapping crewmembers in exchange for ransom – a strategy that is much more profitable (Blanchard et al., 2009). On average, one pirate can earn between $6000 and $10,000 for a $1 million ransom (International Expert Group on Piracy off the Somali Coast, 2008). This constitutes an equivalent of a two- to three-year salary earned from legal activities. However, it must also be noted that those recruited tend to be uneducated. Thus, they only have a minimal chance of finding a legitimate source of income at this level. Although $10,000 constitutes a substantial gain for a Somali pirate, it is only a fraction of a typical ransom. Where does the rest of the money go? In order to secure their activities on land, pirates need the support of local political forces (warlords). Therefore, a large proportion of money often goes to these individuals with their own illegal ventures, such as human trafficking and mining (Murphy, 2009). Significant resources are also 'reinvested'. Fathi Osman Kahir, a piracy 'treasurer' from an offshore town Hobyo, explains: 'When we get more money, we recruit more.... There's up to 500 people working with us in Hobyo, that's 10 per cent of the population and I'm just talking about the people on the ground.... We have a hierarchy. What do you think we do? We pay wages too' (quoted in Mojon, 2010).

The outburst of piracy off the coast of Somalia must be seen as one of many forms of organised violence linked to the fact that Somalia remains a thoroughly failed state. It has no central government possessing control over the territory of the country, or even Somalia's capital Mogadishu. This condition of permanent insecurity contributes to Somalia's disastrous humanitarian situation. In fact, arguably, there is no single state of Somalia to speak of; instead, there are three autonomous regions existing in parallel within the internationally recognised borders of Somalia. This partition of Somalia is the result of a civil war which erupted after the collapse of the Somali central government in 1991. In the north-west of the country, the Somali National Movement successfully established the so-called Somaliland, which has remained *de facto* independent since 1991 (Bryden, 2004). Another nationalist movement, the Somali Salvation Democratic Front, was active around the same time in the north-eastern part of the country; this is where semi-autonomous Puntland was established (Møller, 2009). The central and southern part of Somalia officially remains under the authority of the Transitional Federal Government (TFG). This is also the most violent part of the country. These conditions of instability and the lack of law enforcement have contributed to Somalia (and particularly its coast) developing into a favourable ground for piratical groups to operate. The European Union (EU), the United States and other international actors support the TFG with the hope that it will eventually extend its authority over Mogadishu and the rest of Somalia.

Piracy off the coast of Somalia emerged as a security problem at the beginning of the 1990s, following the collapse of the central government in Mogadishu. While there have been a number of high-profile piratical attacks since then (including the attack on the US-operated cruise liner Seabourn Spirit in 2005), in 2008 the problem expanded and became an ever more urgent security threat (Burnett, 2002; Lehr and Lehmann, 2007; Murphy, 2007, 2009; Lennox, 2008). Despite international mobilisation, the number of attacks off the coast of Somalia increased in 2009 as compared to 2008 (ICC-IMB, 2009). In 2010, 49 vessels and 1016 crew members were taken hostage by Somali-organised gangs, which amount to 92 per cent of all ship seizures that year (ICC-IMB, 2011). In February 2011, four American hostages were killed (NYT, 2011). There is a prevailing international agreement that only by effectively addressing the problem of the failed state of Somalia can security problems in the region, such as maritime piracy, be reliably contained.

As a response to this situation, the United Nations (UN) Security Council urged states and regional organisations to take action. Amongst the actors responding to this request is the EU, launching its first-ever naval mission European Union Naval Force (EUNAVFOR) Atalanta, a Common Security and Defence Policy (CSDP) mission. This chapter contributes to discussions on the EU as a security actor in the external dimension of internal security (of Somalia), that is piracy and organised crime off the coast of Somalia, through analysing different dimensions of the EU's response to this problem. The EU can be conceptualised as an international policeman through its naval capabilities, whereby military forces turn into internal security missions and adopt certain policing and judicial functions. The argument in this chapter unfolds in the following manner. In the first section, the scope of European integration is analysed with respect to tackling a complex form of organised crime, that is Somali maritime piracy. In this context, of particular importance is the CSDP framework, including a number of bodies set in Brussels to coordinate the policies of 27 Member States. The second section examines the capabilities deployed by the EU to counter Somali piracy in the short- to long-term. To strengthen the analysis, the second section has also identified key recommendations by maritime piracy experts, and it assesses the EU's response against these recommendations. Finally, the last section assesses the extent to which the EU has been recognised for its counter-piracy efforts as a security actor.

The EU and Somali piracy: scope of integration

In order to understand the position of the EU as a security actor in countering Somali piracy, it is first important to outline the international context in which the EU has become involved. The EU has responded to the problem of piracy off the coast of Somalia in the legal context of the requests of the UN Security Council. This UN body has condemned piracy off the Somali coast and encouraged states and 'relevant regional organisations' (UNSC, 2009) to deter piracy in this region. In order to allow for a more effective pursuit of suspected pirates, the

UN Security Council has created an exception to the provisions of the international law. The Convention on the High Seas from 1958 defines piracy as 'illegal acts of violence, detention or any act of depredation' (UN, 1958: 5) committed on the high seas, outside the jurisdiction of any state. The Convention also makes explicit that '[t]he right of hot pursuit ceases as soon as the ship pursued enters the territorial sea of its own country or of a third State' (UN, 1958: 7). The 1982 United Nations Convention on the Law of the Sea (UNCLOS) incorporates the provisions on piracy as defined in the Convention, stating that piracy relates to violent acts committed for private ends on the high seas or beyond the jurisdiction of any state. Once within territorial waters, pirates (then defined as armed robbers) are subject to domestic law and law enforcement measures.

Murphy (2009) has identified a number of problems with this provision, including the following: (a) while the perpetrators may be domestic, victims are likely to be international; their freedom of navigation is not defended vigorously enough; (b) states do not want to be recognised as having a piracy problem, thus the temptation to discourage incident reporting; (c) it is likely that states will only undertake action when their own interests are threatened; and (d) some states may be so poor, weak or corrupt that they lack the capabilities to protect transit within their territorial waters. The failed state of Somalia is the case in point and the UN Security Council, after long discussions, recognised the problem. Resolution 1816 from 2008 enabled navy ships of third states to pursue pirates into the territorial waters of Somalia and to use 'all necessary means' to repress piracy. However, in order to underline the undisputed commitment to secure the norm of sovereignty, the same resolution imposed a number of restrictions (Guilfoyle, 2008). Most importantly, the right to enter Somali territorial waters was granted only to states recognised by the TFG as 'cooperating'.

The EU has responded within the framework of the UN Security Council resolutions by deploying capacities available to the EU and Member States within the CSDP framework. The CSDP is a relatively recent institutional framework of the EU. The impetus for its development came from St Malo in France, where in 1998 British Prime Minister Tony Blair and French President Jacques Chirac declared that 'the Union must have the capacity for autonomous action, backed up by credible military forces, the means to decide to use them, and a readiness to do so, in order to respond to international crises' (ISS-EU, 2000). What followed were three important European Council Summits: in Cologne (June 1999), Helsinki (December 1999) and Feira (June 2000), which filled the CSDP with substance, including setting the Helsinki Headline

Goal. The goal was for the EU to establish the European Rapid Reaction Force, capable of deploying 50–60 thousand persons within 60 days for at least one year. This goal was later upgraded through the new Headline Goal 2010, which introduced the idea of smaller and more flexible battle groups (Nugent, 2010). The Lisbon Treaty is the first EU treaty which codifies the CSDP. It is noted in the treaty that '[t]he common security and defence policy shall be an integral part of the common foreign and security policy. It shall provide the Union with an operational capacity drawing on civilian and military assets' (Council, 2008c: 51). With regard to CSDP decision-making, the treaty states: 'Decisions relating to the common security and defence policy, including those initiating a mission as referred to in this Article, shall be adopted by the Council acting unanimously on a proposal from the High Representative of the Union for Foreign Affairs and Security Policy or an initiative from a Member State' (Council, 2008c: 52).

The CSDP is composed of a number of bodies, all of which have been playing a role in developing EU response to Somali piracy. The Political and Security Committee (PSC) is the most important preparatory body of the Council, playing a crucial role in the CSDP institutional structure. It is composed of political directors from the foreign ministries of Member States. It meets at least twice a week, but more often if necessary (Howorth, 2007). The PSC worked on an interim basis from 2000 to 2001, when it was transformed into a permanent body. However, the roots of this EU body date back to the 1970s and the creation of the Political Committee within the EPC framework (Hayes-Renshaw, 2006). The role of the PSC was defined in article 25 of the Treaty of Nice and amended in the Lisbon Treaty, which states:

> Political and Security Committee shall monitor the international situation in the areas covered by the common foreign and security policy and contribute to the definition of policies by delivering opinions to the Council at the request of the Council or of the High Representative of the Union for Foreign Affairs and Security Policy or on its own initiative. It shall also monitor the implementation of agreed policies, without prejudice to the powers of the High Representative.
> (Council, 2008c: 48)

However, the competences of the PSC go beyond monitoring and advisory roles. The Lisbon Treaty also specifies that 'The Council may authorise the Committee, for the purpose and for the duration of a crisis management operation, as determined by the Council, to take the relevant decisions concerning the political control and strategic direction of the operation' (Council, 2008c: 49).

For EUNAVFOR 'Atalanta', the Council, in its Joint Action launching the EU military operation (Council, 2008d), has authorised the PSC to assume a number of responsibilities, most notably to exercise 'political control and strategic direction'. The first decision of the PSC was to appoint Antonios Papaioannou as the EU Force Commander for 'Atalanta' (Political and Security Committee, 2008), a few months later replaced by Captain Garat Caramé (Political and Security Committee, 2009). Among other decisions of the PSC were the acceptance of Norwegian and Croatian contributions to EUNAVFOR 'Atalanta', and the appointment of the new Operational Commander for 'Atalanta' Major General Buster Howe in May 2010, who replaced Rear Admiral Peter Hudson (Political and Security Committee, 2010).

The EU Military Committee (EUMC) is the highest military body of the EU. It is entrusted with advising and providing recommendations of military nature to the PSC. The EUMC is composed of Member States' Chiefs of Defence, but regular meetings are attended by Member States' Military Representatives. The EUMC plays a central role whenever the Council decides on a CSDP military operation. When such a decision is taken, the EUMC is expected to deliver a consensual advice to the PSC on how the operation should be conducted. Howorth (2007) notes strong commonalities between the role of the EUMC and the role of the NATO Military Committee. He identifies the EUMC as key in 'drawing up and evaluating strategic military options, overseeing the elaboration of an operational plan and monitoring operations throughout the mission' (Howorth, 2007: 74). One of the EUMC's roles with respect to EUNAVFOR 'Atalanta' is to maintain ongoing coordination with the EU Force Headquarter (FHQ) in Djibouti and with the EU Operational Headquarter (OHQ) in Northwood. In June 2009, the then EUMC Chairman Gen Henri Bentégeat, along with the military representatives of the two 2009 EU Presidencies, visited Djibouti. They formed the 'EU military' type of troika. The purpose of this visit was to discuss the conduct of 'Atalanta' with the Force Commander, Captain Garat Caramé (EUMC, 2009).

The EU Military Staff, composed of senior officers from EU Member States, is the main supporting body of the EUMC. According to former EUMC Chair Gen Henri Bentégeat, 'all documents, concepts, military advices and matters discussed during the meetings of the EUMC are generally initiated and staffed by the EUMS' (Bentégeat, 2009: 7). The European Union Military Staff (EUMS) works under the political guidance of the PSC and the military guidance of the EUMC (Howorth, 2007). The EUMS is further divided into various Directorates and Cells, such as the Intelligence Directorate (providing intelligence data) and the Civilian-Military Cell (conducting civil-military planning). Some of the activities of the EUMS with regard to planning and executing EUNAVFOR 'Atalanta' include the following (Leakey, 2009): (a) the EUMS Mission Monitoring Team (EUMS MMT) 'Somalia Anti-Piracy' was established; its role was to support the OHQ in Northwood when it was assuming the command of the operation in November 2008; (b) the EUMS MMT helped the EUMC and the OHQ with processing of various planning documents up to the launch of the operation; (c) the EUMS MMT also provided input to drafting the November 2008 Joint Action launching the military mission; and (d) the EUMS MMT remains involved in the operation; it advices the EUMC and supports the OHQ, in particular with regard to the interaction with third states taking part in fighting piracy in the region.

The OHQ is at the heart of any operation involving the deployment of military capacities. NATO has its OHQ at the Supreme Headquarters, Allied Powers Europe (SHAPE) in Mons, Belgium. The EU does not have comparable capacities in this regard, but three options are available for CSDP missions nonetheless. Firstly, in January 2007 the EU has established the so-called 'EU Operations Centre' within the EUMS. It was activated in June 2007, during the second military exercise of the EU, called 'Milex 2007' (Council, 2007d). For the purpose of this exercise, the EU FHQ was located in Sweden. The idea was to train the staff of the Operations Centre to coordinate its actions with the FHQ. As already mentioned, the EU FHQ for 'Atalanta' is located in Djibouti. The EU Operations Centre was particularly designed for short-notice, limited-size operations, requiring civilian-military coordination. The second option for the EU is to utilise one of the five national headquarters. These include (a) the French OHQ in Mont Valérien, Paris; (b) the UK OHQ in Northwood; (c) the German OHQ in Potsdam, Berlin; (d) the Italian OHQ in Rome; and (e) the Greek OHQ in Larissa. Thirdly, under the so-called 'Berlin Plus agreement', the EU can also use the NATO's OHQ in Mons.

None of these options are ideal from the CSDP's operational perspective. Thus, in 2011, five EU countries (France, Germany, Italy, Poland and Spain) requested Catherine Ashton to 'examine all institutional and legal options available to Member States, including permanent structured co-operation, to develop critical CSDP capabilities, notably a permanent planning and conduct capability'. Setting a permanent military headquarter for the EU has been a long ambition of a number of EU Member States, such as Poland and France, but the United Kingdom opposes this idea on the basis that NATO already has necessary capacities for launching and commanding military operations (EUobserver, 2011). Consequently, it appears that if the initiative is successful, it can be implemented through the Lisbon Treaty-based provision for permanent structured cooperation, allowing nine or more Member States to advance integration in a particular policy area without other Members.

Drawing on the above analysis, it could be concluded that the institutional structure of the CSDP is remarkable, considering how recent developments in this intergovernmental area of European integration are. Indeed, it is an indication of a significant progress that the EU has developed institutions allowing it to conduct limited-scale, yet autonomous military operations. However, Howorth (2007) identifies a number of constraints affecting the CSDP. First, he points to the inter-agency competition (or turf wars) between the Council and the Commission, especially in the area of civilian crisis management, where inter-institutional coherence is essential. The Lisbon Treaty aims to address this problem by combining the post of the EU's High Representative with the Vice-President of the European Commission. The reforms also shifted the responsibility for planning civilian crisis management to the European External Action Service (EEAS), which brings together Member States and officials previously working in the Commission and Council Secretariat. Second, the CSDP remains thoroughly intergovernmental, which creates tensions between Member States recognising the need for a better central coordination on the one hand but hesitating to cease control over issues of military security on the other hand. This leads to the third constraint – the long time for processing initiatives, which in the end must represent the lowest denominator of often divergent preferences of Member States. The Lisbon Treaty has not introduced a substantial improvement in this regard, apart from the aforementioned permanent structured cooperation instrument. This, however, raises questions about the capabilities available for the EU within the CSDP if, for example, the United Kingdom chooses to opt-out from further integration.

The EU and Somali piracy: capabilities

The modern-day international security agenda presents states and non-state actors with challenges that are complex and interconnected, requiring a holistic approach. Maritime piracy off the coast of Somalia is an example of such a challenge, because of its multifaceted character. In particular, this means that organised gangs hijacking ships with crews for ransom are one of the many outcomes of the failed state of Somalia, thus linking problems such as the lack of law enforcement, extreme poverty and the lack of effective political governance. Scholars have recognised the complexity of maritime piracy in the Horn of Africa, trying to identify the main causes of piracy in this region, as well as possible solutions. According to Murphy (2009), the following enabling factors are particularly relevant for understanding the outburst of piracy in the Horn of Africa:

(a) Firstly, conflict and disorder create enabling conditions for piracy to thrive. This is at the root of piracy in the Western Indian Ocean and the Gulf of Aden, with conflict and disorder ravaging Somalia for almost two decades.
(b) Secondly, the promise of receiving significant financial rewards, underpinned by extreme poverty, is also a crucial factor. Yet, Burnett (2002: 117) notes that '[p]overty is the driving force behind the increase in piracy, not just off the coast of Africa, but in the Caribbean, South America, India, Bangladesh, and Southeast Asia'.
(c) Thirdly, underfunded law enforcement and inadequate security is a feature at the Horn of Africa more generally, not only in Somalia. Other states in the region, most notably Kenya, Djibouti, Tanzania and Yemen, do not, as yet, have capacities to tackle piracy more effectively either.

Furthermore, the maritime piracy expert Chalk (2008) suggests that the massive increase in commercial maritime traffic and the global proliferation of small arms are additional significant factors enabling piracy. According to this author, ready access to munitions such as pistols, light and heavy machine guns and rocket propelled grenades, amongst others, 'is one of the main factors contributing to the growing level of violence that has come to typify piracy in recent years' (Chalk, 2008: 14). Other reasons for piracy, according to Chalk, include the following: the use by maritime traffic of narrow and congested maritime chokepoints; the Asian financial crisis; external pressure after the September 11 attacks on states to invest in expensive homeland security systems, which had a negative impact on securing territorial waters; the low level of security in ports, leading to harbour thefts (particularly in the Horn of Africa and Southeast Asia); and, finally, corrupted and dysfunctional national criminal justice systems.

Some recommendations on how to best tackle piracy have been formulated, ranging from short-term protective measures to longer-term tackling of the root causes. Vego (2009) argues that, ultimately, the problem of piracy could be resolved only by going ashore. In this scenario, in addition to destroying gangs at sea, it is also of crucial importance to destroy the pirate leadership, their basing areas and their supporting structures. Commander Nakamura (2009: 12), US Naval War College, suggests: 'Coastal pirate bases should be disrupted by coalition military forces in concert with other government agencies. Special operations forces could be used to gather intelligence and employ operational fires to attack bases directly, setting conditions for follow-up conventional forces.'

Moreover, between short-term military action and long-term tackling of the root causes of piracy, there are also a range of activities that help to address piracy in the medium term, both off the coast of Somalia and in other vulnerable regions. Most notably, experts point to enhancing coastal monitoring and interdiction capabilities through training, technical support and deploying appropriate surveillance assets (Chalk, 2008). For example, in Southeast Asia, the Regional Cooperation Agreement on Combating Piracy and Armed Robbery (ReCAAP) created an Information Sharing Centre, aiming to enhance capacities of states in the region to tackle piracy of their coasts (Ho, 2009). A similar instrument is currently being developed for countries around the Gulf of Aden, under the auspices of the International Maritime Organization (IMO). Also, the shipping industry must continuously work to improve the capacities of merchant vessels to defend themselves. To this end, EUNAVFOR 'Atalanta' has been publicising the 'Best Management Practices to Deter Piracy off the Coast of Somalia and in the Arabian Sea Area' (BMP). The BMP is a set of rules developed by the shipping industry in cooperation with the EU and NATO task forces operating in the Gulf of Aden to raise awareness among ship crews on how to avoid piratical attacks and what to do if an attack occurs.

Finally, the scholarship on contemporary piracy, particularly piracy off the coast of Somalia, underlines the importance of long-term, structural solutions. Vego (2009: 178) notes: 'The military action alone cannot resolve the problem of piracy. It must be only a part of a much broader and comprehensive series of actions. The main causes of piracy are predominantly political, economic, and social.' The question of how to improve the situation in Somalia, so piracy can be curbed at its roots, is much more problematic. The EU, as this chapter demonstrates, is an actor involved at different levels in tackling piracy and other forms of

178 The EU as a Global Security Actor

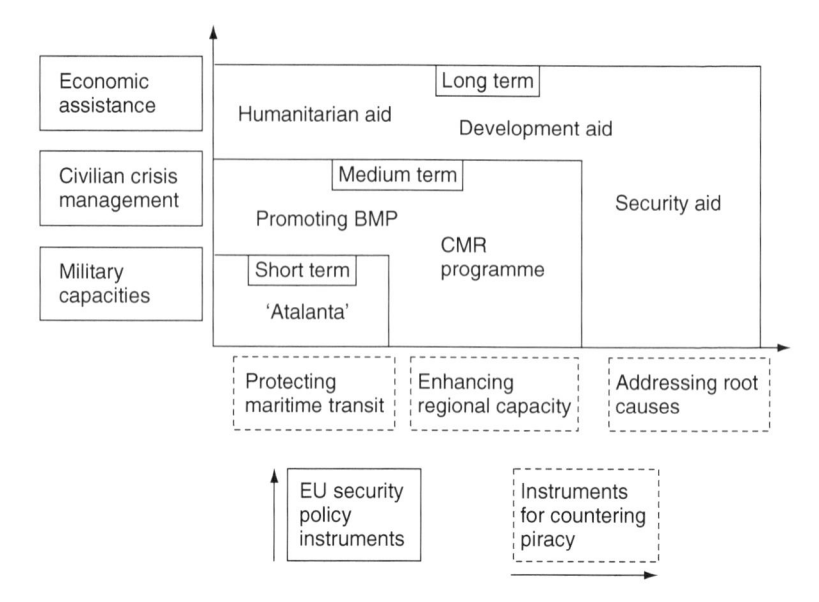

Figure 7.1 The EU as an international security actor in the case of maritime piracy: three categories of instruments

crime in Somalia. The EU's involvement includes deploying not only the largest task force to provide protection for vessels but also the largest and most comprehensive financial assistance with humanitarian, development and security dimensions. Figure 7.1 summarises three different aspects of a comprehensive response to the problem of Somali piracy.

The EU participates in all three types of recommended responses to piracy: (a) protecting maritime transit, (b) enhancing regional capacity and (c) addressing root causes. Table 7.1 summarises the policies and instruments that the EU has deployed up to date. They include not only measures which directly aim to counter the problem of piracy but also measures with broader objectives of improving economic and security conditions in the failed state of Somalia. This suggests that in addressing the security problem of Somali piracy, the EU has to rely exclusively on positive integration instruments, most notably the economic, diplomatic and military resources. As this section demonstrates, each of these resources plays a role in its own right, enabling to engage not only with the root causes of insecurity in the Horn of Africa but also with the direct threat of piratical attacks. The remaining of this section analyses each of the three responses to piracy by the EU.

Table 7.1 EU counter-piracy and long-term, preventive resources

Protecting maritime transit:	(a) EUNAVFOR 'Atalanta military operation (b) Web-based platform Maritime Security Centre: Horn of Africa
Enhancing regional capacities:	(c) Critical Maritime Routes programme (d) Best management practices
Addressing root causes:	(e) Humanitarian assistance (f) Development assistance (g) Security-oriented assistance (h) EUTM training mission in Uganda

This section first outlines the scope of the first-ever EU naval mission EUNAVFOR 'Atalanta', which aims to provide protection for maritime transit through directly engaging suspected pirates. The mission was launched in December 2008, and its mandate was extended until December 2012. Subsequently, this section analyses the EU's efforts aiming to enhance regional capacities, which can be considered a medium-term response. Finally, this section also examines the long-term EU policy on Somalia, aiming to address some of the root causes of piracy and other security problems in this country, such as the lack of effective law enforcement.

Protecting maritime transit

EUNAVFOR 'Atalanta' is the flagship EU response to the problem of piracy off the coast of Somalia. It is also the first EU naval mission. It was launched by the EU Council of Ministers in November 2008. The Council Joint Action from 10 November 2008 provides the legal basis for this CSDP operation, stating that '[t]he European Union (EU) shall conduct a military operation in support of Resolutions 1814 (2008), 1816 (2008) and 1838 (2008)' (Council, 2008d: 35). The purpose of this unprecedented EU operation was defined as twofold: to protect the vessels of the World Food Program delivering aid to Somalia and to protect vulnerable vessels cruising off the coast of Somalia.

EUNAVFOR 'Atalanta' consists of two major components. The first component includes warships, surveillance planes and other military capabilities of EU Member States, commanded by the Operational Commander in Northwood and the Force Commander in Djibouti. The second component includes a web-based platform called the Maritime Security Centre (Horn of Africa). This platform, established by the EU in cooperation with the shipping industry, contributes to the security of maritime transport in the Gulf of Aden through the constant monitoring of registered vessels. In addition, it also allows actors involved in fighting piracy off the Somali coast to coordinate their efforts in a real time.

The total number of EU military units involved in EUNAVFOR 'Atalanta' has changed over the course of the operation, but it includes (a) navy vessels; (b) Maritime Patrol and Reconnaissance Aircrafts; and (c) vessel protection detachment (VPD) teams. In June 2009, there were six of the VPDs available in the region. The budget for 'Atalanta' amounted to €8.4 million for 2010 and over €8 million for 2011. This sum covered mainly expenses related to the functioning of the OHQ in Northwood and the FHQ in Djibouti. It was collected from EU Member States, proportionally to their gross domestic product (GDP). The actual costs of deployments are covered by individual Member States taking part in the operation.

The military capabilities provided by EU Member States constitute just one, albeit the most visible dimension of EUNAVFOR 'Atalanta'. Another important resource allowing the EU to develop its 'actorness' in the area of organised crime off the coast of Somalia is a web-based platform called 'Maritime Security Centre: Horn of Africa' (MSCHOA). An EU Military Staff official explained that the rationale for creating this website was to convince ship owners and insurers that the Gulf of Aden was safe for transport. Otherwise, he pointed out, maritime transit in this region would become too expensive.[1] He also admitted that MSCHOA is 'unprecedented for any military operation in history' (MILSTAFF, 2009). The website has three sections:

(a) an unprotected section, providing general information about EUNAVFOR 'Atalanta', including yachting guidelines;
(b) a password-protected section, explaining how those cruising through the Gulf of Aden can protect themselves, that is what to do if an attack occurs. To this end, the website offers ship owners 'the facility to register their details securely with MSCHOA, update positions of their vessels and receive information and guidance designed to reduce the risk of pirate attacks'. In 2009, there were over 4500 registered users;
(c) an additional-security section, allowing live communication among states and organisations involved in fighting piracy in the region of the Western Indian Ocean and the Gulf of Aden. Some of the international actors that have been using the chat room include EUNAVFOR OHQ and FHQ, Combined Task Force (CTF) 151, China,

NATO, Japan, Russia, South Korea, Malaysia and the Seychelles. An official from the EU Military Staff admitted that 'it is remarkable that our partners really use it' (MILSTAFF, 2009).

The popularity of this platform is indeed an indication of the EU's recognition as a facilitator of the exchange of information among actors fighting piracy off the coast of Somalia. Assistant Chief of Staff (Operations) for the Combined Maritime Forces, Cdr Alistair Clark, envisaged, in June 2009, that MERCURY (the technical name of the chat room) was about to become 'the main means of disseminating unclassified information' (Clark, 2009). Both aspects of EUNAVFOR 'Atalanta', the military and electronic, constitute an important step for the EU to develop a military dimension of its international security 'actorness' in the area of organised crime.

On the one hand, the military operation adds a navy component to the EU experience of working within the framework of the CSDP. Rear Admiral Philip Jones of the UK Ministry of Defence, when examined by the House of Lords, underlined the novelty of 'Atalanta': 'It is the first ever EU maritime operation conducted under ESDP. I am the first ever UK commander of an EU operation under ESDP, so there are two very significant firsts there, and I think that the range of other navies that we are dealing with in the area has been an absolute first' (Great Britain, 2010: 1). The MSCHOA, on the other hand, demonstrates how Internet technologies can be utilised when responding to contemporary security challenges such as organised crime. Admiral Jones notes that the website 'has been one of the unexpected and very significant successes of the operation, where almost all of the shipping companies that transit through the Gulf of Aden register' (Great Britain, 2010: 3).

Enhancing the regional capacity

In order to investigate the EU as a counter-piracy security actor in a comprehensive manner, the analysis must go beyond the military operation and also include longer-term activities. This implies that such an approach requires moving beyond the CSDP, in order to look at all the instruments available to the EU, most notably through the European Commission (and currently the EEAS). While the Commission, traditionally, has not been regarded as important for EU security, over time, this view has begun to be questioned (Kirchner, 2006; Keukeleire and MacNaughtan, 2008; Kaunert, 2010c). In fact, empirically, it has been playing an increasingly significant role in EU security policy, both within and outside the EU borders.

To perform such a role, the Commission has had a number of financial instruments at its disposal, the most important of which is the Instrument for Stability (IfS) (Gänzle, 2009), already introduced in the previous chapter. Following the Lisbon Treaty reforms, the IfS will now be developed by the EEAS and implemented by the European Commission. This instrument, according to the former Member of the European Parliament (MEP) Angelika Beer, constitutes the first attempt to 'define the Grey Zone between the Council's CFSP, ESDP and the Commission's development policy, a step that might complete existing programs and might encourage active conflict prevention' (Beer, 2006). This instrument is designed for the EU to participate in projects aimed at strengthening law enforcement as well as strengthening capacities of judicial and civil authorities in such areas as combating terrorism and organised crime.

In addition to preventing the proliferation of WMDs (Zwolski, 2011a, 2011b), the area in which the EU can get involved through the IfS is 'threats to international transport, energy operations and critical infrastructure, including passenger and freight traffic and energy distribution' (European Parliament and the Council, 2006). This competence enables to utilise the IfS, to address the security problem of maritime piracy off the coast of Somalia. The Critical Maritime Routes (CMR) programme has been developed for this purpose, aiming to finance transnational initiatives enhancing the security of maritime transit, such as the sharing of information amongst states in vulnerable regions. The European Commission, in its IfS Multi-Annual Indicative Program 2009–2011, defined the CMR as the following: 'This program will seek to address a number of risks and threats posed by piracy and armed robbery at sea in a comprehensive and integrated way by bringing together the appropriate legal frameworks, institutional arrangements and operational measures, including capacity building to improve the exchange of information' (European Commission, 2009a).

Although the main geographical focus of the CMR programme is the Horn of Africa, a limited support is also envisaged for combating piracy in South-East Asia. Thus, in order to learn more about desirable responses to piracy in South-East Asia, the Commission arranged a series of high-level expert missions to Singapore, Malaysia and Indonesia. The purpose of these missions was 'to identify, select and recruit experts from EU Member States who would help us to prepare the specific projects in the regions' (COM-F, 2009). In spring 2008, as a result of the sharp increase of piracy in the Western Indian Ocean, the Commission decided that it was also necessary to deploy a similar fact-finding mission to countries around Somalia. A set of visits were conducted to Djibouti, Saudi Arabia and Yemen. Somalia was not included, at the time, due to its lack of institutional capacities to actively engage in the fight against piracy.

Commission-sponsored projects are developed multilaterally under the auspices of the IMO. Of notable importance, in this regard, was the IMO meeting in Djibouti, in January 2009, which the Commission attended as an observer. One major outcome of this meeting was the so-called Code of Conduct (Code of Conduct Concerning the Repression of Piracy and Armed Robbery against Ships in the Western Indian Ocean and the Gulf of Aden), together with the Resolution on Enhancing Training in the Region (IMO, 2009). One of the priorities identified in the Code of Conduct was to enhance the sharing of information amongst the states in the region. To this end, the establishment of 'information exchange centres' was envisaged in Kenya, Tanzania and Yemen (IMO, 2009). The European Commission decided to contribute to the setting up of the centre in Yemen.

An official from DG EuropeAid Co-Operation Office of the European Commission explained that, at the very minimum, the information sharing centres in the Horn of Africa and the Gulf of Aden should mirror those already in place in South-East Asia, established by the ReCAAP (Ho, 2009). The Resolution on Enhancing Training in the Region, another important outcome of the Djibouti meeting in 2009, requests the Secretary General of the IMO to establish a training centre in Djibouti, which will allow a uniform implementation of the Code of Conduct. The European Commission subsequently decided to support this project financially. For the period of 2009–2011 the Commission assigned between €14 and €18 million for the implementation of the CMR program (European Commission, 2009a).

Addressing the root causes

When talking to the EU officials, it appears that addressing the root causes of piracy off the coast of Somalia is very important for the EU. In this context, some observers point to illegal fishing and toxic waste dumping off the coast of Somalia as important reasons for piracy to emerge (Hari, 2009; Tharoor, 2009). These factors have also been identified as root causes of piracy by a Somali government official during a May 2010 informal UN General Assembly meeting on piracy (UN, 2010). However, regardless of the degree to which illegal fishing and toxic waste dumping contributed to piracy off the Somali coast, almost all experts and EU officials agree that the failed state of Somalia constitutes the main root cause of piracy in the Western Indian Ocean and the Gulf of Aden. Extreme poverty, the lack of law enforcement and corrupt officials (warlords) make any anti-piracy task force only a partial solution. In order to address the problem over the long term, structural conditions in Somalia need to improve. Yet, this is easier said than done; this task seems next to impossible in the post-2006 climate of constant violence and humanitarian disaster. Nonetheless, the EU remains the largest donor of official development assistance to Somalia, committed to improving political, economic and security conditions in this country. With regard to the political situation in Somalia, the EU, together with other international actors, continues to support the TFG as the only authority in Somalia considered legitimate by the international Community. In order to enhance security in Somalia, the EU contributes financially to the peace-keeping mission of the African Union (AU), to the Rule of Law Program of the UN Development Programme (UNDP) and, it also started its own training program in Uganda for Somali security forces.

EU development aid to Somalia is guided by the framework prepared jointly by the UN Development Group and the World Bank, upon the request of the TFG. Their work on the Joint Needs Assessment (JNA) for Somalia began in 2005 and resulted in a five-volume document called the Reconstruction and Development Program for Somalia (RDP). The RDP identifies a number of priority needs for Somalia, which were grouped into three broad pillars: (a) deepening peace, improving security and establishing good governance; (b) investing in people through improved social services; and (c) creating enabling environment for private sector-led growth to expand employment and reduce poverty (United Nations and World Bank, 2008). The EU incorporated these pillars into its own development strategy for Somalia for the years 2008–2013 (European Union, 2008). Overall, the EU's long-term engagement in Somalia can be grouped into five categories: (a) EU humanitarian aid, (b) EU development aid, (c) EU support for the Rule of Law program, derived from the UNDP, (d) EU support for African Union Mission in Somalia (AMISOM), the AU peace-keeping mission in Somalia, and (e) EU training missions in Uganda.

EU humanitarian aid to Somalia is managed by the Humanitarian Aid department of the European Commission (ECHO). In Somalia, conditions for delivering humanitarian aid are extremely difficult, with 37 aid workers killed in 2008; this is 66 per cent of all aid workers killed worldwide (Sullivan, 2009). At the same time, Somalia is in a state of a constant humanitarian disaster, with 225 out of 1000 children not reaching the age of five (European Union, 2008). The European Commission increased its humanitarian assistance from €12 million in 2007 to €45.8 million in 2008 (Council, 2010b). In 2010, the Commission allocated not only €35 million for the victims of conflict and natural disasters in Somalia (European Commission, 2010b) but also €15 million for Somalis in Kenya, the location for the world's biggest refugee camp (European Commission, 2010c).

The EU development aid, as opposed to humanitarian assistance, contributes to long-term development projects, aimed at changing the structural conditions in the country. It is constructed around three main focal sectors, reflecting the three pillars identified in the RDP. The focal sectors, identified in the EU's Somalia Joint Strategy Paper for the Period 2008–2013 (European Union, 2008), include the following: (a) Governance: promoting security, supporting reconciliation, strengthening the governance, supporting Somali non-state actors; (b) Education: strengthening and expanding capacity of administrations at all levels, teaching force, access to education and participation of disadvantaged adults; and (c) Economic Development and Food Security: developing the framework for private sector-led growth, supporting the main productive sectors, supporting sustainable management of natural resources, supporting food security and livelihood recovery. The total budget for the EU's long-term development assistance to Somalia for the years 2008–2013 is €215 million.

The EU is also involved in providing a more security-focused assistance. Firstly, the EU contributes to the Rule of Law and Security Program of the UNDP. This initiative aims to improve the security situation in Somalia through projects such as (a) Judiciary/Access to justice – building mobile courts, training professionals, establishing the Women Lawyers' Association in Somalia; (b) Law enforcement – providing training for the police, increasing access for women and children to justice; (c) Community safety – building on the experience of similar projects in Haiti, Colombia and El Salvador; this project supports local communities in organising Local Safety Committees and in developing Community Safety Plans. The EU has been focusing on supporting the development of the police force in Somalia, committing in total €43 million over the last few years (Council, 2010b).

In addition, the EU supports AMISOM, the AU peace-keeping mission in Somalia, launched by the AU Peace and Security Council in January 2007 and authorised by the UN Security Council (UNSC, 2007b). This mission, supported by the EU, the United States and other international donors right from the beginning, aims to fill the vacuum created by the withdrawal of Ethiopian forces, after they removed the Islamic Courts Union (ICU) from power in December 2006. Considering that many defeated Islamist fighters initiated the guerrilla war in Somalia, the AU ministers decided that the existence of the TFG could only be secured by an external peace-keeping mission. AMISOM, although critical for the security of the Somali government, has limited resources. At the same time, al-Shabaab has increased its pressure, trying to capture, for example, the Presidential Palace in May 2010. AU ministers, as a result of Kampala attacks in July 2010, attempted to broaden the mandate of the mission, to include peace enforcement, but such a move was blocked by the United Nations (Kasasira and Muyita, 2010). Since 2007, the EU has committed over €100 million to the support of AMISOM. Most notably, the EU pledged €60 million at the International Donor Conference on Somalia, hosted by the European Commission in April 2009, and co-organised by the United Nation and the AU (European Commission, 2009b).

Moreover, in addition to supporting security in Somalia through other international frameworks, the EU launched its own mission in April 2010, aiming to train 2000 Somali forces in Uganda. The European Union Training Mission (EUTM) Somalia intends to contribute to the security situation in Somalia 'as part of a wider international effort and encompassing inter alia the vetting of trainees, the monitoring and mentoring of the forces once back in Mogadishu and the funding and payment of the salaries of the soldiers' (Council, 2010c). The success of this mission, which has the potential to enhance the quality of the Somali army, will depend on the stability of wages being paid to those who are being trained. In April 2010, media outlets revealed that many Somali soldiers, trained with the support of US funding in Djibouti, deserted (Associated Press and Smith, 2010). While some of them returned to their families, others joined al-Shabaab and now are involved in fighting the TFG and AMISOM forces.

Ultimately, the only long-term solution to piracy off the coast of Somalia is a more stable and lawful state of Somalia. This section demonstrated that the EU remains active in providing long-term assistance. Yet, it remains difficult to assess the effectiveness of the EU's involvement. This is due to the fact that Somalia remains a thoroughly failed state, torn by permanent fights between various clans as well as between Islamist insurgents and the forces supporting the TFG. As a result, it remains almost impossible to assess any progress. As a vivid example, one can note the fact that Somalia has been unable to even deliver data for the UNDP in order to rank the country in the Human Development Index. Over the long term, security and development in Somalia will depend on the ability of the parties in the conflict to reach some sort of agreement, as happened in 2004, when the Transitional Federal Institutions were created. Until then, the EU, through a variety of instruments at its disposal, needs to remain a leading international actor facilitating progress towards this goal.

The EU and Somali piracy: recognition

EUNAVFOR 'Atalanta' constitutes the first naval operation of the EU, which, as such, is generally not considered an actor with significant autonomous military capabilities. In fact, as already noted, the EU does not have its own military capacities; instead, for its operations, it relies exclusively on the contributions of Member States, with the exception of the limited Brussels-based headquarter capability (EU Operations Centre). To what extent is the EU recognised for its counter-piracy efforts? Within the UN framework, the EU became recognised as a valuable contributor to international counter-piracy efforts. For example, in Resolution 1838 the EU was 'commended' for setting up a coordination unit supporting the surveillance off the Somali coast[2] (UNSC, 2008a). In Resolution 1846, the UN Security Council welcomed the efforts of international and regional organisations, including NATO and 'in particular' the decision of the EU to launch EUNAVFOR 'Atalanta' (UNSC, 2008b). Apart from the UN Security Council, states in the region of the Horn of Africa and the Gulf of Aden have also recognised the EU in the context of its anti-piracy measures. For example, an agreement was concluded between the EU and the Republic of Djibouti, concerning the presence of EU military forces on the territory of Djibouti (The EU and the Republic of Djibouti, 2010). Similarly, in the exchange of letters between Kenya and the EU, the former agreed to conditions proposed by the EU regarding the detention of suspected pirates on Kenyan territory (The EU and the Government of Kenya, 2009).

The prosecution of suspected pirates has been a contentious issue for states and organisations deterring piracy off the coast of Somalia. The reason for this is that, on the one hand, Somalia does not have the capacity to prosecute and, on the other hand, actors involved in fighting piracy in this region are reluctant to transfer suspects to their home countries. Thus, international actors have been trying to secure agreements with states in the region, allowing the prosecution and detention of suspected pirates in these states. The EU successfully achieved this goal in March 2009, when it reached an agreement with Kenya (The EU and the Government of Kenya, 2009). In June 2009, one EU official observed that, at that time, NATO still did not have a similar agreement, which made the EU a more attractive framework for states to get involved in fighting piracy off the coast of Somalia (MILSTAFF, 2009).

Politically, 'Atalanta' enjoys rather high recognition, partially due to its consistent publicity efforts, raising awareness of the EU's involvement in the Horn of Africa. This is done, for example, through a dedicated website 'European Union Naval Force Somalia – Operation Atalanta' (eunavfor.eu). Unsurprisingly, EU officials, in general, tend to agree that EUNAVFOR 'Atalanta' is strongly recognised for its anti-piracy efforts. One official from the Unit Africa of the Council Secretariat observes: 'Our naval operation is widely known in the region [Western Indian Ocean and the Gulf of Aden]. I would say that we are the most prominent actor there' (CON-B, 2009). Another official, from DG MARE of the European Commission, notes that 'Atalanta' is strongly recognised because, for example, it has a system of fast exchange of information with the vessels of other actors involved in fighting piracy off the coast of Somalia. The official also notes that 'Atalanta' is more welcome in the region than the involvement of the United States, because with the involvement of the EU 'there is no "war on terror" rhetoric associated with the operation; it is perceived as a policing mission' (COM-C, 2009).

As part of research, a number of interviews were conducted with actors in the region. They seem to corroborate that, indeed, the EU has acquired high level of recognition for its counter-piracy mission in the Gulf of Aden and Western Indian Ocean. For example, a founder and president of Nairobi-based Somali Think-Tank Abdullahi M. Aden noted in 2009: 'Already in November 2008, we heard that the EU's mission against Somali piracy is directed towards the coast of Somalia. We knew that it was a deployment by the EU and not individual countries. We also knew that the European naval operation off the coast of Somalia was led by the UK and it was based on UN Resolution 1838.' A Turkish navy officer, directly involved in fighting piracy in the Gulf of Aden, also underlined the visibility of the EU in the region:

> Operation ATALANTA is well visible in the area from the points of deterring and disrupting piracy. Every operation conducted by the EU, NATO or Coalition Forces are very well coordinated. Exchanging intelligence and region coverage are well organised by three headquarters. (...) As far as I have observed, all EU countries which have

the capability to send naval forces, either frigates or marine patrolling aircrafts to operate in this region, do their best to contribute to this operation.

(NAVY1, 2010)

Perhaps this is the highest level of recognition the EU has achieved among other actors involved in countering piracy off the Somali coast, including both state- and non-state actors. This recognition is mainly facilitated through the aforementioned MSCHOA, constituting an important part of EUNAVFOR 'Atalanta'. One of the functions of this electronic platform is to provide a secure chat room for states and international organisations which have deployed military capacities off the coast of Somalia. This is how one EU official, involved in conducting EUNAVFOR 'Atalanta', explains the role of this chat room: 'It is a secure but unclassified facility and we have there Russians, NATO, Chinese, Indians, and all the other partners communicating with each other on a minute-to-minute basis' (MILSTAFF, 2009). Indeed, the fact that other states and organisations take advantage of this EU-facilitated instrument, in order to coordinate their decisions, is important. It indicates a high level of the recognition of the EU as an international security actor or even as a leading security actor in this particular case.

Conclusion

In recent years, the internal security problem of Somalia has become an external security problem for the entire international Community with the UN Security Council urging its Member States and regional organisations to combat piracy. This chapter demonstrated how the EU has managed to construct an important role for itself in emerging new security areas, such as the external dimension of Somalia's internal security problem. To this end, the chapter assessed the scope of European integration in CSDP, the capabilities at the EU's disposal and the extent to which it has been recognised for its counter-piracy efforts. In the context of planning and executing EUNAVFOR 'Atalanta', the institutional setup of the CSDP has been assessed, ranging from high-level bodies of political importance, such as the PSC, to the headquarters, necessary for any mission involving the deployment of military capacities. It has been noted that this institutional setup is rather remarkable, considering its recent development and the fact that there is no agreement among Member States about the extent to which the EU should develop its military muscle. At the same time, important limitations have been identified, most notably the exclusively intergovernmental character of the EU's cooperation in this policy area, necessarily affecting the scope of integration.

With regard to the EU's capabilities, this chapter analysed three types of EU policies, aiming to respond to Somali piracy directly and indirectly; these include (1) the policies aiming to protect maritime transport, primarily EUNAVFOR 'Atalanta'; (2) the policies aiming to enhance regional capacities, such as the CMR programme and the promotion of the BMP; and (3) the efforts to address the root causes of insecurities in Somalia and off its coast, through the variety of assistance and training programmes. We conclude that whilst the EU's efforts to address the problem of maritime piracy as such are important and can be considered to some degree successful, longer-term policies aiming at improving the structural conditions in Somalia have not yet achieved visible positive outcomes. Finally, this chapter has also suggested that the EU has acquired high recognition for its counter-piracy measures, even though, in general, the EU is not considered a 'hard security' actor.

Somalia has often been mentioned as the first failed state; in fact, its overall security situation is probably worse than anywhere else in the world. More recently, some authors have even raised questions over the strategy of supporting the TFG, identifying such a strategy as unsustainable in the long run. For example, Bruton (2009) advocates strategic disengagement of the United States and the international Community from supporting the Somali government. This support should be replaced, in her view, with a decentralised approach focused on providing aid to the society, even at the expense of Islamists taking the leadership of the country. If this would prove to be the only available option in the long term, given the fact that the country, according to some authors, is 'beyond repair' (Tannock, 2009), then clearly the EU's security-oriented assistance to Somalia would be shown as, ultimately, a waste of money and, in the end, doomed to fail. However, this chapter does not provide any evidence to support this notion.

At present, empirical research is unable to really assess the effectiveness of any actor in Somalia. This also constitutes an important limitation to assessing the role of the EU as a security actor in the case of Somali piracy, particularly with regard to the long-term structural component of this role. Reliable data from Somalia is scarce. This means that we are unable to empirically assess the effectiveness of the EU's policies, but, equally, we are also unable to assess other international actors, whether the United States, the United Nations, or the AU in terms of effectiveness. As a result, it is necessary to measure alternative dimensions to international counter-piracy efforts, such as the comprehensiveness of such efforts. In this regard, one can note that the EU's efforts are reasonably successful in that they are sufficiently comprehensive.

Conclusion

This book contributes to the flourishing strand of literature concerned with the role of the European Union (EU) as an actor in international security policy. This literature, in turn, is part of a broader research agenda on European foreign policy, which includes questions concerning the institutional structure of the EU's external relations, problems of coherence and Europeanisation, the challenge of applying European integration and/or International Relations (IR) theories to explain the EU's external role as well as uncertainties surrounding the EU's civilian/normative power status. Traditionally, and in particular since the Maastricht Treaty, the analysis of the EU's foreign policy has been almost exclusively confined to the developments in what has become the second pillar of the newly established Union, defined by Title V of the Treaty on the European Union (TEU) as the Common Foreign and Security Policy (CFSP). The CFSP marked the first such important effort on the part of European Economic Community (EEC) Member States to give European integration a more political character. These empirical developments were quickly recognised by scholars who already in the 1990s began to analyse and assess the nature, structure and performance of the Union as a political actor in its own right. Some of the key authors of that time, who largely set the research agenda for studying the CFSP, include Christopher Hill (1993, 1998), David Allen (1998), Michael Smith (1998), Helene Sjursen (1998) and Peterson and Sjursen (1998).

Furthermore, the debate on the role of the EU in IR, including security policy, has become framed into a number of key themes. The first of these themes concerned the discrepancy between the ambitious provisions of Title V and the actual role of the Union as a foreign policy actor. This discrepancy was quickly captured by Hill (1993, 1998), who framed it as the 'capability–expectations gap' in European foreign policy, that is the situation in which expectations towards the EU's performance on the world scene surpass the actual capabilities of the EU to meet such expectations. This argument has not lost much of its relevance 20 years after the CFSP was established. The EU Member States still struggle to speak with one voice on matters of concern for the EU as a whole. In fact, the institutional reforms of the Lisbon Treaty may, paradoxically, further exacerbate the gap between the EU's capabilities and expectations towards its global role. This is because, on the one hand, the provisions of the Lisbon Treaty truly equip the EU with the *potential* to become a coherent global player, providing new structures such as the European External Action Service (EEAS). Yet, on the other hand, European capitals are still cautious when it comes to channelling their foreign policies through Brussels rather than developing autonomous actions.

Another important theme in studying the EU's global role was framed by Michael Smith (1998), who questioned the overarching focus on the CFSP. He argued that, in fact, it is the EC's extensive external economic role which must be taken into account more seriously by scholars of European foreign policy. This view was even contested in the same edited volume in which it was introduced (Peterson and Sjursen, 1998). Dave Allen (1998) was quick to point out that although the external relations of the European Commission are important, they must be seen as just one element of European foreign policy. Europe's external economic role is no substitution for the political and strategic role, and neither the European Commission nor the Council acting separately can advance the EU's position on the world stage.

This theme of the European Commission's role in IR continued to evolve (Marsh and Mackenstein, 2005; Kaunert, 2007, 2009a, 2010a, 2010b, 2010c; Zwolski, 2011a, 2011b, 2012a, 2012b) and, as this book has demonstrated, also remains important in the field of security policy. Indeed, the Commission's growing importance on the world stage provided a key impetus for reforming the structure of the EU's foreign policy apparatus in order to bring the former European Community (EC) pillar and the CFSP closer together. As the external responsibilities of the Commission continued to grow alongside the slowly progressing integration of the Union in the second pillar, Member States recognised that the Union's global role will be seriously hampered if the first and second pillars remain separated by two different leadership and institutional structures. As a result, the Lisbon Treaty merged the post of the EU's High Representative with that of the Vice President of the European Commission. Furthermore, external relations bureaucracies from the Commission and the Council General Secretariat were moved *en bloc* to the newly established EEAS. The full effect of these reforms is yet to be seen, but this book has contributed to the debate by emphasising the foreign and security policy instruments and resources which used to belong to the EC pillar of the EU and now are managed jointly by the EEAS and the Commission. This analysis, of course, relates to the broader question of the nature of international security and the evolution of the 'security' concept after the Cold War. In this context, the book argues that incorporating the broadened approach to security, as dominant in the security studies literature (Krause and Williams, 1997; Collins, 2007; McInnes, 2008; Thomas, 2008; Dalby, 2009; Smith, 2010), necessitates broadening the scope of EU policies, instruments and resources which are considered relevant for assessing the EU's global security role.

Bringing closer together the instruments of a more economic nature and those more political and security-oriented may contribute to developing further the EU as a strategic and comprehensive security actor. However, it raises some challenges of its own. Most notably, pursuing the norm of a more holistic, strategic international security policy has arguably threatened a key norm which contributes to the EU's normative identity, namely the apolitical character of its aid. In other words, the same consolidation that can turn the EU into a more strategic and effective security actor raises strong objections from those concerned with the impartiality of its aid. What is at stake, according to the sceptics, is the credibility of the EU as a provider of development and humanitarian assistance (Zwolski, 2012b). The friction in the EU between the norms of the strategic and holistic approach to international security policy, and the apolitical character of the EU's development assistance, has long been inevitable. Notably, the EU has long been criticised for a lack of coherency in its external policies, which has been caused by the formal separation, post-Maastricht, of the instruments of the Commission from the policies of the Council. This separation has often been reflected and reinforced in the design of scholarly literature on the EU's external policy, which tended to analyse the policies of the first and second pillars separately (Knodt and Princen, 2003: 2–3) – a separation which this book has attempted to overcome.

It could be argued that a more strategic and holistic approach from the EU to its international security policy is inevitable. This is due to a number of factors, including the discourse emphasising 'comprehensiveness' and security–development nexus in the EU's international policy, which is constantly repeated in strategic documents on the role of the EU in international security and its development policy, and the direction of institutional reforms in the EU, most notably the location of external assistance instruments of the EU under the overall responsibility of the High Representative, assisted by the EEAS. Of course, much will depend on the position which the EEAS will develop for itself over time vis-à-vis Member States and other institutions and on the leadership role provided by the High Representative.

A more recent theme in literature concerns the external face of European internal security, that is the process of a growing external dimension of the Area of Freedom, Security and Justice (AFSJ). European cooperation on transnational matters of internal security dates back to the framework of the European Political Cooperation (EPC) in the 1970s. Initially confined to coordinating counter-terrorism measures, this policy area became institutionalised alongside the first and the second pillar of the newly established EU in 1993 and became known as the third pillar of the EU – Justice and Home Affairs (JHA). The progress of integration in this policy field was slow and difficult throughout the 1990s – just as it was in the CFSP. However, soon thereafter, the AFSJ – as re-named by the Treaty of Amsterdam – became one of the fastest growing and most dynamic areas of European integration. This was especially prompted by shocking external events, that is the 11 September attacks in the United States and subsequent attacks in London and Madrid. As a consequence, what was originally the framework for dealing with European internal security problems increasingly became a policy area challenging the traditional internal–external security divide. In response to external demands for policy coordination, the AFSJ has become a policy area with an important and still expanding external security dimension, most notably through European counter-terrorism cooperation with the United States, as this book has demonstrated. This trend, naturally, became recognised in the literature and soon developed into a new 'theme' in studies of the EU's role as a global security actor. On the one hand, scholars interested in European internal security have started integrating the external dimension into their research (Mitsilegas et al., 2003; Occhipinti, 2003; Balzacq and Carrera, 2005, 2006; Friedrichs, 2005; Kaunert, 2007, 2009a, 2010a, 2010b, 2010c; Bossong, 2008). On the other hand, scholars primarily interested in European foreign policy have started including an analysis of the AFSJ as another policy framework through which the EU pursues its global security objectives (Keukeleire and MacNaughtan, 2008). The argument of this book is that the external dimension of the AFSJ must be integrated into any analysis of the EU's role as a global security actor which aims to approach the topic in a comprehensive manner.

All these themes have emerged as part of the latest research on European foreign policy in response to empirical developments in the EU. They remain relevant and this book has engaged with them in various ways. At the same time, a significant strand of literature emerged towards the end of 1990s and in the 2000s, focusing specifically on the role of the EU as a global *security* actor. Rather unsurprisingly, just like the broader European foreign policy literature tended to focus on the CFSP, the literature on European external security policy typically narrowly confined its analysis to the European Security and Defence Policy (ESDP), as discussed in the Introduction.

In this book, the position of the ESDP (and now the Common Security and Defence Policy (CSDP)) framework in the EU's global security role is put in perspective – as one of the many different kinds of instruments and resources at the disposal of the EU. Notably, most of the case studies in this book do not require the deployment by the EU of military capacities. In fact, military capacities would be inappropriate as a response to problems such as those occurring to refugees or even those due to climate change. Moreover, even in cases where the military has a role to play, such as the problem of Somali maritime piracy, those who are actually involved on the ground in protecting maritime traffic argue that the military will not solve the piracy problem. Instead, they point out that the economic and political situation on land has to improve, and for this a different set of capabilities is more relevant. As a result, while the CSDP must be taken into account when studying the EU as a global security actor, this framework should only be seen as one of the EU's many instruments – and often not even the most important, or, indeed, most relevant one.

Revisiting the aims of this book

This book aimed to assess, in a comprehensive manner, the role of the EU as an international security actor. This led to a number of objectives which were examined in the theoretical component of this volume. Firstly, it has been necessary to address the question of the EU as an international actor: is it possible for a non-state entity, such as the EU, to be considered an international actor? Building on the research examined in Chapter 1, this book has suggested that there are no inevitable theoretical difficulties in conceptualising the EU as an actor if a set of criteria for assessing such 'actorness' is defined. These criteria have been grounded in the literature on the EU as a *sui generis* international actor, explained in the theoretical chapter and applied to the analysis of the empirical case studies.

Secondly, it has been necessary to justify the comprehensive approach to security adopted in this book. To this end, the theoretical part has integrated the conceptualisation of security as widely discussed in scholarly research on contemporary security studies. For the most part, this book has argued that the literature on the EU's role as an international/global security adopts an implicitly narrow understanding of security, mainly limited to the problems of a military nature. While more traditional security problems and instruments are still relevant and important, this book has argued that significant developments in security studies must be taken into account when analysing the EU's role as a global security actor. In this literature, scholars, for the most part, demonstrate how the 'security' concept had been understood too narrowly without taking into consideration important security concerns of non-state referent objects (Krause and Williams, 1997; Collins, 2007; McInnes, 2008; Thomas, 2008; Dalby, 2009; Smith, 2010).

Related to this aspect, we also argued that a comprehensive approach entails studying EU instruments and policies beyond the CFSP/CSDP framework. When incorporating a broader understanding of security, as dominating security studies research, it becomes apparent that the EU has been playing a significant security policy role through its long-term capacity-building relationship with third countries, complemented by a range of short- to long-term financial instruments. Furthermore, as this book has demonstrated, non-CFSP measures have also been utilised in addressing more traditional security problems, such as the non-proliferation of chemical, biological, radiological and nuclear (CBRN) materials.

These objectives served the purpose of addressing the main research question of this volume, that is 'to what extent has the EU developed as an international security actor?' In order to address this question in a way which is congruent with the theoretical framework set in Chapter 1, the empirical component was structured around criteria for assessing international 'actorness' of an entity such as the EU. These criteria included the scope of integration, capabilities and recognition. Furthermore, the empirical analysis of the EU policy has not been limited to the instruments and resources available within the framework of the CFSP/CSDP. Whereas these EU policy frameworks play a key role in the EU's international security policy, it was demonstrated that the European Commission has its own instruments, important for addressing some of the contemporary security challenges. Some of these instruments, such as the Instrument for Stability (IfS), are now a shared competence with the EEAS, and it remains to be seen what kind of inter-institutional balance emerges in this respect. In order to address the problem of a gap between the approach to security in the European studies literature and literature on contemporary security studies, a varied sample of contemporary security challenges was introduced into the empirical part of this book. These case studies include the following:

(a) The EU and climate change as one of the so-called 'non-traditional' security issues. It has been noted that there already is a wide array of studies on the EU and climate change policy. However, these contributions, while valuable in explaining various aspects of the EU environmental policy, do not explicitly contribute to a better understanding of the EU as an international security actor. Moreover, the EU recently began to develop a separate policy, aiming to address specifically the security dimension of climate change. This recent development has not been acknowledged in the literature yet.

(b) The terrorist attacks of 11 September 2001 in the United States as well as a series of subsequent terrorist attacks in Europe prompted the EU to integrate and become a stronger actor in counter-terrorism policy. As a result, empirical developments of the last decade seem to suggest an ever increasing role of terrorism on the security agenda of the EU. Interestingly, it was the threat of ideological terrorism which prompted European cooperation on internal security in the 1970s within the EPC framework, and it is also terrorism (although of a very different kind, nowadays primarily Islamist terrorism) which is a key driving force for further integration within the AFSJ.

(c) The case study concerning the EU's security 'actorness' in relation to asylum and refugees is to some degree similar to the climate security case in that there is debate in the academic and the policy world over whether these challenges should be linked to security, that is whether they should be securitised. In contrast to the case of climate change, however, framing the issue of asylum and refugees as security problems has been resisted by central EU institutions, even in the face of attempts by Member States to do the opposite.

(d) The EU and the danger of the proliferation of weapons of mass destruction (WMDs), particularly from Russia and the former Soviet Union. There was a considerable threat of an unauthorised access to the large stockpiles of nuclear and chemical weapons in this geographical region after the collapse of the Soviet Union. The

EU, together with the United States and other international actors, played an important role in preventing this danger from materialising. Again, the 9/11 attacks raised the concerns of terrorist groups gaining access to WMD stockpiles in Russia. The EU is one of the international actors which became involved in addressing this challenge.

(e) The EU and piracy off the coast of Somalia is considered in this volume the most-traditional security problem due to the type of solution that it requires. Whereas the previous two cases require almost exclusively political, economic and diplomatic resources, the problem of piracy actually requires a limited military response as part of the solution. The EU was one of the first international actors to respond to the calls by the UN Security Council. It remains involved in fighting piracy in the short term, through its military mission, but is also active in addressing the root causes of piracy and other forms of organised crime, through long-term development and security aid to Somalia.

The results of the case study analysis

A comprehensive approach to analysing the role of the EU as an international security actor allows obtaining a more accurate picture of such a role. This section first outlines the findings of the individual case studies. In the second part, it refers back to the criteria of 'actorness', in order to draw more general conclusions, based on the analysis of all five case studies.

Each of the five case studies selected for this book can be considered a separate contribution to studying the role of the EU as an international security actor. First, the case study examining EU 'actorness' in the area of climate security highlighted the EU's role in developing the international security dimension of climate change. It was not until a few years ago that state- and non-state actors began conceptualising climate change in the context of international security. However, this trend is uneven. At the global level, states such as China, Pakistan and many other developing countries object to broadening the scope of the UN Security Council by debating challenges posed by climate change. In this context, as the book demonstrated, the EU attempts to act as a 'norm entrepreneur', promoting the broader, more inclusive international security agenda at the global level. Within the EU, the process was launched in 2007 and 2008, leading to the adoption of some guiding documents on climate security policy and incorporating climate security into the European Security Strategies of 2003 and 2008. This process was mainly facilitated by the so-called Steering Group on Climate Change and International Security (Zwolski and Kaunert, 2011). In the wake of the Lisbon Treaty reforms, the bureaucratic units responsible for developing this agenda were moved to the EEAS. Thus, the position of climate change on the EU *security* agenda and consequently the determination of the EU to promote climate security globally will largely depend on the leadership of the High Representative.

Second, the EU's role as an actor in asylum policy has a number of qualities. First, the EU has achieved a significant degree of scope of integration and, furthermore, quite significant capabilities in this policy area. While the EU has obviously not achieved a full harmonisation of asylum policy across the 27 Member States, it has nonetheless obtained important minimum standards for refugees across the EU. Despite fears to the contrary, the Commission, in particular, managed to anchor asylum policy within internationally accepted standards, such as the Geneva Convention. It has thus acquired significant capabilities as an actor in refugee policy worldwide. The EU has been clearly visible in its actions towards asylum seekers and refugees. Yet, in terms of recognition, it must be noted that the central EU institutions, most notably the Commission, have successfully blocked the recognition of the EU as a *security* actor in this policy area, despite the preferences of some Member States to the contrary. The Commission as well as the European Parliament aimed to maintain the EU's image of a humanitarian, rather than security actor in asylum and refugee policy, and have largely succeeded, despite setbacks on the way.

Third, the empirical evidence suggests that the EU has achieved a significant degree of global security 'actorness' in counter-terrorism policy. It has attained a high degree of integration in this policy area, primarily in response to the tragic events of the terrorist attacks in the United States and in Europe. In response to these attacks, the European Commission has taken up a leading role, which can be conceptualised as that of a policy entrepreneur, in establishing common capabilities and pushing for mutual recognition of national legal systems, exemplified by high-profile initiatives, such as the European Arrest Warrant. Importantly, the EU has become recognised as a crucial partner in counter-terrorism by the United States, in spite of the widely publicised transatlantic divergences over the war in Iraq and even during the presidency of George W. Bush. With more integration regarding internal security measures inside the EU, the United States became increasingly interested in cooperating with the EU. An additional consequence of the high degree of integration in EU counter-terrorism has been the increasingly close relationship with the world's only remaining superpower – the United States. This area can clearly be seen as a strong success story in terms of acquiring international security 'actorness' for the EU.

Fourth, the case study concerning preventing the proliferation of WMDs from Russia and the former Soviet Union has demonstrated that, even though the EU is not highly recognised as an actor in this area, there are some significant (even surprising) developments taking place at the EU level. Most notably, the European Commission continues to play an important role in the EU non-proliferation policy, through utilising a variety of instruments. In the 1990s, the policy of the Commission focused exclusively on the former Soviet Union and was delivered through the Technical Assistance to the Commonwealth of Independent States (TACIS) programme. In 2007, two new instruments replaced TACIS. One of these new instruments, the IfS, identified non-proliferation as one of the key security priorities for the European Commission. As a result, even though the policies of the EU (including the Commission and the Council) became overshadowed by the activities of individual EU Member States working within international frameworks outside the EU, central EU bureaucracies continue to develop the non-proliferation policy of the EU. Interestingly, this policy even begins to move beyond the geographical area of the former Soviet Union; the EEAS and the Commission extend their activities to the Middle East, Africa and Asia.

Fifth, the chapter on the problem of piracy off the coast of Somalia examined the EU efforts to counter this threat in the short, medium and long term. In the short term, this volume discussed the first-ever EU naval operation, deployed to protect vulnerable vessels in the Western Indian Ocean and the Gulf of Aden. Apart from being the first naval mission of the EU, EUNAVFOR 'Atalanta' is also an operation which has achieved a high level of recognition. Perhaps, it is the most widely recognised CSDP operation deployed to date. In the medium term, the European Commission participates in implementing the Djibouti Code of Conduct. To this end, the Commission has utilised the IfS. In the long term, the EU has been active in providing various forms of aid to Somalia. The EU assistance ranges from humanitarian relief to long-term projects aiming to enhance development and security in Somalia. These activities address some of the root causes of piracy off the coast of Somalia and other forms of organised crime. This case study particularly indicated the importance of assessing the security 'actorness' of the EU in a comprehensive manner. This means that, in addition to analysing the most immediate EU response, that is the CSDP mission 'Atalanta', it is important to investigate longer-term EU actions, even though the link between these actions and fighting piracy is often indirect and sometimes remote.

All five case studies represent different kinds of contemporary security challenges. Thus, they require different policies when developing an appropriate response. However, at least two similarities can be observed in the way in which the EU aims to respond to these challenges. Firstly, in all five case studies, the EU attempts to develop its policies within a broader, multilateral framework. In the area of climate security and terrorism, the EU has been primarily active within and reactive to the UN General Assembly and the UN Security Council. With regard to refugees, the EU has been primarily active within, but also confined by, the boundaries of the Geneva Convention and the United Nations High Commissioner for Refugees (UNHCR). In terms of non-proliferation, the EU has been primarily active within the G8 Global Partnership framework. Other frameworks, such as the Committee 1540 are also important for guiding the EU activities. Finally, in order to address piracy off the coast of Somalia, the EU has been developing its responses within the framework of the UN Security Council resolutions (for short-term solutions), within the International Maritime Organization (IMO) framework (for medium-term solutions) and within the framework of the Joint Needs Assessment for Somalia (for a more long-term solution).

Secondly, in most of the case studies, the EU financial instruments and technical assistance are playing an important role. In the case of climate security, funding for adaptation to climate change in developing countries has been at the core of EU response. In the case of non-proliferation with a particular focus on Russia, the EU has been channelling its assistance through TACIS, the IfS and the Instrument for Nuclear Safety Cooperation (INSC), in addition to financial and technical contributions of EU Member States. In the case of piracy off the coast of Somalia, the EU has deployed a mixture of military and financial instruments, with Critical Maritime Routes (CMR) programme and the EU's development aid at the core of the EU's longer-term policy. This book suggests that, although harder to assess, a medium- and long-term approach is crucial to tackle systematically most of the contemporary international security challenges.

The empirical analysis of the EU's international security 'actorness' has corroborated the observation that whereas negative integration instruments are more appropriate for tackling security problems of a relatively more internal character, positive integration instruments are important for security problems that are primarily, or exclusively, external in their nature. However, this distinction is not as clear-cut as it may seem. Importantly, the theoretical framework for this book has further divided positive integration instruments into regulations, that is (a) harmonisation of policies in a given policy area and (b) capacity-building and intervention that entail short- to long-term utilisation of the EU's capabilities. In this context, two extremes can be identified. On the one hand, the case study on counter-terrorism, as well as the case study on refugees and asylum, to a lesser extent, has demonstrated the importance and relevance of negative integration instruments, that is the mutual recognition of the EU's legal systems and standards, together with the first type of positive integration instruments, that is the regulation and harmonisation of EU policies. On the other hand, the case studies of climate security, non-proliferation and particularly Somali piracy have demonstrated the importance of positive integration instruments, particularly those of the second type, including diplomatic capacities, financial resources, technical assistance and military means.

The research presented in this book also allows assessing the degree to which the case studies illuminate the criteria of 'actorness' as defined in Chapter 1. The theory chapter explained that the scope of integration refers to 'the procedures according to which policy decisions are taken focusing on the involvement of supranational bodies and Council voting rules' (Börzel, 2005: 220). It is informed by autonomy and authority – two criteria of 'actorness' identified by Jupille and Caporaso (1998). Whereas autonomy implies a degree of distinctiveness (or independence) of the EU from its Member States, authority relates to the EU's legal competence to act in a given subject matter. Capabilities were operationalised as resources, instruments and cohesiveness (Hill, 1988) and recognition was incorporated as a criterion in order to reflect the social constructivist nature of the social world.

Concerning the scope of integration, the EU now has authority and institutional capacities to undertake actions at the international level in the area of security policy. Importantly, even though the EU is sometimes criticised for its extensive bureaucracy, its institutions contribute to the development of EU 'actorness' in the area of international security. In particular, two institutions have played key roles: the Council of the European Union (including its General Secretariat) and the European Commission. While it does not come as a surprise that EU Member States work within the Council on the EU's common foreign and security policies, this book has also highlighted the role of the Commission in this policy area, an institution that, traditionally, has been associated exclusively with economic policy. This book makes an original contribution by demonstrating the role of the Commission in international security policy of the EU, which includes, importantly, the so-called 'non-traditional' security challenges as well as more traditional ones, such as the proliferation of WMDs.

The Lisbon Treaty reforms the institutional structure of the EU's external action, including its security policy. However, it is too early to assess whether the scope of integration will be affected significantly as a result of these reforms. What is certain at this point is that, for the foreseeable future, the scope of integration will remain differentiated. This means that more traditional security policies based primarily on diplomacy and developed within the CFSP framework will remain intergovernmental to a much higher extent than policies concerning mostly non-traditional (new) security problems, which, to a large degree, have been incorporated into 'normal' EU policy-making. This also concerns the policies initially dealt with through the third pillar of the EU, that is counter-terrorism, as well as asylum and refugee policy, which have gradually been communitarised. Since the Lisbon Treaty, they are subject to the ordinary legislative procedure as part of the EU's unified legal framework.

Concerning capabilities, the EU has a growing number of short- and long-term resources, allowing it to address contemporary security challenges from different angles. The case of piracy off the coast of Somalia is instructive in this respect. In order to address the problem of piracy, the EU has deployed its first-ever naval operation, within the framework of the CSDP. However, limiting the analysis of EU policy to EUNAVFOR 'Atalanta' would lead to the omission of other EU policies. Most notably, it would exclude the medium- and long-term involvement of the European Commission. As a medium-term solution, the Commission has launched its CMR programme, within the framework of the IfS. This instrument, which replaced the Rapid Reaction Mechanism in 2007, allows the Commission to address a range of contemporary security challenges. The EU's contribution aims to enhance the capacities of states in the region to be able to tackle maritime piracy more effectively. As a long-term solution, the Commission is also involved in addressing some of the root causes of organised crime in Somalia, by providing development and security aid to this country.

Finally, the EU tends to be recognised as an international actor, once it gets involved in a certain security policy area. This book has demonstrated a high level of EU recognition in the area of counter-terrorism, climate security and countering piracy off the Somali coast. In these cases, the EU is recognised and considered an important, if not the leading, actor. In the case of counter-terrorism, the EU is recognised by the most important actor on the global stage, the United States. Such a finding of a high degree of recognition is particularly interesting in the case of maritime piracy, because addressing this challenge involves deploying military capabilities. Even though the EU has not developed into a powerful military actor, its military mission off the coast of Somalia is recognised in the region and among other actors involved in fighting piracy in the Western Indian Ocean and the Gulf of Aden. Admittedly, the EU does not tend to be recognised as an actor in the area of non-proliferation, alongside its unwillingness to be recognised as a security actor in refugee policy. Overall, however, this provides for a more significant external recognition of the EU than what might have been expected. It also provides a very strong baseline for the EU to continue to develop in the future.

The empirical findings presented in this book invite to reflect back on the theoretical framework and the criteria utilised to assess the 'actorness' of the EU in international security policy. As explained in Chapter 1, scholars have been attempting to understand and assess the nature of the EEC/EU in IR since the early 1970s. For this purpose, a new body of literature emerged, in which authors have been treating the EEC/EU as a *sui generis* actor. In this literature, typically, scholars would identify a set of criteria which allow drawing conclusions about the nature of this new beast. In this book, we drew on this body of scholarship and we can reinforce the understanding of the EU as a *sui generis* international actor, which is neither a state nor an inter-governmental organisation. Importantly, this observation is also relevant in the area of international security, where some policies remain mostly intergovernmental (military security), whilst others are partially supranationalised (external financial instruments, the AFSJ).

The criteria of 'actorness' adopted in this book proved valuable in eliciting the key aspects of the EU's role as a security actor. They allowed for a more rigorous comparison between the case studies, shedding light on similarities and differences in the EU's performance across different security challenges. With regard to the scope of integration, this book demonstrated that not only is this criterion affected by the type of the security challenge ('soft' vs 'hard' security issues) but it can also be differentiated within any single case study. This differentiation within a single case study was best reflected in the EU's counter-piracy policy, involving not only intergovernmental framework of the CSDP but also more supranational instruments relating to capacity building.

Whilst the scope of integration is particularly relevant for analysing a non-state international entity, the capabilities and recognition as criteria of 'actorness' can be equally applied to states, to assess their performance in international security. Capabilities, in this book, have been understood broadly, to include resources, instruments and cohesiveness. The resources are most relevant for external security problems, while legal instruments are mainly appropriate for the AFSJ, including its external dimension. It would be difficult to imagine any framework for analysing international 'actorness' of a state or non-state entity without taking account of its capabilities in a broad sense. Similarly, recognition has proven valuable not only for assessing the position of the EU in international security both in general terms but also to compare between the case studies. Influenced by social constructivist approaches, this criterion enabled us to conclude that the EU tends to be recognised by other international actors (states, organisations, experts), which further strengthens the construction of the EU as an important actor.

Global picture

How do the findings of this book relate to broader developments in international security governance? At this point of European integration in the area of international security policy, EU Member States do not manifest a desire for the EU to replace other regional security organisations, most notably the Organisation for Security and Cooperation in Europe (OSCE) and NATO. It is certain that a number of EU Member States would firmly oppose such a goal. Instead, the EU develops its international security capabilities only in addition to its more prominently developed economic policies. In fact, this strong economic dimension of European integration is one of the reasons that the international security policy of the EU so heavily relies on financial instruments. As a result, some scholars (for example, Drozdiak, 2010) have been arguing that, in order for the West to tackle contemporary security challenges effectively, it is necessary to merge the 'hard power' of NATO and the 'soft power' of the EU. This idea is not new, but neither EU Member States nor the United States seems to be interested in such defined transatlantic burden-sharing. For the EU, to rely on NATO in 'hard security' would mean to abandon its CSDP or to transform it into something reminiscent of the European Security and Defence Identity of the 1990s. There does not seem to be such desire, particularly after launching EUNAVFOR 'Atalanta', which in Brussels is considered a spectacular success of the CSDP. Whitman (2004) suggests another kind of division of labour, structured around the area of involvement. According to him, while the EU is more comfortable operating closer to its borders, 'NATO has evolved into a "wider-European" pluralistic security community embracing states across the Eurasian landmass in a network of structured relations' (Whitman, 2004: 448). It is too early to assess the viability of this observation, but the CSDP operation in Congo and now off the coast of Somalia suggests that the EU may be in the process of enlarging its 'security comfort zone'.

Regardless of the range of CSDP operations, the EU remains a unique international security actor. On the one hand, there is no strong desire among EU Member States for the EU to match the capabilities of NATO in the area of 'hard security'. The EU was created for entirely different purposes than NATO. On the other hand, the EU has *some* capabilities in crisis management (both civilian and military), which will probably continue to grow steadily, judging by the growing CFSP budget. On top of its modest military capabilities, the EU has considerable economic and financial security instruments – an asset which other regional security organisations do not have.

An important question is whether this unique character of EU international security 'actorness' is well suited to tackle *effectively* contemporary security challenges. This book has demonstrated that the EU has the potential to address not only the challenges which require a predominantly financial response, such as climate change, but also the challenges requiring a mixed military and non-military response. The extent to which EU efforts can be effective depends on a variety of factors, such as coherence among EU Member States and the nature of the security problem. For example, Russia remains a difficult partner for the EU, particularly in the area of 'hard security' and WMDs. Similarly, the United States and China remain difficult partners in discussions on climate change. This undermines the effectiveness of EU efforts. On the other hand, the United States has been a very strong partner of the EU in counter-terrorism. This is precisely the reality in which the EU has to operate, which diverges from issue to issue, from institutional framework to framework and from cooperating partner to cooperating partner.

It is sometimes argued that the EU would be a more effective security actor if its policy was backed by more robust military capabilities (Bailes, 2008; Menon, 2009). This argument is difficult to sustain. Firstly, developing such military capabilities would undermine a strong normative dimension of the EU as a 'force for good'. This unique normative dimension to EU international security policy, even if modest, contributes to the credibility of the EU on the international stage. In other words, there is a danger that, to paraphrase Robert Kagan (2003), if the EU acquires a better hammer, more international problems will start looking like nails. Secondly, there are already international security actors with very well-developed 'hard security' capabilities, yet they struggle to address effectively some of the contemporary security challenges (such as the threat of the proliferation of WMDs), just like the EU does. Thus, provided that there is enough political will, the EU will remain a unique international security actor. Its success will largely depend on the ability to align its short-, medium- and long-term policies and instruments.

Limitations of the study

This book has demonstrated that the EU can be an important international security actor. It is capable of acting in a unified manner when developing international security policies (in some cases more than others) and it has acquired considerable capabilities; these are primarily financial and technical in nature but also include some limited military means. However, as the first decade of the 21st century demonstrated, there may be obstacles for the EU to fulfil its role as a meaningful security actor on the world scene. Most notably, such 'actorness' is unlikely to occur when EU Member States have diverging initial preferences with regard to the matter in question. In many case studies identified for this book, EU Member States have had largely overlapping preferences. There was a general agreement among the Member States that the EU should develop a policy with respect to all five contemporary security challenges discussed in this volume. Whenever differences occurred, Member States managed eventually to reach consensus, albeit sometimes with derogations and exceptions, such as in EU asylum policy. On the other hand, there are examples of international policy events, when the EU was not able to act as an actor. Most notably, the EU was divided in relation to the US military campaign in Iraq in 2003. Some EU Member States were utterly against the invasion, while others supported it and even joined US efforts.

However, there are two caveats as regards the particular case of Iraq. Firstly, it would be inaccurate to draw too far-reaching conclusions about the EU's inability to be a security actor as a result of disagreements over the Iraqi campaign. Already in December 2003 the EU adopted its first-ever security strategy, and in the same year it launched its first CSDP mission – operation Concordia in Macedonia (Menon, 2004). Whitman (2006: 113) actually calls 'remarkable' the fact that 'the status quo in the

EU's foreign, security and defence policy remained largely unaffected by the war in Iraq'. Secondly, the 'default' pro-American stance of some EU countries should not be taken for granted. In Central and Eastern Europe, it may shift as a result of the process of Europeanisation of foreign policies of these countries (Pomorska, 2007). Furthermore, such a pro-American stance may decline if the US Administration continues to demonstrate a rather ambivalent stance towards Europe (Demes et al., 2009; Shapiro and Witney, 2009; Stelzenmüller, 2010). In addition to these observations, Longhurst and Zaborowski (2004: 391) note that Iraqi experience was so traumatic for Europe that it 'may have marked the first and the last occurrence of the old and new Europe divide'. While this did not end up being the last occurrence of a divide within the EU, given the fact that there was also no unity over the military campaign in Libya in 2011, with France and the United Kingdom involved in the fighting and Germany on the sidelines, this book demonstrated the wide scope of security 'actorness' of the EU even in times when it can be divided: the war on Iraq did not prevent the EU from developing very strong counter-terrorism relations with the United States. Thus, while there may be many more Libya-style disagreements in the future, the EU is likely to be a strong security actor in many other areas, particularly those that fall under the radar-screen of most tabloid newspapers. We should continue to investigate all of these areas, even when newspapers do not.

Notes

Introduction

1. While the 'European Economic Community' in this book refers to the period before 1993, the 'European Community' refers to the first pillar of the EU between 1993 and 2009.
2. The 'CSDP' in this book refers to the European Security and Defence Policy (ESDP). The Lisbon Treaty has changed the name of ESDP to CSDP.
3. Human security, as a distinctive conceptualisation of security, was institutionalised in 1994 by the United Nations Development Programme (UNDP) in its 1994 *Human Development Report* (UNDP, 1994).

6 The EU and Non-proliferation: The Case of Russia

1. According Ms Giannella, the main reason for the delay was that her office was awaiting more details concerning the EU's Joint Diplomatic Service (see Great Britain 2005: 39).

7 The EU and Somali Piracy

1. So far, most shipping companies have continued to calculate the odds in terms of transiting the Gulf of Aden, reasoning that the cost of diverting to alternative routes far exceeds the risk of attack.
2. Before launching EUNAVFOR 'Atalanta', the EU established EUNAVCO with the goal to support EU Member States, which decided to deploy military assets off the coast of Somalia.

Bibliography

Ackers, D. (2005) 'The Negotiations on the Asylum Procedures Directive', *European Journal of Migration and Law*, 7(1), 1–33.

Adler, E. (2003) 'Constructivism and International Relations', in W. Carlsnaes, T. Risse and B. Simmons (eds) *Handbook of International Relations* (London: Sage), pp. 95–118.

Alibek, K. (2000) *Biohazard* (London: Arrow Books).

Allen, D. (1998) ' "Who Speaks for Europe?": The Search for an Effective and Coherent External Policy', in J. Peterson and H. Sjursen (eds) *A Common Foreign Policy for Europe? Competing Visions of the CFSP* (London: Routledge), pp. 41–58.

Allen, D. and Smith, M. (1990) 'Western Europe's Presence in the Contemporary International Arena', *Review of International Studies*, 16(1), 19–37.

Alvarez, J.E. (2003) 'Hegemonic International Law Revisited', *The American Journal of International Law*, 97(4), 873–88.

Amnesty International (2003) 'UK/EU/UNHCR. Unlawful and Unworkable – Amnesty International's Views on Proposals for Extra-territorial Processing of Asylum Claims', 18 June, http://web.amnesty.org (home page) (date accessed 15 April 2012).

Anderson, S.B. (2008) *Crafting EU Security Policy: In Pursuit of a European Identity* (Boulder, CO: Lynne Rienner Publishers).

Annan, K. (2005) ' "In Larger Freedom": Decision Time at the UN', *Foreign Affairs*, 84(3), 63–74.

Anthony, I. (2004) 'Reducing Threats at the Source: A European Perspective on Cooperative Threat Reduction', SIPRI Research Report No. 19 (Oxford: Oxford University Press).

Argomaniz, J. (2009) 'When the EU is the "Norm-Taker": The Passenger Name Records Agreement and the EU's Internalization of US Border Security Norms', *Journal of European integration*, 31(1), 119–36.

Associated Press and Smith, D. (2010) 'US-trained Somali Soldiers Defect to al-Qaeda', *The Guardian*, 28 April.

Bagoyoko, N. and Gibert, M.V. (2009) 'The Linkage Between Security, Governance and Development: The European Union in Africa', *Journal of Development Studies*, 45(5), 789–814.

Bailes, A.J. (2008) 'The EU and a "Better World": What Role for the European Security and Defence Policy?', *International Affairs*, 84(1), 115–30.

Baker, H. and Cutler, L. (2000) 'A Report Card on the Department of Energy's Nonproliferation Programs with Russia', The Russia Task Force of the Secretary of Energy Advisory Board, 10 January.

Ball, D.Y. and Gerber, T.P. (2004) 'Will Russian Scientists Go Rogue? A Survey on the Threat and the Impact of Western Assistance', *PONARS Policy Memo*, 357, November.

Balzacq, T. and Carrera, S. (eds) (2005) *Migration, Border and Asylum – Trends and Vulnerabilities in EU Policy* (Brussels: Centre for European Policy Studies).

Balzacq, T. and Carrera, S. (eds) (2006) *Security Versus Freedom? A Challenge for Europe's Future* (Aldershot: Ashgate).
Barnett, J. (2003) 'Security and Climate Change', *Global Environmental Change* 13(1), 7–17.
Barnett, J. (2007) 'Environmental Security', in A. Collins (ed) *Contemporary Security Studies* (Oxford: Oxford University Press), pp. 182–203.
BBC News (2001a) 'Text of Bush's Act of War Statement', 12 September, http://www.bbc.co.uk (home page) (date accessed 15 April 2012).
BBC News (2001b) 'Schroeder Issues EU Rallying Cry', 18 October, http://www.bbc.co.uk (home page) (date accessed 15 April 2012).
BBC News (2003a), 'Setback for UK at EU Summit', 19 June, http://www.bbc.co.uk (home page) (date accessed 15 April 2012).
BBC News (2003b), 'Croatia Asylum Camp for "UK Refugees"', 15 June, http://www.bbc.co.uk (home page) (date accessed 15 April 2012).
Beer, A. (2006) 'Final Report. Conference on Greening Foreign and Security Policy: The Role of Europe', European Parliament, 6 and 7, http://www.envirosecurity.org (home page) (date accessed 15 April 2012).
Bentégeat, H. (2009) 'Diplomat and Commander', *Impetus (EU Military Staff magazine)*, November.
Berthelet, P. (2003) *Le Droit Institutionnel de la Sécurité Intérieure Européenne* (Bruxelles: Presses Interuniversitaires Européennes – Peter Lang).
Beyer, C. (2008) 'The European Union as a Security Policy Actor: The Case of Counterterrorism', *European Foreign Affairs Review*, 13(3), 293–315.
Bigo, D. (1996) *Polices En Réseaux. L'Expérience Européenne* (Paris: Presses de Sciences Po).
Bigo, D. (1998a) 'L'Europe De La Sécurité Intérieure: Penser Autrement La Sécurité', in A.-M. Le Gloannec (ed) *Entre Union Et Nations. L'Etat En Europe* (Paris: Presses de Sciences Po), pp. 55–90.
Bigo, D. (1998b) 'Europe Passoire Et Europe Forteresse: La Sécurisation/Humanitarisation De L'Immigration', in A. Rea (ed) *Immigration Et racisme En Europe* (Bruxelles: Complexe), pp. 203–41.
Bigo, D. (1998c) 'L'immigration À La Croisée Des Chemins Sécuritaires', *Revue Européenne Des Migrations Internationales*, 14(1), 25–46.
Bigo, D. (2001) 'Migration and Security', in V. Guiraudon and C. Joppke (eds) *Controlling a New Migration World* (London: Routledge), pp. 121–49.
Bigo, D. (2002) 'Security and Immigration: Toward a Critique of the Governmentality of Unease', *Alternatives*, 27(Special Issue), 63–92.
Biscop, S. (2008) 'The European Security Strategy in Context: A Comprehensive Trend', in S. Biscop and J.J. Andersson (eds) *The EU and the European Security Strategy: Forging a Global Europe* (London: Routledge), pp. 5–20.
Biscop, S. (2009) 'The Value of Power, the Power of Values: A Call for an EU Grand Strategy', *Egmont – The Royal Institute for International Relations*, Egmont Paper 33 (Gent: Academia Press).
Biscop, S. and Andersson, J.J. (eds) (2007) *The EU and the European Security Strategy: Forging a Global Europe* (London: Routledge).
Blanchard, C., King, R., Mason, R., Ploch, L. and O'Rourke, R. (2009) *Piracy off the Horn of Africa* (Washington, DC: Congressional Research Service).
Börzel, T. (2003) *Environmental Leaders and Laggards in Europe: Why There Is (not) a Southern Problem* (Aldershot: Ashgate).

Börzel, T.A. (2005) 'Mind the Gap! European Integration Between Level and Scope', *Journal of European Public Policy*, 12(2), 217–36.

Bossong, R. (2008) 'The Action Plan on Combating Terrorism: A Flawed Instrument of EU Security Governance', *Journal of Common Market Studies*, 46(1), 27–48.

Boswell, C. (2003a) 'The "External Dimension" of EU immigration and Asylum Policy', *International Affairs*, 79(3): 619–38.

Boswell, C. (2003b) *European Migration Policies in Flux. Changing Patterns of Inclusion and Exclusion* (London: Royal Institute of International Affairs).

Boswell, C. (2007) 'Migration Control in Europe after 9/11: Explaining the Absence of Securitization', *Journal of Common Market Studies*, 45(3), 589–610.

Boswell, C. (2008) 'Evasion, Reinterpretation and Decoupling: European Commission Responses to the "External Dimension" of Immigration and Asylum', *West European Politics*, 31(3), 491–512.

Boswell, C. and Geddes, A. (2011) *Migration and Mobility in the European Union* (Basingstoke: Palgrave Macmillan).

Bretherton, C. and Vogler, J. (1999) *The European Union as a Global Actor* (London: Routledge).

Bretherton, C. and Vogler, J. (2006) *The European Union as a Global Actor*, 2nd edn (London: Routledge).

Brouwer, E. (2009) 'The EU Passenger Name Record (PNR) System and Human Rights: Transferring Passenger Data or Passenger Freedom?' CEPS Working Document No. 320 (Brussels: Centre for European Policy Studies).

Brown, L. (1977) *Worldwatch Paper 14: Redefining National security* (Washington, DC: Worldwatch Institute).

Brown, O., Hammill, A. and McLeman, R. (2007) 'Climate Change as the "New" Security Threat: Implications to Africa', *International Affairs*, 83, 1141–54.

Bruter, M. (1999) 'Diplomacy Without a State: The External Delegations of the European Commission', *Journal of European Public Policy*, 6(2), 183–205.

Bruton, B. (2009) 'In the Quicksands of Somalia', *Foreign Affairs*, 88(6), 79–94.

Bryden, M. (2004) 'Somalia and Somaliland: Envisioning a Dialogue on the Question of Somali Unity', *African Security Review*, 13(2), 23–33.

Bull, H. (1982) 'Civilian Power Europe: A Contradiction in Terms?', *Journal of Common Market Studies*, 21, 149–70.

Bulletin Quotidien Europe (2004), 'Débat Et Explications Sur Les Camps De Réfugiés Et La Politique Européenne D'Asile Au Conseil Informel Jeudi Et Vendredi', 29 September.

Bunn, M. (2010) 'Securing the Bomb 2010: Securing All Nuclear Materials in Four Years', *Belfer Center for Science and International Affairs*, April 2010.

Bures, O. (2006) 'EU Counter-Terrorism: A Paper Tiger', *Terrorism and Political Violence*, 18(1), 57–87.

Bures, O. (2011) *EU Counterterrorism Policy: A Paper Tiger?* (Farnham: Ashgate).

Burnett, J. (2002) *Dangerous Waters: Modern Piracy and Terror on High Seas* (New York: Plume).

Burnham, P., Gilland, K., Grant, W. and Layton-Henry, Z. (2004) *Research Methods in Politics* (Basingstoke: Palgrave Macmillan).

Busby, J.W. (2008) 'Who Cares about the Weather? Climate Change and U.S. National Security', *Security Studies*, 17(3), 468–504.

Busch, N.E. and Holmes, J.R. (2009) 'Russia's Nuclear Security Culture', in N.E. Busch and D.H. Joyner (eds) *Combating Weapons of Mass Destruction: The Future of International Nonproliferation Policy* (Athens, GA: University of Georgia Press), pp. 325–42.

Busch, N.E. and Joyner, D.H. (eds) (2009) *Combating Weapons of Mass Destruction: The Future of International Nonproliferation Policy* (Athens, GA: University of Georgia Press).

Buzan, B. (1983) *People, States and Fear* (Brighton: Wheatsheaf).

Buzan, B. (1991) *People, States and Fear – An Agenda for International Security Studies in the Post-Cold War Era*, 2nd edn (London: Harvester Wheatsheaf).

Buzan, B. and Hansen, L. (2009) *The Evolution of International Security Studies* (Cambridge: Cambridge University Press).

Buzan, B., Wæver, O. and de Wilde, J. (1998) *Security – A New Framework for Analysis* (London: Lynne Rienner).

Byrne, R. (2005) 'Remedies of Limited Effect: Appeals under the forthcoming Directive on EU Minimum Standards on Procedures', *European Journal of Migration and Law*, 7(1), 71–86.

Calvocoressi, P. (1977) *World Politics since 1945* (London: Longman Group Limited).

Cameron, F. (2007a) *An Introduction to European Foreign Policy* (New York: Routledge).

Cameron, F. (2007b) 'Transatlantic Relations and Terrorism', in D. Spence (ed) *The European Union and Terrorism* (London: John Harper Publishing), pp. 124–42.

Campbell, K.M. and Parthemore, C. (2008) 'National Security and Climate Change in Perspective', in K.M. Campbell (ed) *Climatic Cataclysm: The Foreign Policy and National Security Implications of Climate Change* (Washington, DC: Brookings Institution Press), pp. 1–25.

Carrera, S. and Geyer, F. (2008) 'The Reform Treaty and Justice and Home Affairs: Implications for the Common Area of Freedom, Security and Justice', in E. Guild and F. Geyer (eds) *Security versus Justice? Police and Judicial Cooperation in the European Union* (Aldershot: Ashgate), pp. 289–308.

Ceyhan, A. and Tsoukala, A. (2002) 'The Securitization of Migration in Western Societies: Ambivalent Discourses and Policies', *Alternatives*, 27, 21–39.

Chalk, P. (2008) *The Maritime Dimension of International Security Terrorism, Piracy, and Challenges for the United States* (Santa Monica, CA: Rand Corporation).

Christiansen, T. (2001) 'Intra-Institutional Politics and Inter-Institutional Relations in the EU: Towards Coherent Governance?', *Journal of European Public Policy*, 8(5), 747–69.

Clark, A. (2009) *Counter Piracy Operations, Challenges, Shortfalls and Lessons Learned*. Combined Maritime Forces (CMF) Cdr Alastair Clark RN CMF ACOS (OPS), 4 June, http://www.nato.int (home page) (date accessed 15 April 2012).

Collins, A. (ed) (2007) *Contemporary Security Studies* (Oxford: Oxford University Press).

Commission (1985) 'Completing the Internal Market: White Paper from the Commission to the European Council, Milan, 28–29 June 1985', COM(85) 310 final, 14 June (Brussels: Commission of the European Communities).

Commission (1993) 'TACIS: Annual Report from the Commission, 1991 and 1992', COM(93) 362 final, 28 July (Brussels: Commission of the European Communities).

Comte, F. (2010) 'A New Agency is Born in the European Union: The European Asylum Support Office', *European Journal of Migration and Law*, 12, 373–405.

Cosgrove, C. and Twitchett, K. (eds) (1970) *The New International Actors: The UN and the EEC* (London: Macmillan).

Costello, C. (2005) 'The Asylum Procedures Directive and the Proliferation of Safe Country Practices: Deterrence, Deflection and The Dismantling of International Protection', *European Journal of Migration and Law*, 7(1), 35–69.

Cottey, A. (2007) *Security in the New Europe* (Basingstoke: Palgrave Macmillan).

Council (1994) 'Decision 94/509/CFSP Concerning the Joint Action Regarding Preparation for the 1995 Conference of the States Parties to the Treaty on the Non-proliferation of Nuclear Weapons', OJ L 205, 25 July (Brussels: General Secretariat of the Council).

Council (1999) 'Council Joint Action of 17 December 1999 Establishing a European Union Cooperation Programme for Non-proliferation and Disarmament in the Russian Federation', 1999/878/CFSP, 23 December (Brussels: General Secretariat of the Council).

Council (2001) 'Conclusions Adopted By the Council (Justice and Home Affairs)', Doc. SN 3926/6/01, 20 September (Brussels: General Secretariat of the Council).

Council (2002) 'Council Decision of 28 February Setting Up Eurojust with a View to Reinforcing the Fight Against Serious Crime', 2002/187/JHA, 6 March 2002 (Brussels: General Secretariat of the Council).

Council (2003a) 'A Secure Europe in a Better World: European Security Strategy', Report No. 15895/03, 8 December (Brussels: General Secretariat of the Council).

Council (2003b) 'Presidency Conclusions of the Brussels European Council, 20–21 March 2003', Doc. 8410/3 POLGEN 29, 5 May (Brussels: General Secretariat of the Council).

Council (2003c) 'Presidency Conclusions of the Thessaloniki European Council, 19–20 June 2003', Doc. 11638/03 POLGEN 55, 1 October (Brussels: General Secretariat of the Council).

Council (2003d) 'Fight Against the Proliferation of Weapons of Mass Destruction – Mainstreaming Non-proliferation Policies into the EU's Wider Relations with Third Countries', 14997/03, 19 November (Brussels: General Secretariat of the Council).

Council (2004) 'Council Joint Action 2004/796/CFSP of 22 November 2004 for the Support of the Physical Protection of a Nuclear Site in the Russian Federation', L 349 (OJEU), 25 November (Brussels: General Secretariat of the Council).

Council (2006a) 'Fight against Terrorism: Six-monthly Report', Doc. 16370/06, 06 December (Brussels: General Secretariat of the Council).

Council (2006b) 'EU Strategy against the Proliferation of WMD: Monitoring and Enhancing Consistent Implementation', 16694/06, 12 December (Brussels: General Secretariat of the Council).

Council (2007a) 'Presidency Conclusions of the Brussels European Council, 21 and 22 June 2007', 11177/1/07 REV 1, 20July (Brussels: General Secretariat of the Council).

Council (2007b) 'Fight Against Terrorism: Six-Monthly Report', Doc. 11948/2/07, 5 October 2007 (Brussels: General Secretariat of the Council).

Council (2007c) 'Council Joint Action 2007/178/CFSP of 19 March 2007 in Support of Chemical Weapons Destruction in the Russian Federation in the Framework of the EU Strategy against Proliferation of Weapons of Mass Destruction', L 81 (OJEU), 22 March (Brussels: General Secretariat of the Council).

Council (2007d) 'Press Release Concerning EU Military Exercise 2007 (MILEX 07) to be Conducted from 7–15 July 2007', 8 June (Brussels: General Secretariat of the Council).

Council (2008a) 'Climate Change and Security: Recommendations of the High Representative on follow-up to the High Representative and Commission report on Climate Change and International Security', 16994/1/08 REV1, 12 December (Brussels: General Secretariat of the Council).

Council (2008b) 'Press Release: 2917th Meeting of the Council Agriculture and Fisheries, Brussels', Report No. 16916/1/08 REV 1 (Presse 361), 18–19 December (Brussels: General Secretariat of the Council).

Council (2008c) 'Consolidated Versions of the Treaty on European Union and the Treaty on the, Functioning of the European Union', 6655/08, 15 April (Brussels: General Secretariat of the Council).

Council (2008d) 'Council Joint Action 2008/851/CFSP of 10 November 2008 on a European Union Military Operation to Contribute to the Deterrence, Prevention and Repression of Acts of Piracy and Armed Robbery Off the Somali Coast', L 301 (OJEU), 12 November (Brussels: General Secretariat of the Council).

Council (2009) 'Joint Progress Report and Follow-Up Recommendations on Climate Change and International Security (CCIS) to the Council', 166645/09, 25 November (Brussels: General Secretariat of the Council).

Council (2010a) 'Council Decision of 26 July 2010 Establishing the Organisation and Functioning of the European External Action Service (2010/427/EU)', L 201 (OJEU), 3 August (Brussels: General Secretariat of the Council).

Council (2010b) 'EU Engagement in Somalia', February, http://www.consilium.europa.eu (home page) (Brussels: General Secretariat of the Council).

Council (2010c) 'Council Decision 2010/197/CFSP of 31 March 2010 on the Launch of a European Union Military Mission to Contribute to the Training of Somali Security Forces', L 87 (OJEU), 7 April (Brussels: General Secretariat of the Council).

Council (2011) '2010 CFSP Budget – Final Update of the 2010 CFSP Budget', 5230/11, 12 January (Brussels: General Secretariat of the Council).

Cremona, M. (2009) 'EC Competence, "Smart Sanctions", and the Kadi Case', *Yearbook of European Law*, 28(1), 559–92.

Dabelko, G.D. (2009) 'Planning for Climate Change: The Security Community's Precautionary Principle: An Editorial Comment', *Climatic Change*, 96(1–2), 13–21.

Dalby, S. (2009) *Security and Environmental Change* (Cambridge: Polity).

Da Lomba, S. (2004) *The Right to Seek Refugee Status in the European Union* (Antwerp: Intersentia).

Dannreuther, R. (2007) *International Security: The Contemporary Agenda* (Cambridge: Polity).

de Hert, P. and de Schutter, B. (2008) 'International Transfer of Data in the Field of JHA: The Lessons of Europol, PNR and Swift', in B. Martenczuck and S. van Thiel (eds) *Justice, Liberty and Security – New Challenges for EU External Relations* (Brussels: VUB Press, Brussels University Press), pp. 303–40.

De Jong, S., Sterkx, S and Wouters, J. (2010) 'The EU as a Regional Actor: Weapons of Mass Destruction', *Working Paper* No. 10, EU-GRASP.
De Lobkowicz, W. (2002) *L'Europe Et la Sécurité Intérieure* (Paris: La Documentation française).
De Wilde, J.H. (2008) 'Environmental Security Deconstructed' in H.G. Brauch, C. Mesjasz, J. Grin, P. Dunay, Ú.O. Spring, B. Chourou, P. Kameri-Mbote, P.H. Liotta and N.C. Behera (eds) *Globalization and Environmental Challenges: Reconceptualizing Security in the 21st Century* (Berlin: Springer), pp. 595–602.
Deflem, M. (2006) 'Europol and the Policing of International Terrorism: Counter-Terrorism in a Global Perspective', *Justice Quarterly*, 23(3), 336–59.
Deighton, A. (2002) 'The European Security and Defence Policy', *Journal of Common Market Studies*, 40(4), 719–41.
Demes, P., Gyarmati, I., Krastev, I., Liik, K., Rotfeld, A. and Vondra, A. (2009) 'Why the Obama Administration Should Not Take Central and Eastern Europe for Granted', *The German Marshall Fund of the United States*, Policy Brief, 13 July.
Den Boer, M., Hillebrand C. and Noelke, A. (2008) 'Legitimacy under Pressure: The European Web of Counter-Terrorism Networks', *Journal of Common Market Studies*, 46(1), 101–24.
Den Boer, M. and Monar, J., (2002) 'Keynote Article: 11 September and the Challenge of Global Terrorism to the EU as a Security Actor', *Journal of common Market Studies*, 40(4), 11–28.
Denza, E. (2005) 'Non-proliferation of Nuclear Weapons: The European Union and Iran', *European Foreign Affairs Review*, 10(3), 289–311.
Diez, T. (2005) 'Constructing the Self and Changing Other: Reconsidering "Normative Power Europe"', *Millennium*, 33(3), 613–36.
Diez, T. and Manners, I. (2007) 'Reflecting on Normative Power Europe', in F. Berenskoetter and M.J. Williams (eds) *Power in World Politics* (London: Routledge), pp. 173–88.
Dijkstra, H. (2009) 'Commission versus Council Secretariat: An Analysis of Bureaucratic Rivalry in European Foreign Policy', *European Foreign Affairs Review*, 14(3), 431–50.
Douglas-Scott, S. (2004) 'The Rule of Law in The European Union – Putting the Security into the Area of Freedom, Security and Justice', *European Law Review*, 29(2), pp. 219–42.
Draghici, C. (2009) 'International Organisations and Anti-Terrorist Sanctions: No Accountability for Human Rights Violations?', *Critical Studies on Terrorism* 2(2), 293–312.
Drozdiak, W. (2010) 'The Brussels Wall', *Foreign Affairs*, 89(3), 7–12.
Dryburgh, L. (2008) 'The EU as a Global Actor? EU Policy towards Iran', *European Security*, 17(2), 253–71.
Dubois, D. (2002) 'The Attacks of 11 September: EU-US Cooperation Against Terrorism in the Field of Justice and Home Affairs', *European Foreign Affairs Review*, 7(3), 317–55.
Duchêne, F. (1972) 'Europe's Role in World Peace', in R. Mayne (ed) *Europe Tomorrow: Sixteen European Looks Ahead* (London Fontana), pp. 32–47.
Duke, S. (2000) *The Elusive Quest for European Security: From EDC to CFSP* (Basingstoke: Palgrave Macmillan).
Easton, D. (1979) *A Systems Analysis of Political Life* (Chicago: The University of Chicago Press).

Eckes, C. (2009) *EU Counter-Terrorist Policies and Fundamental Rights* (Oxford: Oxford University Press).
Edwards, G. and Meyer, C. (2008) 'Introduction: Charting a Contested Transformation', *Journal of Common Market Studies*, 46(1), 1–25.
Elbe, S. (2007) 'Health and Security', in A. Collins (ed) *Contemporary Security Studies* (Oxford: Oxford University Press), pp. 413–27.
El-Enany, N. (2008) 'Who Is the New European Refugee?', *European Law Review*, 33(3), 313–35.
El-Enany, N. and Thielemann, E. (2011) 'The Impact of EU Asylum Policy on National Asylum Regimes', in S. Wolff et al. (eds) *Freedom, Security and Justice after Lisbon and Stockholm* (The Hague: T.M.C. Asser Press), pp. 97–116.
Eling, K. (2007) 'The EU, Terrorism and Effective Multilateralism', in D. Spence (ed) *The European Union and Terrorism* (London: John Harper), pp. 105–23.
Ellermann, A. (2008) 'The Limits of Unilateral Immigration Control: Deportation and Inter-State Cooperation', *Government and Opposition*, 43(2), 168–89.
EUMC (European Union Military Committee) (2009) 'Chairman EUMC Visited EUNAVFOR Somalia Force Headquarters (FHQ) in Djibouti and Met Local Authorities', 17 and 18 June, http://www.consilium.europa.eu/ (home page) (date accessed 15 April 2012).
EUobserver (2003) 'Asylum Seekers to Wait in Croatia', 16 June, http://www.euobserver.com (home page) (date accessed 15 April 2012).
EUobserver (2011) 'Group of Five Calls for EU Military Headquarters', 9 September.
European Commission (2001a) 'Communication from the Commission to the Council and the European Parliament on a Common Policy on Illegal Immigration', COM (2001) 672, 15 November (Brussels: European Commission).
European Commission (2001b) 'TACIS Regional Cooperation: Strategic Considerations 2002–2006 and Indicative Programme 2002–2003. Annex C: The ICTC/STCU Indicative Programmes for 2003–2003', 27 December (Brussels: European Commission).
European Commission (2003a) 'Communication from the Commission to the Council and the European Parliament "Towards More Accessible, Equitable and Managed Asylum Systems"', COM(2003) 315 final, 3 June (Brussels: European Commission).
European Commission (2003b) 'TACIS ISTC/STCU Action Programme 2003', http://ec.europa.eu/europeaid/ (home page) (date accessed 15 April 2012).
European Commission (2004a) 'Proposal for a Regulation of the Council Establishing an Instrument for Stability', COM(2004) 630 Final, 29 September (Brussels: European Commission).
European Commission (2004b) 'Commission Decision 2004/535/EC on the Adequate Protection of Personal Data Contained in the Passenger Name Record of Air Passengers Transferred to the United States' Bureau of Customs and Border Protection', OJ L 235, 6 July (Brussels: European Commission).
European Commission (2005) 'Communication from the Commission to the Council and the European Parliament on Regional Protection Programmes', 1 September (Brussels: European Commission).

European Commission (2007a) 'The Instrument for Stability: Strategy Paper 2007-2011', http://ec.europa.eu/europeaid/ (home page) (date accessed 15 April 2012).
European Commission (2007b) 'Communication from the Commission to the Council, the European Parliament, the European Economic and Social Committee and the Committee of the Regions. A European Strategic Energy Technology Plan (SET-Plan): Towards a Low Carbon Future', COM(2007) 723 final, 22 November (Brussels: European Commission).
European Commission (2007c) 'Commission activities in the Fight Against Terrorism', MEMO/07/08 (Brussels: European Commission).
European Commission (2007d) 'Commission Staff Working Document Accompanying the Communication from The Commission to the European Parliament, the Council, the European Economic and Social Committee and the Committee of the Regions Towards a Common Immigration Policy: Interim Report on the Global Approach to Migration', SEC(2007) 1632, 5 December (Brussels: European Commission).
European Commission (2007e) 'Nuclear Safety Strategy for Community Cooperation Programmes 2007-2013 and Indicative Programme for 2007-2009', Revision 17, 4 July (Brussels: European Commission).
European Commission (2007f) *The European Union and Russia: Close Neighbours, Global Players, Strategic Partner* (Luxemburg: Office for Official Publications of the European Communities).
European Commission (2008) 'Communication from the Commission to the European Parliament, the Council, the European Economic and Social Committee and the Committee of the Regions – Preparing the Next Steps in Border Management in the European Union', SEC (2008) 153, SEC (2008) 154 9 (Brussels: European Commission).
European Commission (2009a) 'The Instrument for Stability – Multi-Annual Indicative Programme 2009-2011', C(2009)2641, 8 April (Brussels: European Commission).
European Commission (2009b) 'International Donor Conference on Somalia Security – European Commission Pledges to Commit 72 Million Euros', IP/09/633, 23 April (Brussels: European Commission).
European Commission (2010a) 'Second Revision of the Cotonou Agreement – Consolidated Agreed Texts', 19 March (Brussels: European Commission).
European Commission (2010b) 'European Commission Allocates €35 Million for Victims of Conflict and Natural Disasters in Somalia', IP/10/1012, 27 July (Brussels: European Commission).
European Commission (2010c) 'Kenya: Commission Allocates €15 Million to Bring Relief to World's Biggest Refugee Camps', IP/10/1020, 2 August (Brussels: European Commission).
European Commission (2011) 'Proposal for a Directive of the European Parliament and of the Council on the use of Passenger Name Record Data for the Prevention, Detection, Investigation and Prosecution of Terrorist Offences and Serious Crime', SEC(2011) 132 final, SEC(2011) 133 final (Brussels: European Commission).
European Commission/Danish Centre for Human Rights (2003) 'Study on the Feasibility of Processing Asylum Claims Outside the EU against the Background

of the Common European Asylum System and the Goal of a Common Asylum Procedure' (Luxembourg: Office for Official Publications of the European Communities).
European Council (1999a) 'Presidency Conclusions of the Tampere European Council (1999)', SN 200/99, 15–16 October (Brussels: General Secretariat of the Council).
European Council (1999b) 'Common Strategy of the European Union of 4 June 1999 on Russia', 1999/414/CFSP, 4 June (Brussels: General Secretariat of the Council).
European Council (2001) 'Conclusions and Plan of Action of the Extraordinary Meeting on 21 September', SN140/01 (Brussels: General Secretariat of the Council).
European Council (2003) 'Fight Against the Proliferation of Weapons of Mass Destruction – EU Strategy Against Proliferation of Weapons of Mass Destruction', 15708/03, 10 December (Brussels: General Secretariat of the Council).
European Council (2006) 'The European Consensus on Development', OJEU C46 (Brussels: General Secretariat of the Council).
European Council (2008) 'European Security Strategy: Report on the Implementation of the European Security Strategy – Providing Security in a Changing World' (Brussels: General Secretariat of the Council).
European Parliament (1999) 'Report on the Environment, Security and Foreign Policy', 14 January (Brussels: European Parliament).
European Parliament (2007) 'Resolution of 14 February 2007 on SWIFT, the PNR Agreement and the Transatlantic Dialogue on these Issues', P6_TA(2007)0039 (Brussels: European Parliament).
European Parliament and the Council (2006) 'Regulation (EC) no 1717/2006 of the European Parliament and the Council of 15 November 2006 Establishing an Instrument for Stability', L 327 (OJEU), 24 November.
European Union (2008) 'Somalia Joint Strategy Paper for the Period 2008–2013', http://ec.europa.eu (home page) (date accessed 15 April 2012).
European Union (2009) 'EU contribution to the UN Secretary General's Report on Climate Change and International Security', http://www.un.org (home page) (date accessed 29 March 2012).
European Voice (2001) 'Justice Chief Warns Against Rushing EU Arrest Warrant', *European Voice*, 27 September 2001, 7(35), 1–3.
Europol (2011) 'EU Terrorism Situation and Trend Report' (The Hague: Europol).
Faist, T. (2004) 'The Migration-Security Nexus. International Migration and Security before and after 9/11', *Willy Brandt Series of Working Papers in International Migration and Ethnic Relations 4/03* (Malmö: Malmö University).
Falk, R. (1971) *This Endangered Planet: Prospects and Proposals for Human Survival* (New York: Random House).
Financial Times (2003a) 'UK Asylum Proposals Draw Mixed Response', 28 March, http://www.ft.com (home page) (date accessed 11 February 2010).
Financial Times (2003b) 'UK Moots "Zones of Protection" for Refugees', 16 June, http://www.ft.com (home page) (date accessed 11 February 2010).
Finnemore, M. and Sikkink, K. (1998) 'International Norm Dynamics and Political Change', *International Organization*, 52(4), 887–917.
Floyd, R. (2008) 'The Environmental Security Debate and its Significance for Climate Change', *The International Spectator*, 43(3), 51–65.

Francesco, S. (2007) 'Climate Change: A Security (Council) Issue?', *The Carbon & Climate Law Review*, 1(1), 29–44.
Frankel, J. (1979) *International Relations in a Changing World* (Oxford: Oxford University Press).
Freeman, G. (1998) 'The Decline of Sovereignty? Politics and Immigration Restriction in Liberal States', in C. Joppke (ed) *Challenge to the Nation State: Immigration in Western Europe and The United States* (Oxford: Oxford University Press), pp. 86–108.
Friedrichs, J. (2005) *Fighting Terrorism and Drugs* (London: Routledge).
Fullerton, M. (2005) 'Inadmissible in Iberia: The Fate of Asylum Seekers in Spain and Portugal', *International Journal of Refugee Law*, 17(4), 659–87.
G8 (2002) 'Statement by G8 Leaders: The G8 Global Partnership against the Spread of Weapons and Materials of Mass Destruction', 27 June, http://www.g7.utoronto.ca/ (home page) (date accessed 15 April 2012).
G8 Information Centre (2009) '2008 Hokkaido-Toyako G8 Summit Final Compliance Report, Covering the Period 10 July 2008 to 26 June 2009', 30 June, http://www.g7.utoronto.ca/ (home page) (date accessed 15 April 2012).
Galtung, J. (1973) *The European Community: A Superpower in the Making?* (London: Allen and Unwin).
Gänzle, S. (2009) *Coping with the 'Security-Development Nexus': The European Community's Instrument for Stability – Rationale and Potential* (Bonn: German Development Institute).
Gänzle S. and Sens, A. (eds) (2007) *The Changing Politics of European Security: Europe Alone?* (Basingstoke: Palgrave Macmillan).
Garlick, M. (2006) 'Asylum Legislation in the European Community and the 1951 Convention', in T. Balzacq and S. Carrera (eds) *Security Versus Freedom? A Challenge for Europe's Future* (Aldershot: Ashgate), pp. 45–60.
Garlick, M.V. (2010) 'The Common European Asylum System and the European Court of Justice: New Jurisdiction and New Challenges', in E. Guild, S. Carrera and A. Eggenschwiler (eds) *The Area of Freedom, Security and Justice Ten Years on: Successes and Future Challenges under the Stockholm Programme* (Brussels: Centre for European Policy Studies), pp. 49–62.
Gärtner, H. (2003) 'European Security: The End of Territorial Defence', *Brown Journal of World Affairs*, 9(2), 135–47.
Geddes, A. (2000) *Immigration and European Integration. Towards Fortress Europe?* (Manchester: Manchester University Press).
Geddes, A. (2001) 'International Migration and State Sovereignty in an Integrating Europe', *International Migration*, 39(6), 21–39.
Geddes, A. (2008) *Immigration and European Integration: Towards Fortress Europe*, 2nd edn (Manchester: Manchester University Press).
Germond, B. (2010) 'From Frontier to Boundary and Back Again: The European Union's Maritime margins', *European Foreign Affairs Review*, 15(1), 39–55.
Gettleman, J. (2010) 'In Somalia Civil War, Both Sides Embrace Pirates', *The New York Times*, 1 September.
Ginsberg, R. (2001) *The European Union in World Politics: Baptism by Fire* (Oxford: Rowman & Littlefield Publishers).
Glarbo, K. (1999) 'Wide-Awake Diplomacy: Reconstructing the Common Foreign and Security Policy of the European Union', *Journal of European Public Policy*, 6(4), 634–51.

Goens, J. (1987) 'The Opportunities and Limits of European Co-operation in the Area of Non-proliferation', in H. Müller (ed) *A European Nonproliferation Policy* (Oxford: Clarendon Press), pp. 31–70.

Great Britain (2005) Parliament. House of Lords. *Preventing Proliferation of Weapons of Mass Destruction: The EU Contribution*, HL Paper 96, 13th Report of Session 2004–2005 (London: Stationery Office Limited).

Great Britain (2006) Parliament. House of Commons. *Piracy*, HC 1026, Eighth Report of Session 2005–2006 (London: Stationery Office Limited).

Great Britain (2010) Parliament. House of Lords. *Combating Somali Piracy: The EU's Naval Operation Atalanta*, HL Paper 103, 12th Report of Session 2009–10 (London: Stationery Office Limited).

Gregory, F. (2005) 'The EU's Response to 9/11: A Case Study of Institutional Roles and Policy Processes with Special Reference to Issues of Accountability and Human Rights', *Terrorism and Violence*, 17, 105–23.

Groenleer, M. and Van Shaik, L. (2007) 'United We Stand? The European Union's International Actorness in the Cases of the International Criminal Court and the Kyoto Protocol', *Journal of Common Market Studies*, 45(5), 969–98.

Guardian (2003a) 'EU Rejects Asylum Camps Plan', 20 June, http://www.guardian.co.uk (home page) (date accessed 11 February 2010).

Guardian (2003b) 'Britain Wavers on Asylum Plans', 16 June, http://www.guardian.co.uk (home page) (date accessed 11 February 2010).

Guild, E. (1999) 'The Impetus to Harmonise: Asylum Policy in the European Union', in F. Nicholson and P. Twomey (eds) *Refugee Rights and Realities. Evolving International Concepts and Regimes* (Cambridge: Cambridge University Press), pp. 313–35.

Guild, E. (2002) 'Between Persecution and Protection – Refugees and the New European Asylum Policy', in *Cambridge Yearbook of European Legal Studies*, (Oxford: Hart), pp. 169–97.

Guild, E. (2003a) 'International Terrorism and EU Immigration, Asylum and Borders Policy: The Unexpected Victims of 11 September 2001', *European Foreign Affairs Review*, 8(3), 331–46.

Guild, E. (2003b) 'The Face of Securitas: Redefining the Relationship of Security and Foreigners in Europe', in P. Craig and R. Rawlings (eds) *Law and Administration in Europe: Essays in Honour of Carol Harlow* (Oxford: Oxford University Press), pp. 139–53.

Guild, E. (2004) 'Seeking Asylum: Stormy Clouds between International Commitments and EU Legislative Measures', *European Law Review*, 29(2), 198–218.

Guild, E. (2006) 'The Europeanisation of Europe's Asylum Policy', *International Journal of Refugee Law*, 18, 630–51.

Guild, E. (2009) *Security and Migration in the 21st Century Polity* (Cambridge: Cambridge University Press).

Guild, E. and Brouwer, E. (2006) 'The Political Life of Data: The ECJ Decision on the PNR Agreement Between the EU and the US', *CEPS Policy Brief 109* (Brussels: Centre for European Policy Studies).

Guilfoyle, D. (2008) 'Piracy off Somalia: UN Security Council Resolution 1816 and IMO Regional Counter-Piracy Efforts', *International and Comparative Law Quarterly*, 57, 690–99.

Guiraudon, V. (2000) 'European Integration and Migration Policy: Vertical Policy-Making as Venue Shopping', *Journal of Common Market Studies*, 38(2), 251–71.

Guiraudon, V. (2003) 'The Constitution of a European Immigration Policy Domain: A Political Sociology Approach', *Journal of European Public Policy*, 10(2), 263-82.

Guiraudon, V. and Joppke, C. (eds) (2001) *Controlling a New Migration World* (London: Routledge).

Haas, P.M. (1992) 'Introduction: Epistemic Communities and International Policy Coordination', *International Organization*, 46(1), 1-35.

Hadfield, A. (2007) 'Janus Advances? An Analysis of EC Development Policy and the 2005 Amended Cotonou Partnership Agreement', *European Foreign Affairs Review*, 12(1), 39-66.

Hailbronner, K. (2004) 'Asylum Law in the Context of a European Migration Policy', in Walker, N. (ed) *Europe's Area of Freedom, Security and Justice* (Oxford: Oxford University Press), pp. 41-88.

Hailbronner, K. (2008) 'Minimum Standards relating to the Eligibility for Refugee Status or International Protection and Content of these Status – Assessment (Summary) of the Implementation of the 2004 Directive and Proposals for a Common European Regime of Asylum', European Parliament Briefing Note, No. PE 393.293.

Hailbronner, K. (2009) 'Towards a Common European Asylum System – Assessments and Proposals', European Parliament Briefing Paper.

Hailbronner, K., Papakonstantinou, V. and Kau, M. (2008) 'The Agreement on Passenger-Data Transfers (PNR) and the EU-US Cooperation in Data Communication', *International Migration*, 46(2), 187-97.

Haldén, P. (2007) *The Geopolitics of Climate Change* (Stockholm: FOI Swedish Defence Research Agency).

Hari, J. (2009) 'Johann Hari: You Are Being Lied to about Pirates', *The Independent*, 5 January.

Harnish, S. (2007) 'Minilateral Cooperation and Transatlantic Coalition-Building: The E3/EU-3 Iran Initiative', *European Security*, 16(1), 1-27.

Hayes-Renshaw, F. (2006) 'The Council of Ministers', in J. Peterson and M. Shackleton (eds) *The Institutions of the European Union* (Oxford: Oxford University Press), pp. 60-80.

Hayes-Renshaw, F. and Wallace, H. (2006) *The Council of Ministers* (Basingstoke: Palgrave Macmillan).

Helmberg, M. (2007) 'Eurojust and Joint Investigation Teams: How Eurojust Can Support JITs', *ERA Forum*, 8, 245-51.

Hill, C. (1988) 'European Preoccupations with Terrorism', in A. Pijpers, E. Regelsberger and W. Wessels (eds) *European Political Cooperation in the 1980s: A Common Foreign Policy for Western Europe?* (Dordrecht: Martinus Nijhoff Publishers), pp. 166-93.

Hill, C. (1993) 'The Capability-Expectations Gap, or Conceptualizing Europe's International Role', *Journal of Common Market Studies*, 31(3), 305-28.

Hill, C. (1998) 'Closing the Capabilities-Expectations Gap?', in J. Peterson and H. Sjursen (eds) *A Common Foreign Policy for Europe? Competing Visions of the CFSP* (London: Routledge), pp. 18-38.

Hill, C. and Smith, M. (eds) (2010) *International Relations and the European Union* (Oxford: Oxford University Press).

Hintermeier, S. (2008) 'Reconceptualization of External Security in the European Union', in H.G. Brauch, C. Mesjasz, J. Grin, P. Dunay, Ú.O. Spring, B. Chourou,

P. Kameri-Mbote, P.H. Liotta and N.C. Behera (eds) *Globalization and Environmental Challenges: Reconceptualizing Security in the 21st Century* (Berlin: Springer), pp. 659–76.

Ho, J. (2009) 'Combating Piracy and Armed Robbery in Asia: The ReCAAP Information Sharing Centre (ISC)', *Marine Policy*, 33(2), 432–34.

Hoffman, B. (2006) *Inside Terrorism*, 2nd edn (New York: Columbia University Press).

Hoffman, S. (2000) 'Towards a Common European Foreign and Security Policy', *Journal of Common Market Studies*, 38(2), 189–98.

Hoffmann, L. (2009) 'Don't let the sun go down on me: The German Constitutional Court and its Lisbon judgement', *Journal of Contemporary European Research*, 5(3), 482–90.

Höhl, K., Müller, H., Schaper, A. and Schmitt, B. (2003) 'EU Cooperative Threat Reduction Activities in Russia', *Institute for Security Studies*, Chaillot Papers No. 61, June.

Homer-Dixon, T.F. (1994) 'Environmental Scarcities and Violent Conflict: Evidence from Cases', *International Security*, 19(1), 5–40.

Hough, P. (2004) *Understanding Global Security* (London: Routledge).

Hout,W. (2010) 'Between Development and Security: the European Union, Governance and Fragile States', *Third World Quarterly*, 31(1), 141–57.

Howlett, D. (2011) 'Nuclear Proliferation', in J. Baylis, S. Smith and P. Owens (eds) *The Globalization of World Politics: An Introduction to International Relations* (Oxford: Oxford University Press), pp. 382–97.

Howorth, J. (2007) *Security and Defence Policy in the European Union* (Basingstoke: Palgrave Macmillan).

Howorth, J. (2010) 'The EU as a Global Actor: Grand Strategy for a Global Grand Bargain?', *Journal of Common Market Studies*, 48(3), 455–74.

HR and European Commission (2008) 'Climate Change and International Security', S113/08, 14 March (Brussels: High Representative and European Commission).

Hulme M., Neufeldt H. and Colyer H. (eds) (2009) 'Adaptation and Mitigation Strategies: Supporting European Climate Policy. The Final Report from the ADAM Project. Revised June 2009', *Tyndall Centre for Climate Change Research* (Norwich: University of East Anglia).

Huysmans, J. (2000) 'The European Union and the Securitization of Migration', *Journal of Common Market Studies*, 38, 751–77.

Huysmans, J. (2004) 'A Foucaultian View on Spill-Over: Freedom and Security in the EU', *Journal of International Relations and Development*, 7(3), 294–318.

Huysmans, J. (2006) *The Politics of Insecurity: Fear, Migration and Asylum in the European Union* (London: Routledge).

Hyde-Price, A. (2004) 'European Security, Strategic Culture, and the Use of Force', *European Security*, 13(4), 323–43.

ICC-IMB (International Chamber of Commerce International Maritime Bureau) (2009) 'Piracy Figures for 2009 Surpass those for Previous Year', 23 September.

ICC-IMB (International Chamber of Commerce International Maritime Bureau) (2011) 'Hostage-taking at sea rises to record levels, says IMB', 17 January.

IMO (International Maritime Organisation) (2009) 'Record of the Meeting', Djibouti, 26–29 January, http://www.fco.gov.uk (home page) (date accessed 15 April 2012).

Bibliography 225

Independent (2003) 'Europe Lukewarm on Asylum Centre Plans', 29 March, http://www.independent.co.uk (home page) (date accessed 11 February 2010).

International Expert Group on Piracy off the Somali Coast (2008) 'Piracy off the Somali Coast', Workshop Commissioned by the Special Representative of the Secretary General of the UN to Somalia Ambassador Ahmedou Ould-Abdallah, Nairobi, 10–21 November.

IPCC (Intergovernmental Panel on Climate Change) (2007) *The Fourth Assessment Report* (Geneva: IPCC).

ISS-EU (2000) *Joint Declaration Issued at the British-French Summitt, Saint Malo, France*, 3–4 December 1998, http://www.consilium.europa.eu/uedocs/cmsUpload/French-British%20Summit%20Declaration,%20Saint-Malo,%2019 98%20-%20EN.pdf (accessed 8 September 2012)

Jachtenfuchs, M. (2010) 'The Institutional Framework of the European Union', in H. Enderlein, S. Wälti and M. Zürn (eds) *Handbook on Multi-level Governance* (Cheltenham: Edward Elgar), pp. 203–13.

Joly, D. (1996) *Haven or Hell? Asylum Policies and Refuges in Europe* (Basingstoke: Palgrave Macmillan).

Joppke, C. (ed) (1998) *Challenge to the Nation-State: Immigration in Western Europe and the United States* (Oxford: Oxford University Press).

Joppke, C. (2001) 'The Legal-Domestic Sources of Immigrant Rights: The United States, Germany and the European Union', *Comparative Political Studies*, 34(4), 339–366.

Jupille, J. and Caporaso, J. (1998) 'States, Agency, and Rules: The European Union in Global Environmental Politics', in C. Rhodes (ed) *The European Union in the World Community* (Boulder, CO: Lynne Rienner), pp. 213–29.

Kagan, R. (2003) *Of Paradise and Power: America and Europe in the New World Order* (New York: Alfred A. Knopf).

Kaldor, M., Martin, M. and Selchow, S. (2007) 'Human Security: A New Strategic Narrative for Europe', *International Affairs*, 83(2), 273–88.

Karl, R., Melillo, J. and Peterson, T. (eds) (2009) *Global Climate Change Impacts in the United States* (Cambridge: Cambridge University Press).

Karyotis, G. (2003) *European Migration Policy in the aftermath of September 11: The Security-Migration Nexus*, Paper prepared for presentation at the second workshop of the UACES Study Group 'The Evolving European Migration Law and Policy', Manchester, 11–12 April 2003.

Kasasira, R. and Muyita, S. (2010) 'United Nations Blocks Change of AMISOM Mandate', *Daily Monitor*, 28 July.

Katsioulis, C. and Mölling, C. (2010) *NPT Review 2010: What Role for the EU?* (Berlin: Friedrich Ebert Stiftung).

Kaunert, C. (2005) 'The Area of Freedom, Security and Justice: the construction of a "European public order"', *European Security*, 14(4), 459–83.

Kaunert, C. (2007) ' "Without the Power of Purse or Sword": The European Arrest Warrant and the Role of the Commission', *Journal of European Integration*, 29(4), 387–404.

Kaunert, C. (2009a) 'Liberty versus Security?: EU Asylum Policy and the European Commission', *Journal of Contemporary European Research*, 5(2), pp. 148–70.

Kaunert, C. (2009b) 'The Lisbon Treaty and the Constitutionalization of the EU', *Journal of Contemporary European Research*, 5(3), 465–71.

Kaunert, C. (2010a) 'The External Dimension of EU Counterterrorism Relations: Competences, Interests, and Institutions', *Terrorism and Political Violence*, 22(1), 41–61.

Kaunert, C. (2010b) 'Europol and EU Counterterrorism: International Security Actorness in the External Dimension', *Studies in Conflict and Terrorism*, 33(7), 652–71.

Kaunert, C. (2010c) *European Internal Security: Towards Supranational Governance in the Area of Freedom, Security and Justice?* (Manchester: Manchester University Press).

Kaunert, C. (2010d) 'The Area of Freedom, Security and Justice in the Lisbon Treaty: Commission Policy Entrepreneurship?', *European Security*, 19(2), 169–89.

Kaunert, C. and Della Giovanna, M. (2010) 'Post 9/11 EU Counter-Terrorist Financing Cooperation: Differentiating Supranational Policy Entrepreneurship by the Commission and the Council Secretariat', *European Security*, 19(2), 275–95.

Kaunert, C. and Léonard, S. (eds) (2010) After the Stockholm Programme: An Area of Freedom, Security and Justice in the European Union?, Special Issue of *European Security*, 19(2), 143–49.

Kaunert, C. and Léonard, S. (2011a) 'The EU Asylum Policy: Towards a Common Area of Protection and Solidarity?' in S. Wolff, F. Goudappel and J. de Zwaan (eds) *The Area of Freedom, Security and Justice after Lisbon and Stockholm. From Myth to Reality* (The Hague: T.M.C. Asser Press), pp. 79–95.

Kaunert, C. and Léonard, S. (2011b) 'Counter-Terrorism in the European Neighbourhood Policy', *Terrorism and Political Violence*, 23(2), 286–30.

Kaunert, C., Léonard, S. and Pawlak, P. (2012) *European Homeland Security: A European Strategy in the Making?* (London: Routledge).

Keohane, R.O. and Nye, J.S. (1974) 'Transgovernmental and International Organizations', *World Politics*, 27(1), 39–62.

Keukeleire, S. and MacNaughtan, J. (2008) *The Foreign Policy of the European Union* (Basingstoke: Palgrave Macmillan).

Kile, S. (2005) *Europe and Iran: Perspectives on Non-Proliferation*, SIPRI Research Report No. 21 (Oxford: Oxford University Press).

Kiliam, B. and Elgström, O. (2010) 'Still a Green Leader? The European Union's Role in International Climate Negotiations', *Cooperation and Conflict*, 45(3), 255–73.

Kimble, M. (2005) 'Climate Change: Emerging Insecurities', in F. Dodds and T. Pippard (eds) *Human and Environmental Security: An Agenda for Change* (London: Earthscan), pp. 103–14.

Kirchner, E. (2006) 'The Challenge of European Union Security Governance', *Journal of Common Market Studies*, 44(5), 947–68.

Knodt, M. and Princen, S. (2003) 'Introduction: Puzzles and Prospects in Theorizing EU's External Relations', in M. Knodt and S. Princen (eds) *Understanding the European Union's External Relations* (London: Routledge), pp. 1–16.

Kostakopolou, T. (2000) 'The Protective Union: Change and Continuity in Migration Law and Policy in Post-Amsterdam Europe', *Journal of Common Market Studies*, 38(3), 497–518.

Kratochvil, P. and Braun, M. (2009) 'The Lisbon Treaty and the Czech Republic: Past Imperfect, Future Uncertain', *Journal of Contemporary European Research*, 5(3), 498–504.

Krause, K. and Williams, M. (eds) (1997) *Critical Security Studies: Concepts and Cases* (London: UCL Press).

Lacasta, N., Dessai, S. and Powroslo E. (2002) 'Consensus among Many Voices: Articulating the European Union's Position on Climate Change', *Golden Gate University Law Review*, 32, 351–414.

Laïdi, Z. (2010) 'Europe as a Risk Averse Power: A Hypothesis', Garnet Policy Brief 11 (Paris: SciencesPo).

Lamy, S. (2008) 'Contemporary Mainstream Approaches: Neo-realism and Neoliberalism', in J. Baylis, S. Smith and P. Owens (eds) *The Globalization of World Politics: An Introduction to International Relations* (Oxford: Oxford University Press), pp. 114–29.

Larsen, H. (2002) 'The EU: A Global Military Actor?', *Cooperation and Conflict*, 37(3), 283–302.

Larsen, H. (2003) 'Still a National Residue in Small State Foreign Policy? Danish Foreign Policy in an EU Context', 2003 EUSA Conference, Nashville, Tennessee, 27–29 March 2003.

Lavenex, S. (1998) 'Transgressing Borders: The Emergent European Refugee Regime and "Safe Third Countries"' in Cafruny, A. and P. Peters (eds) *The Union and The World. The Political Economy of a Common European Foreign Policy* (The Hague: Kluwer Law International), pp. 113–32.

Lavenex, S. (1999) *Safe Third Countries. Extending the EU Asylum and Immigration Policies to Central and Eastern Europe* (Budapest and New York: Central European University Press).

Lavenex, S. (2001a) 'The Europeanization of Refugee Policies: Normative Challenges and Institutional Legacies', *Journal of Common Market Studies*, 39(5), 851–74.

Lavenex, S. (2001b) *The Europeanisation of Refugee Policies. Between Human Rights and Internal Security* (Aldershot: Ashgate).

Lavenex, S. (2004) 'EU External Governance in "Wider Europe"', *Journal of European Public Policy*, 11(4), 680–700.

Lavenex, S. (2006) 'Shifting Up and Out: The Foreign Policy of European Immigration Control', *West European Politics*, 29(2): pp. 329–50.

Leakey, D. (2009) 'Progress Report', *Impetus (EU Military Staff magazine)*, Issue 7, Spring/Summer.

Lebl, L.S. (2006) 'Working with the European Union', *Orbis*, Winter 2006.

Lee, J.R. (2009) *Climate Change and Armed Conflict: How and Cold Wars* (London: Routledge).

Lehr, P. and Lehmann, H. (2007) 'Somalia – Pirates' New Paradise', in P. Lehr (ed) *Violence at Sea: Piracy in the Age of Global Terrorism* (New York: Routledge), pp. 1–22.

Lennox, P. (2008) *Contemporary Piracy off the Horn of Africa* (Calgary: Canadian Defence & Foreign Affairs Institute).

Leonard, M. (2005) *Can EU Diplomacy Stop Iran's Nuclear Programme?* (London: Centre for European Reform).

Léonard, S. (2009) 'The Creation of FRONTEX and the Politics of Institutionalisation in the European Union External Borders Policy', *Journal of Contemporary European Research*, 5(3), 371–88.

Léonard, S. (2010a) 'The Use and Effectiveness of Migration Controls as a Counter-Terrorism Instrument in the European Union', *Central European Journal of International and Security Studies*, 4(1), 32–50.

Léonard, S. (2010b) 'EU Border Security and Migration into the European Union: FRONTEX and Securitization through Practices', *European Security*, 19(2), 231–54.

Levy, C. (2005) 'The European Union after 9/11: the Demise of a Liberal Democratic Asylum Regime?', *Government and Opposition*, 40(1), 26–59.

Levy, C. (2010) 'Refugees, Europe, Camps/State of Exception', *Refugee Survey Quarterly*, 29(1), 92–119.

Loescher, G. (1989) 'The European Community and Refugees', *International Affairs*, 65(4), 617–36.

Loescher, G. (1992) 'Refugee Movements and International Security', *Adelphi Paper 268* (London: The International Institute for Strategic Studies).

Loescher, G. (1993) *Beyond Charity – International Cooperation and the Global Refugee Crisis* (Oxford: Oxford University Press).

Loescher, G. (1995) 'International Security and Population Movements', in R. Cohen (ed) *The Cambridge Survey of World Migration* (Cambridge: Cambridge University Press), pp. 557–60.

Loescher, G. (2004) 'Refugee Protection and State Security: Towards a Greater Convergence', in R.M. Price and M.W. Zacher (eds) *The United Nations and Global Security* (Basingstoke: Palgrave Macmillan), pp. 161–76.

Longhurst, K. and Zaborowski, M. (2004) 'The Future of European Security', *European Security*, 13(4), 381–91.

MacKenzie, A. (2010) 'The EU's Increasing Role in Foreign Policy Counter-Terrorism', *Journal of Contemporary European Research*, 6(2), 147–63.

Majone, G. (2010) 'Harmonization and Mutual Recognition in an Enlarged European Union', in M.H. Guimarães, A.P. Faria and P. Ghauri (eds) *Product Market Integration: A Multifaceted Approach* (Bingley: Emerald Group Publishing), pp. 13–36.

Manners, I. (2002) 'Normative Power Europe: A Contradiction in Terms?', *Journal of Common Market Studies*, 40(2), 235–58.

Manners, I. (2006a) 'The European Union as Normative Power: A Response to Thomas Diez', *Millennium*, 35(1), 167–80.

Manners, I. (2006b) 'Normative Power Europe Reconsidered: Beyond the Crossroads', *Journal of European Public Policy*, 13(2), 182–99.

Manners, I. (2011) 'The European Union's Normative Power: Critical Perspectives and Perspectives on the Critical', in Whitman, R. (ed) *Normative Power Europe: Empirical and Theoretical Perspectives* (Basingstoke: Palgrave Macmillan), pp. 226–47.

Manners, I. and Whitman, R. (2003) 'The "Difference Engine": Constructing and Representing the International Identity of the European Union', *Journal of European Public Policy*, 10(3), 380–404.

Marrus, M.R. (1985) *The Unwanted. European Refugees in the Twentieth Century* (Oxford: Oxford University Press).

Marrus, M.R. (1988) 'Introduction', in A.C. Bramwell (ed) *Refugees in the Age of Total War* (London: Unwin Hyman), pp. 1–6.

Marsh, S. and Mackenstein, H. (2005) *The International Relations of the European Union* (London: Pearson Longman).
Matlary, J.H. (2008) 'Much Ado about Little: The EU and Human Security', *International Affairs*, 84(1), 131–43.
Mattiussi, J. (2006) 'External Relations Perspectives', Informal Seminar on Biopreparedness of the European Union, Brussels, 24–25 July 2006, http://www.ebsaweb.eu/ebsa_media/Downloads/EUSeminar/Mattiussi.pdf (date accessed 15 April 2012).
McAdam, J. (2005) 'The European Union Qualification Directive: The Creation of a Subsidiary Protection Regime', *International Journal of Refugee Law*, 17(3), 461–516.
McCormick, J. (2001) *Environmental Policy in the European Union* (Basingstoke: Palgrave Macmillan).
McDonald, M. (2002) 'Human Security and the Construction of Security', *Global Society*, 16(3), 277–95.
McGrew, A. (2008) 'Globalization and Global Politics', in J. Baylis, S. Smith and P. Owens (eds) *The Globalization of World Politics: An Introduction to International Relations*. (Oxford: Oxford University Press), pp. 14–33.
McInnes, C. (2008) 'Health', in P.D. Williams (ed) *Security Studies: An Introduction* (London: Routledge), pp. 274–86.
Mendelsohn, B. (2009) *Combating Jihadism: American Hegemony and Interstate Cooperation in the War on Terrorism* (Chicago: The University of Chicago Press).
Menon, A. (2004) 'From Crisis to Catharsis: ESDP after Iraq', *International Affairs*, 80(4), 631–48.
Menon, A. (2009) 'Empowering Paradise? The ESDP at Ten', *International Affairs*, 85(2), 227–46.
Missiroli, A. (2001) 'European Security Policy: The Challenge of Coherence', *European Foreign Affairs Review*, 6(2), 177–96.
Missiroli, A. (2010) 'The New EU "Foreign Policy" System after Lisbon: A Work in Progress', *European Foreign Affair Review*, 15(4), 427–52.
Mitsilegas, V. (2003) 'The New EU-USA Cooperation on Extradition, Mutual Legal Assistance and the Exchange of Police Data', *European Foreign Affairs Review*, 8, 515–36.
Mitsilegas, V. and Gilmore, B. (2007) 'The EU Legislative Framework against Money Laundering and Terrorist Finance: A Critical Analysis in the Light of Evolving Global Standards', *International and Comparative Law Quarterly*, 56, 119–41.
Mitsilegas, V., Monar, J. and Rees, W. (2003) *The European Union and Internal Security – Guardian of the People* (Basingstoke: Palgrave Macmillan).
Mojon, J.-M. (2010) 'In the Heart of a Somali Pirates' Lair', *AFP*, 1 September.
Møller, B. (2009) *The Somali Conflict: The Role of External Actors* (Copenhagen: Danish Institute for International Studies).
Monar, J. (1999) 'An Emerging Regime of European Governance for Freedom, Security and Justice', ESRC One Europe of Several? Programme Briefing Note 2/99.
Monar, J. (2005) 'A New Area of Freedom, Security and Justice for the Enlarged EU? The Results of the European Convention', in K. Henderson (ed) *The Area of Freedom, Security and Justice in the Enlarged Europe* (Basingstoke: Palgrave Macmillan), pp. 110–34.

Moschini, R.M. (2008) 'The Comprehensive Security Concept of the European Union', in H.G. Brauch, C. Mesjasz, J. Grin, P. Dunay, Ú.O. Spring, B. Chourou, P. Kameri-Mbote, P.H. Liotta and N.C. Behera (eds) *Globalization and Environmental Challenges: Reconceptualizing Security in the 21st Century* (Berlin: Springer), pp. 651–57.

MSNBC.com, (2008) 'Piracy Threat Hikes Insurance Premiums', 20 November.

Müller, H. (2005) *The 2005 NPT Review Conference: Reasons and Consequences of Failure and Options for Repair* (Stockholm: The Secretariat of the Weapons of Mass Destruction Commission).

Müller, H. (2007) 'Europe and the Proliferation of Weapons of Mass Destruction', in P. Foradori, P. Rosa and R. Scartezzini (eds) *Managing Multilevel Foreign Policy* (Lanhan: Lexington Books), pp. 181–200.

Müller-Wille, B. (2008) 'The Effect of International Terrorism on EU Intelligence Co-operation', *Journal of Common Market Studies*, 46(1), 49–73.

Murphy, M. (2007) *Contemporary Piracy and Maritime Terrorism: The Threat to International Security* (London: The International Institute for Strategic Studies).

Murphy, M. (2009) *Small Boats, Weak States, Dirty Money* (London: Hurst & Company).

Nakamura, M. (2009) *Piracy off the Horn of Africa: What is the Most Effective Method of Repression*, Naval War College, 4 May.

Nicolaïdis, C. and Howse, R. (2003) 'This Is My EUtopia...: Narrative as Power', in J.H.H. Weiler, I. Begg and J. Peterson (eds) *Integration in an Expanding European Union* (Oxford: Blackwell), pp. 341–66.

Niemann, A. (2008) 'Dynamics and Countervailing Pressures of Visa, Asylum and Immigration Policy Treaty Revision: Explaining Change and Stagnation from the Amsterdam IGC to the IGC 2003–2004', *Journal of Common Market Studies*, 46(3), 559–91.

Noll, G. (2000) *Negotiating Asylum – The EU Acquis, Extraterritorial Protection and the Common Market of Deflection* (The Hague: Martinus Nijhoff Publishers).

Norman, P. (2001) 'Common Criminals', *Financial Times*, 6 December 2001.

Nugent, N. (2003) *The Government and Politics of the European Union*, 5th edn (Basingstoke: Palgrave Macmillan).

Nugent, N. (2010) *The Government and Politics of the European Union*, 7th edn (Basingstoke: Palgrave Macmillan).

Nuttall, S. (2000) *European Foreign Policy* (Oxford: Oxford University Press).

Nuttall, S. (2005) 'Coherence and Consistency', in C. Hill and M. Smith (eds) *International Relations and the European Union* (Oxford: Oxford University Press), pp. 91–112.

NYT (2011) Suddenly, A Rise in Piracy's Price. *The New York Times*, 26 February.

Observer (2003), 'Secret Balkan Camp Built to Hold UK Asylum Seekers', 15 June.

Occhipinti, J. (2003) *The Politics of EU Police Cooperation – Towards A European FBI?* (Boulder, CO: Lynne Rienner Publishers).

Occhipinti, J. (2008) *Progress Amid Difference: The EU and US Counter-Terrorism*, paper presented at the Annual Conference of the International Studies Association (ISA), San Francisco, CA, USA, 29 March 2008.

Orbie, J. (2008) *Europe's Global Role: External Policies of the European Union* (Farnham: Ashgate).

Overhaus, M. (2007) *Analysis: European Diplomacy and the Conflict over Iran's Nuclear Programme*, 19 July, http://www.deutsche-aussenpolitik.de/ (home page) (date accessed 15 April 2012).
Oxfam (2011) 'Whose Aid Is it Anyway?', 145 Oxfam Briefing Paper (Oxford: Oxfam).
Pal Singh Sidhu, W. (2008) 'Nuclear Proliferation', in P. Williams (ed) *Security Studies: An Introduction* (London: Routledge), pp. 361–72.
Parker, C. and Karlsson, C. (2010) 'Climate Change and the European Union's Leadership Moment: An Inconvenient Truth?', *Journal of Common Market Studies*, 48(4), 923–43.
Peers, S. (2000) *EU Justice and Home Affairs Law* (London: Longman).
Peers, S. (2001) 'Proposed Framework Decision on European Arrest Warrants', *Statewatch Post-11.09.01 Analyses*, No. 3, http://www.statewatch.org (home page) (date accessed 11 February 2010).
Peers, S. (2002) 'Key Legislative Developments on Migration in the European Union', *European Journal of Migration and Law*, 4(1), 85–126.
Peers, S. (2004) 'Irregular Immigration and EU External Relations', in B. Bogusz, R. Cholewinski, A. Cygan and E. Szyszczak (eds) *Irregular Migration and Human Rights. Theoretical, European and International Perspectives* (Leiden and Boston, MA: Martinus Nijhoff Publishers), 193–219.
Peers, S. (2005) 'The Future of the EU Judicial System and EC Immigration and Asylum Law', *European Journal of Migration and Law*, 7(3), 263–74.
Peers, S. (2006) *EU Justice and Home Affairs Law*, 2nd edn (Clarendon: Oxford University Press).
Peers, S. (2007) 'The Jurisdiction of the Court of Justice over EC Immigration and Asylum Law: Time for a Change?', in A. Baldaccini et al. (eds) *Whose Freedom, Security and Justice? EU Immigration and Asylum Law and Policy* (Oxford: Hart), pp. 85–108.
Peers, S. and Rogers, N. (eds) (2006) *EU Asylum and Migration Law: Text and Commentary* (Leiden: Martinus Nijhoff).
Penny, C.K. (2007) 'Greening the Security Council: Climate Change as an Emerging "Threat to International Peace and Security"', *International Environmental Agreements*, 7(1), 35–71.
Peters, D. (2010) *Constrained Balancing: The EU's Security Policy* (Basingstoke: Palgrave Macmillan).
Petersen, N. (1993) 'The European Union and Foreign and Security Policy', in O. Nørgaard, T. Pedersen and N. Petersen (eds) *The European Community in World Politics* (London: Pinter Publishers), pp. 31–51.
Peterson, J. and Shackleton, M. (2006) 'The EU's Institutions: An Overview', in J. Peterson and M. Shackleton (eds) *The Institutions of the European Union* (Oxford: Oxford University Press), pp. 1–16.
Peterson, J. and Sjursen, H. (eds) (1998) *A Common Foreign Policy for Europe? Competing Visions of the CFSP* (London: Routledge).
Political and Security Committee (2008) 'Political and Security Committee Decision Atalanta//1/2008 of 18 November 2008 on the Appointment of an EU Force Commander for the European Union Military Operation to Contribute to the Deterrence, Prevention and Repression of Acts of Piracy and Armed Robbery off the Somali Coast (Atalanta) (2008/888/CFSP)', L 317 (OJEU), 27 November (Brussels: General Secretariat of the Council).

Political and Security Committee (2009) Political and Security Committee Decision Atalanta/6/2009 of 22 July 2009 on the Appointment of an EU Force Commander for the European Union military Operation to Contribute to the Deterrence, Prevention and Repression of Acts of Piracy and Armed Robbery off the Somalia Coast (Atalanta) (2009/559/CFSP)', L 192 (OJEU), 24 July (Brussels: General Secretariat of the Council).

Political and Security Committee (2010) 'Political and Security Committee Decision Atalanta//3/2010 of 28 May 2010 on the appointment of an EU Operation Commander for the European Union Military Operation to Contribute to the Deterrence, Prevention and Repression of Acts of Piracy and Armed Robbery off the Somali Coast (Atalanta) (2010/317/CFSP)', L 142 (OJEU), 10 June (Brussels: General Secretariat of the Council).

Pomorska, K. (2007) 'The Impact of Enlargement: Europeanization of Polish Foreign Policy? Tracking Adaptation and Change in the Polish Ministry of Foreign Affairs', *The Hague Journal of Diplomacy*, 2, 25–51.

Pryce, R. (1972) 'The Politics of Co-operation and Integration in Western Europe', in R. Morgan (ed) *The Study of International Affairs: Essays in Honour of Kenneth Younger* (Oxford: Oxford University Press), pp. 175–96.

Rees, W. (2006) *Transatlantic Counter-Terrorism Cooperation: The New Imperative* (London: Routledge).

Reinares, F. (ed) (2000) *European Democracies against Terrorrism – Government Policies and Intergovernmental Cooperation* (Aldershot: Ashgate).

Reynolds, P.A. (1971) *An Introduction to International Relations* (London: Longman).

Rieker, P. (2009) 'The EU – A Capable Security Actor? Developing Administrative Capabilities', *Journal of European Integration*, 31(6), 703–19.

Rogers, J. (2009) 'From "Civilian Power" to "Global Power": Explicating the European Union's "Grand Strategy" Through the Articulation of Discourse Theory', *Journal of Common Market Studies*, 47(4), 831–62.

Rogers, P. (2008) 'Terrorism', in P.D. Williams (ed) *Security Studies: An Introduction* (London: Routledge), pp. 171–84.

Rosand, E. (2003) 'Security Council Resolution 1373, the Counter-terrorism Committee, and the Fight against Terrorism', *The American Journal of International Law*, 97(2), 333–41.

Rosand, E. (2004) 'The Security Council's Efforts to Monitor the Implementation of Al Qaeda/Taliban Sanctions', *The American Journal of International Law*, 98(4), 745–63.

Rosecrance, R. (1998) 'The European Union: A New Type of International Actor', in J. Zielonka (ed) *Paradoxes of European Foreign Policy* (The Hague: Kluwer Law International), pp. 15–23.

Salmon, T. (2005) 'The European Security and Defence Policy: Built on Rocks or Sand?', *European Foreign Affairs Review*, 10(3), 359–80.

Sauer, T. (2003) 'How "common" Is European Nuclear Non-proliferation Policy', Joint Session of Workshops of the European Consortium for Political Research. Edinburgh, 28 March–2 April.

Schmitt, B. (2005) 'Introduction', in B. Schmitt (ed) *Effective Non-Proliferation: The European Union and the 2005 NPT Review Conference*, Institute for Security Studies, Tshwane, *Chaillot Papers* No. 77, April, pp. 7–8.

Schreurs, M. and Tiberghien, Y. (2007) 'Multi-Level Reinforcement: Explaining European Union Leadership in Climate Change Mitigation', *Global Environmental Politics*, 7(4), 19–46.

Scott, S.V. (2009) 'Securitizing Climate Change: International Legal Implications and Obstacles', in P.G. Harris (ed) *The Politics of Climate Change: Environmental Dynamics in International Affairs* (New York: Routledge), pp. 147–63.

Shapiro, J and Witney, N. (2009) 'Towards a Post-American Europe: A Power Audit of EU–US Relations', *European Council on Foreign Relations*, October.

Sherman, P. (2004) 'Reconceptualizing Security after 9/11', in P. Shearman and M. Sussex (eds) *European Security after 9/11* (Aldershot: Ashgate), pp. 11–27.

Shearman, P. and Sussex, M. (eds) (2004) *European Security after 9/11* (Aldershot: Ashgate).

Sherrington, P. (2000) 'Shaping the Policy Agenda: Think Tank Activity in the European Union', *Global Society*, 14(2), 173–89.

Sidorenko, O.F. (2007) *The Common European Asylum System: Background, Current State of Affairs, Future Direction* (The Hague: T.M.C. Asser Press).

Simpson, G. (1999) 'Asylum and Immigration in The European Union After the Treaty of Amsterdam', *European Public Law*, 5(1), 91–124.

Sindico, F. (2007) 'Climate Change: A Security (Council) Issue?', *The Carbon & Climate Law Review*, 1(1), pp. 29–44.

Sjöstedt, G. (1977) *The External Role of the European Community* (Westmead: Saxon House).

Sjursen, H. (1998) 'Missed Opportunity or Eternal Fantasy?: The Idea of a European Security and Defence Policy', in J. Peterson and H. Sjursen (eds) *A Common Foreign Policy for Europe? Competing Visions of the CFSP* (London: Routledge), pp. 95–112.

Sjursen, H. (2004) 'Security and Defence', in W. Carlsnaes, H. Sjursen and B. White (eds) *Contemporary European Foreign Policy* (London: Sage Publishers), pp. 59–74.

Sjursen, H. (2006a) 'What Kind of Power: European Foreign Policy in Perspective', *Journal of European Public Policy*, 13(2), 169–81.

Sjursen, H. (ed) (2006b) *Questioning EU Enlargement. Europe in Search of Identity* (London: Routledge).

Smith, H. (2002) *European Union Foreign Policy: What it Is and What it Does* (London: Pluto Press).

Smith, K. (2008) *European Union Foreign Policy in a Changing World* (Malden, MA: Polity).

Smith, M. (1998) 'Does the Flag Follow Trade?: "Politicisation" and the Emergence of European Foreign Policy', in J. Peterson and H. Sjursen (eds) *A Common Foreign Policy for Europe? Competing Visions of the CFSP* (London: Routledge), pp. 77–94.

Smith, M.E. (2004) *Europe's Foreign and Security Policy: The Institutionalization of Cooperation* (Cambridge: Cambridge University Press).

Smith, M.E. (2010) *International Security: Politics, Policy, Prospects* (Basingstoke: Palgrave Macmillan).

Sodupe, K. and Benito, E. (1998) 'The Evolution of the European Union's TACIS Programme, 1991–96', *Journal of Communist Studies and Transition Politics*, 14(4), 51–68.

Solana, J. (2004) 'Preface', in N. Gnesotto (ed) *EU Security and Defence Policy: The First Five Years (1999–2004)* (Paris: Institute for European Studies), pp. 5–10.

Solana, J. (2009) *Climate Change and Security* (Denmark: Danish Ministry of Foreign Affairs).
Spence, D. (ed) (2007) *The European Union and Terrorism* (London: John Harper Publishing).
Spencer, T. (2006) 'Final Report. Conference on Greening Foreign and Security Policy: The Role of Europe', European Parliament, 6 and 7 December 2006, http://www.envirosecurity.org/ges/conference/report.pdf (date accessed 17 September 2011).
Stelzenmüller, C. (2010) 'End of a Honeymoon: Obama and Europe, One Year Later', *The German Marshall Fund of the United States*, Brussels Forum Paper Series, March.
Stern, N. (2007) *The Economics of Climate Change: The Stern Review* (Cambridge: Cambridge University Press).
Stessens, G. (2008) 'The EU-US Agreements on Extradition and on Mutual Legal Assistance', in Martenczuck and S. van Thiel (eds) *Justice, Liberty and Security – New Challenges for EU External Relations* (Brussels: VUB Press, Brussels University Press).
Stetter, S. (2000) 'Regulating Migration: Authority Delegation in Justice and Home Affairs', *Journal of European Public Policy*, 7(1), 80–103.
Stetter, S. (2007) *EU Foreign and Interior Policies: Cross-Pillar Politics and the Social Construction of Sovereignty* (New York: Routledge).
Storey, H. (2008) 'EU Refugee Qualification Directive: A Brave New World?', *International Journal of Refugee Law*, 20(1), 1–49.
Stromseth, J.E. (2003) 'The Security Council's Counter-terrorism Role: Continuity and Innovation', *Proceedings of the American Society of International Law*, 97, 41–5.
Sullivan, A. (2009) *Interview with Aadrian Sullivan, the head of the Somalia office at the European Commission's Humanitarian Aid department (ECHO)*, http://ec.europa.eu/echo (home page) (date accessed 15 April 2012).
Talmon, S. (2005) 'The Security Council as World Legislature', *The American Journal of International Law*, 97(4), 873–88.
Tannock, C. (2009) 'How to Stabilise Horn of Africa', *Business Daily*, 29 October.
Tappeiner, I. (2005) 'The Fight against Terrorism: The Lists and the Gaps', *Utrecht Law Review*, 1(1), 97–125.
Tharoor, I. (2009) 'How Somalia's Fishermen Became Pirates', *Time*, 18 April.
The EU and the Government of Kenya (2009) 'Exchange of Letters between the European Union and the Government of Kenya on the conditions and modalities for the transfer of persons suspected of having committed acts of piracy and detained by the European Union-led naval force (EUNAVFOR), and seized property in the possession of EUNAVFOR, from EUNAVFOR to Kenya and for their treatment after such transfer', L 79 (OJEU), 25 March.
The EU and the Republic of Djibouti (2010) 'Agreement between the European Union and the Republic of Djibouti on the status of the European Union-led forces in the Republic of Djibouti in the framework of the EU military operation Atalanta', L 33 (OJEU), 3 February.
Thielemann, E. (2001a) 'The Soft Europeanisation of Migration Policy: European Integration and Domestic Policy Change', Paper prepared for the ECSA 7th Biennial International Conference, May 31–June 2, 2001, Madison, Wisconsin.

Thielemann, E. (2001b) 'The Evolution of a European Asylum Policy: Escaping International and Domestic Constraints', in S. Oppermann (ed) *Magnet Societies: Immigration in Deutschland Und IN Den USA* (Rehburg-Loccum: Evangelische Adademie), pp. 49–80.

Thielemann, E. (2004) 'Why European Policy Harmonization Undermines Refugee Burden-Sharing, *European Journal of Migration and Law*, 6(1), 43–61.

Thielemann, E. (2005) 'Symbolic Politics or Effective Burden-Sharing? Redistribution, Side-Payments and the European Refugee Fund', *Journal of Common Market Studies*, 43(4), 807–24.

Thielemann, E. (2006) 'The Effectiveness of Governments' Attempts to Control Unwanted Migration', in C. Parsons and T. Smeeding (eds) *Immigration and the Transformation of Europe* (Cambridge: Cambridge University Press), pp. 442–72.

Thielemann, E. and Dewan, T. (2006) 'The Myth of Free-Riding: Refugee Protection and Implicit Burden-Sharing', *West European Politics*, 29(2), 351–69.

Thomas, C. (2008) 'Poverty', in P.D. Williams (ed) *Security Studies: An Introduction*. (London: Routledge), pp. 244–59.

Tietje, C. (1997) 'The Concept of Coherence in the Treaty on European Union and the Common Foreign and Security Policy', *European Foreign Affairs Review*, 2(2), 211–33.

Toje, A. (2011) 'The European Union as a Small Power', *Journal of Common Market Studies*, 49(1), 43–60.

Tonra, B. (2009) 'The 2009 Irish Referendum on the Lisbon Treaty', *Journal of Contemporary European Research*, 5(3), 472–79.

Trombetta, M.J. (2009) 'Environmental Security and Climate Change: Analysing the Discourse' in P.G. Harris (ed) *The Politics of Climate Change: Environmental Dynamics in International Affairs* (New York: Routledge), pp. 129–46.

Turpen, E. and Finlay, B. (2009) 'US-Russia Cooperative Nonproliferation', in N.E. Busch and D.H. Joyner (eds) *Combating Weapons of Mass Destruction: The Future of International Nonproliferation Policy* (Athens, GA: University of Georgia Press), pp. 302–24.

UK Government (2003) *New International Approaches to Asylum Processing and Protection*, http://www.statewatch.org (home page) (date accessed 11 February 2010).

Ullman, R. (1983) 'Redefining Security', *International Security*, 8(1), 129–53.

UN (1958) 'Convention on the High Seas', 29 April (Geneva: United Nations).

UN (2010) 'Informal meeting of the General Assembly Plenary on Piracy, 14 May (New York: United Nations Headquarters).

UNDP (United Nations Development Program) (1994) *Human Development Report 1994* (New York: Oxford University Press).

UNDP (United Nations Development Program) (2007) *Human Development Report 2007/2008. Fighting Climate Change: Human Solidarity in a Changing World* (New York: Palgrave Macmillan).

UNGA (2009) 'Sixty-third Session, Agenda item 107. Follow-up to the Outcome of the Millennium Summit', A/63/L.8/Rev.1, 18 May (New York: United Nations General Assembly).

UNHCR (2003) Summary of UNHCR Proposals to Complement National Asylum Systems Through New Multilateral Approaches', *UNHCR Working Paper*, http://www.statewatch.org (home page) (date accessed 11 February 2010).

United Nations and World Bank (2008) 'Somali Reconstruction and Development Programme. Deepening Peace and Reducing Poverty', Volume 1, January.

UNSC (2004) 'Resolution 1540 (2004) Adopted by the Security Council at its 4956th Meeting, on 28 April 2004', S/RES/1540, 28 April (New York: United Nations Security Council).

UNSC (2007a) 'Security Council Holds First-Ever Debate on Impact of Climate Change on Peace, Security, Hearing over 50 Speakers', 5663rd Meeting, 17 April (New York: United Nations Security Council).

UNSC (2007b) 'Resolution 1744 (2007) Adopted by the Security Council at its 5633rd Meeting, on 20 February 2007'. S/RES/1744, 21 February (New York: United Nations Security Council).

UNSC (2008a) 'Resolution 1838 (2008) Adopted by the Security Council at its 5987th Meeting, on 7 October 2008', S/RES/1838, 7 October (New York: United Nations Security Council).

UNSC (2008b) 'Resolution 1846 (2008) Adopted by the Security Council at its 6026th Meeting, on 2 December 2008', S/RES/1846, 2 December (New York: United Nations Security Council).

UNSC (2009) 'Resolution 1816 (2008) Adopted by the Security Council at its 5902nd Meeting on 2 June 2008' S/RES/1816, 2 June (New York: United Nations Security Council).

Van Elsuwege, P. (2010) 'EU External Action after the Collapse of the Pillar Structure: in Search of a New Balance between Delimitation and Consistency', *Common Market Law Review*, 47(4), 987–1019.

Vanhoonacker, S. (2011) 'The Institutional Framework', in C. Hill and M. Smith (eds) *International Relations and the European Union* (Oxford: Oxford University Press), pp. 75–100.

Vanhoonacker, S. and Reslow, N. (2010) 'The European External Action Service: Living Forwards by Understanding Backwards', *European Foreign Affairs Review*, 15(1), 1–18.

Van Selm, J. (2002) 'Immigration and Asylum or Foreign Policy: The EU's Approach to Migrants and their Countries of Origin', in S. Lavenex and E. Uçarer (eds) *Migration and the Externalities of European Integration* (Lanham, MD: Lexington Books), pp. 143–56.

Van Selm, J. (2003) 'Refugee Protection in Europe and the US after 9/11', in N. Steiner, M. Gibney and G. Loescher (eds) *Problems of Protection – The UNHCR, Refugees and Human Rights* (New York and London: Routledge), pp. 237–61.

Vego, M. (2009) 'Counter-Piracy: An Operational Perspective', *Tidskrift i Sjöväsendet*, Issue 3, 169–80.

Vogel, B. (2007) 'Climate Change Creates Security Challenge "More Complex than Cold War"', http://www.globalclimatesecurity.org (home page) (date accessed 29 March 2012).

Vogel, J. (2001) 'Abschaffung der Auslieferung? Kritische Anmerkungen zur Reform des Auslieferungsrechts in der Europäischen Union', *Juristenzeitung*, 56(19), 937–43.

Vogler, J. (2002) 'The European Union and the Securitisation of the Environment', in E.A. Page and M. Redclift (eds) *Human Security and the Environment* (Cheltenham: Edward Elgar), pp. 179–98.

Vogler, J. (2005) 'The European Contribution to Global Environmental Governance', *International Affairs*, 81(4), 835–50.

Wæver, O. (1995) 'Securitization and Desecuritization', in R.D. Lipschutz (ed) *On Security* (New York: Columbia University Press), pp. 46–86.
Wæver, O., Buzan, B., Kelstrup, M. and Lemaitre, P. (1993) *Identity, Migration and the New Security Agenda in Europe* (London: Pinter).
Wagner, W. (2003a) 'Analysing the European Politics of Internal Security', *Journal of European Public Policy*, 10(6), 1033–39.
Wagner, W. (2003b) 'Building an Internal Security Community: The Democratic Peace and the Politics of Extradition in Western Europe', *Journal of Peace Research*, 40(6), 695–712.
Wagner, W. (2011) 'Negative and Positive Integration in EU Criminal Law Co-operation', Paper prepared for presentation at the Workshop 'Policy Change in EU Internal Security' European University Institute Florence, Italy, 12–13 May.
Walton, C.D. and Gray, C.S. (2007) 'The Second Nuclear Age: Nuclear Weapons in the Twenty-first Century', in J. Baylis, J. Wirtz, C.S. Gray and E. Cohen (eds) *Strategy in the Contemporary World* (Oxford: Oxford University Press), pp. 209–27.
Washington Post (2009) 'Copenhagen Climate Deal Shows New World Order May be Led by U.S., China', 20 December, p. A01.
WBGU (German Advisory Council on Global Change) (2007) *Climate Change as a Security Risk* (London: Earthscan).
WCED (World Commission on Environment and Development) (1987) *Our Common Future* (Oxford: Oxford University Press).
Wendt, A. (1999) *Social Theory of International Politics* (Cambridge: Cambridge University Press).
Westing, A.H. (1989) 'The Environmental Component of Comprehensive Security', *Security Dialogue*, 20(2), 129–34.
White, B. (2001) *Understanding European Foreign Policy* (Basingstoke: Palgrave Macmillan).
White, B. (2004) 'Foreign Policy Analysis and the New Europe', in W. Carlsnaes, H. Sjursen and B. White (eds) *Contemporary European Foreign Policy* (London: Sage), pp. 11–31.
Whitman, R. (1998a) 'Creating a Foreign Policy for Europe? Implementing Common Foreign and Security Policy from Maastricht to Amsterdam', *Australian Journal of International Affairs*, 52(2), 165–83.
Whitman, R. (1998b) *From Civilian Power to Superpower? The International Identity of the European Union* (Basingstoke: Palgrave Macmillan).
Whitman, R. (2002) 'The Development of the Common European Security and Defence Policy', in J. Gower (ed) *The European Union Handbook* (London: Fitzroy Dearborn Publishers), pp. 285–300.
Whitman, R. (2004) 'NATO, the EU and ESDP: An Emerging Division of Labour?', *Contemporary Security Policy*, 25(3), 430–51.
Whitman, R. (2006) 'Muscles from Brussels: The Demise of Civilian Power Europe?', in O. Elgström and M. Smith (eds) *The European Union's Roles in International Relations*. (Abingdon: Routledge), pp. 101–17.
Whitman, R. (2011) *The Rise of the European External Action Service: Putting the Strategy into EU Diplomacy?*, http://www.euce.org/eusa/2011/papers/8l_whitman.pdf (date accessed 2 April 2011).
Whitman, R. and Juncos, A. (2009) 'The Lisbon Treaty and the Foreign, Security and Defence Policy: Reforms, Implementation and the Consequences of (Non-)Ratification', *European Foreign Affairs Review*, 14(1), 25–46.

Wilkinson, P. (2006) *Terrorism versus Democracy: The Liberal State Response* (London: Routledge).
Williams, P.D. (2008) 'Security Studies: An introduction', in P.D. Williams (ed) *Security Studies: An Introduction* (London: Routledge), pp. 1–12.
Wirtz, J.J. (2007) 'Weapons of Mass Destruction', in A. Collins (ed) *Contemporary Security Studies* (Oxford: Oxford University Press), pp. 320–37.
Wurzel, R. and Connelly, J. (eds) (2010) *The European Union as a Leader in International Climate Change Politics* (London: Routledge).
Wyn Rees, G. (2006) *Transatlantic Counter-Terrorism Cooperation* (London: Routledge).
Young, O.R. (1972) 'The Actors in World Politics', in J.N. Rosenau, V. Davis and M.A. East (eds) *The Analysis of International Politics* (London: The Free Press), pp. 125–45.
Youngs, R. (2008) 'Fusing Security and Development: Just Another Euro-Platitude?', *European Integration*, 30(3), 419–37.
Zimmermann, D. (2006) 'The European Union and Post-9/11 Counterterrorism: A Reappraisal', *Studies in Conflict and Terrorism*, 29(1), 123–45.
Zwolski, K. (2009) 'Euthanasia, Gay Marriage and Sovereignty: The Polish Ratification of the Lisbon Treaty', *Journal of Contemporary European Research*, 5(3), 489–97.
Zwolski, K. (2011a) 'Unrecognised and Unwelcome? The Role of the EU in Preventing the Proliferation of CBRN Weapons, Materials and Knowledge', *Perspectives on European Politics and Society*, 12(4), 477–92.
Zwolski, K. (2011b) 'The External Dimension of the EU's Non-proliferation Policy: Overcoming Inter-institutional Competition', *European Foreign Affairs Review*, 16(3), 325–340.
Zwolski, K. (2012a) 'The EU as an International Security Actor after Lisbon: Finally a Green Light for a Holistic Approach?', *Cooperation and Conflict*, 47(3), 68–87.
Zwolski, K. (2012b) 'The EU and a Holistic Security Approach after Lisbon: Competing Norms and the Power of the Dominant Discourse', *Journal of European Public Policy*, 19(7), 988–1005.
Zwolski, K. and Kaunert, C. (2011) 'The EU and Climate Security: The Case of Successful Norm Entrepreneurship?', *European Security*, 20(1), 21–43.

Interviews

The European Commission: first set of 25 interviews from 01.04.04 until 01.08.04 (COM1 to COM25); second set of 12 interviews from 01.04.09 until February 2010 (COM-A, COM-B, COM-C, COM-D, COM-E, COM-F, COM-G, COM-H, COM-I, COM-J, COM-K, COM-L).
The European Council Secretariat: first set of 9 interviews from 01.04.04 until 01.08.04 (CON1 to CON9); second set of 6 interviews from 01.04.09 until February 2010 (CON-A, CON-B, CON-C, CON-D, CON-E, CON-F, CON-G).
The European Parliament: 5 interviews from 01.04.04 until 01.08.04 (EP1 to EP5).
MILSTAFF1 (2009) Research Interview in the Council of the European Union, June 2009.
NAVY1 (2010) Research interview with a Turkish Navy officer involved in fighting off pira-cy off the Somali coast, January 2010.

Non-Governmental Organisations (NGOs) and Intergovernmental Organisations (IGOs) first set of 11 interviews from 01.04.04 until 01.08.04 (NGO1 – NGO10 & IGO1); second set of 2 interviews from during April 2009 (NGO-A, NGO-B).

The Permanent Representations of the Member States and the Missions to the EU of Candidate Countries: 26 interviews from 01.04.04 until 01.08.04 (PR1 to PR26).

ShipInd (2009) Research interview with the representative of European shipping industry, April 2009.

WMDExp1 (2009) Phone research interview with an expert in the area of WMDs, April 2009.

WMDExp2 (2009) Phone research interview with an expert in the area of WMDs, April 2009.

WMDExp3 (2009) Phone research interview with an expert in the area of WMDs, April 2009.

WMDExp4 (2009) Phone research interview with an expert in the area of WMDs, May 2009.

WMDExp5 (2009) Phone research interview with an expert in the area of WMDs, May 2009.

Index

Note: The letter 'n' followed by the locator refers to notes in the text.

Advanced Passenger Information, *see* API
Afghanistan, 15, 25, 88, 139
African Union, 184–6
African Union Mission in Somalia, *see* AMISOM
AFSJ, 3–4, 9, 14, 21, 45, 47, 50–2, 57–61, 64–7, 91, 109–11, 113, 122, 195, 198, 205–6
agencies, 21, 48, 66, 92, 101–3, 118
Algeria, 138
Al-Qaeda, 104–5
AMISOM, 184–6
Amsterdam Treaty, 3, 54, 56–9, 60, 62, 73, 95, 120–2, 195
API, 100
Area of Freedom, Security and Justice, *see* AFSJ
Ashton, C., 174
asylum, 11, 16, 56, 58, 59, 65, 91, 116–43, 198, 200, 203–4, 208
Australia, 80, 84, 99, 101

Balkans, 2
Bin Laden, 15, 88–9, 104–6, 143
Bush, G. W., 110, 113, 200

Canada, 78, 99, 101, 155, 160–2
CBRN, 17, 144–66, 197
Central Asia, 68, 84, 154
CFSP, 1–2, 4–5, 9, 10, 14, 28, 43, 47, 50–64, 74, 104–6, 121, 148–51, 157–9, 164, 182, 192–3, 195–7, 204, 207
Chemical, Biological, Radiological and Nuclear weapons, *see* CBRN
China, 34, 80, 82, 84, 180, 199, 207

climate security, 1, 16, 26, 46, 49, 68–71
the EU and climate security, 68–87, 198–200, 202–4
CMR, 182–3, 190, 202, 204
Committee of Permanent Representatives, *see* COREPER
Common Foreign and Security Policy, *see* CFSP
Common Security and Defence Policy, *see* CSDP
communitarisation, 65, 121
consistency, 19, 24, 26, 29–31, 37, 48, 54, 57, 63–4, 148, 151–3
Container Security Initiative, *see* CSI
Cooperative Threat Reduction, 158
COREPER, 73, 152
Council Secretariat, 55, 57, 63, 73–6, 148, 151–3, 164, 194, 203
Counter-terrorism Strategy, 46
crisis management, 29, 63, 152, 172, 175, 178, 207
Critical Maritime Routes, *see* CMR
cross-pillar, 104
CSDP, 1–4, 8–10, 20–1, 27–30, 47–8, 61, 74, 152, 170–5, 179, 181, 189, 196–7, 201–2, 204–8, 210n2
CSI, 97, 112–13

data protection, 98–100, 103, 108, 113
EAW, 45–6, 91–3, 95–6, 109–15, 140
EEAS, 28, 30–1, 42, 63–4, 72–3, 75–6, 86, 148, 151–4, 156, 162, 164–5, 175, 181–2, 193–5, 198, 200–1
effectiveness, 43, 55, 123, 151, 165, 186, 190–1
enlargement, 28, 59
epistemic community, 72, 85–6

ESDP, 6–8, 10, 27–8, 43, 60–1, 63, 181–2, 196, 210n2
ESS, 3, 22–3, 25, 29, 68, 71, 144, 163, 200
  Report on the Implementation of the ESS, 69, 71, 145, 168
EUMC, 61, 173–4
EUMS, 173–4
EUNAVFOR 'Atalanta', 29, 47, 170, 173–4, 177, 179–81, 187–90, 201, 204, 206, 210n2
Eurojust, 47, 97, 108, 115
European Arrest Warrant, *see* EAW
European Court of Justice, 52, 93, 95, 121
European External Action Service, *see* EEAS
European Parliament, 7, 12, 28, 52, 54–6, 58, 65–6, 98–100, 108, 111, 121–2, 141, 156, 166, 182, 200
European Police Office, *see* Europol
European Political Cooperation, 2, 14, 50–1, 52–3, 54–6, 61, 148–9, 172, 195, 198
European Security and Defence Policy, *see* ESDP
European Security Strategy, *see* ESS
European Union Military Committee, *see* EUMC
European Union Military Staff, *see* EUMS
European Union Naval Force 'Atalanta', *see* EUNAVFOR 'Atalanta'
Europol, 11, 15, 21, 47, 88, 97, 101–3, 109, 114–15
extradition, 45–6, 92–7, 107, 109, 113

Force Headquarter, 173–4, 180
Foreign policy analysis, 9
France, 15, 32, 53, 60, 88, 89, 93, 112, 119, 125, 127, 150, 163, 171, 174–5, 209
Frontex, 21, 47

G8 Global Partnership, 17, 145, 147, 161, 163–4, 202
Germany, 13, 15, 32, 53–4, 72, 76, 88–9, 110, 112, 119, 125, 127, 135–6, 150, 158, 160, 174, 209

High Representative, 22, 30–1, 41, 57, 62–3, 64, 66, 71, 74–6, 86–7, 150–1, 162, 164–5, 172, 175, 193, 195, 200

INSC, 29, 153–4, 156–7, 164, 202
Institute for Environmental Security, 75
Instrument for Nuclear Safety Cooperation, *see* INSC
Instrument for Stability, 3, 20, 24, 28–9, 43, 150–1, 153–4, 156–7, 164, 182, 198, 201–2, 204
intelligence, 15, 76–7, 90, 97, 100, 110, 152, 174, 177, 188
Internal Security Strategy, *see* ISS
International Science and Technology Centre, *see* ISTC
Iraq, 15, 25, 88, 146, 200, 208–9
ISS, 103
ISTC, 155–6
Italy, 89, 93, 112, 133, 174

judicial cooperation, 21, 58, 91, 107

Kenya, 176, 183, 185, 187–8

legitimacy, 131, 141, 164
Libya, 138, 162, 209
Lisbon Treaty, 2–4, 14, 27, 29, 30–1, 41, 48, 51, 54, 57, 60, 61–7, 75–6, 86–7, 91, 99–101, 103, 122–3, 141–2, 148, 151–2, 162, 164–5, 172, 175, 182, 193, 200, 204, 210n2
London, 3, 15, 88–9, 133, 140, 195

Maastricht Treaty, 3, 4, 8, 14, 21, 43, 50–2, 54–6, 57–9, 62, 65–6, 91, 93, 98, 103, 107, 120–2, 123, 148–9, 151, 158, 192, 194
Madrid, 3, 89, 140, 195

maritime piracy, 11–13, 17–18, 20, 29–31, 44, 46, 167–91, 196, 199, 201–5
Maritime Security Centre: Horn of Africa, *see* MSCHOA
Mediterranean, 25, 84
Middle East, 68, 84, 89, 145, 154, 156, 164–5, 201
migration, 4, 9, 11, 12, 15–17, 20, 25, 44, 55–6, 58–9, 65, 71, 77–8, 116–43
Mogadishu, 169, 186
Monar, 3, 65
Morocco, 138
MSCHOA, 180–1, 189

NATO, 35, 54, 66, 70, 163, 173–5, 177, 181, 187–9, 206–7
Non-Proliferation Treaty, 17, 148–9, 157

Operational Headquarter, 173–4, 180
Organisation for Security and Cooperation in Europe, *see* OSCE
OSCE, 71, 206

passenger name record, *see* PNR
pillars, 2–4, 8, 21, 30–1, 50–1, 55–8, 60–2, 65, 91, 95, 98–9, 103–4, 121, 148, 150–1, 184–5, 192–5, 204, 210n1
  see also cross-pillar
PNR, 97–101
Poland, 26, 66, 174–5
police cooperation, 53, 56, 97, 102, 104
Political and Security Committee, 61, 73, 172–4, 189

QMV, 42, 57–8, 65, 92, 118
qualified majority voting, *see* QMV

Rapid Reaction Mechanism, 3, 28
Russia, 11, 17, 26, 28–9, 46–7, 80, 84, 144–66, 181, 189, 198–9, 201–2, 207, 210n1

Schengen, 53, 59, 92, 95, 119–20
Schengen Information System (SIS), 53
Science and Technology Centre in Ukraine, *see* STCU
security culture, 146–7
Single European Act, 53–4, 151
Solana, J., 22, 27, 62, 74, 150, 164
solidarity, 7, 66, 102, 107, 124, 128
  clause, 66
Somalia, 11–13, 15, 18, 20, 29–31, 46, 88, 167–91, 199, 201–2, 204–5, 207, 210n2
sovereignty, 7, 32–3, 44–5, 109–10, 119, 171
STCU, 155–6
Steering Group on Climate Change and International Security, 26, 72, 76, 83–4, 86, 200
Stockholm Programme, 100, 142

TACIS (Technical Assistance for the Commonwealth of Independent States), 29, 149, 155–7, 164, 201–2, 214
Tampere Programme, 120, 130, 141
technical assistance, 28, 126, 128, 144, 148, 202–3
  see also TACIS
TEU, 17, 54–6, 65–6, 93, 98, 103, 107, 122, 148–9, 158
Transitional Federal Government, 169, 171, 184, 186, 190
transparency, 106
Treaty on the European Union, *see* TEU
Tunisia, 138
Turkey, 188

UK, 15, 78, 88, 135, 140, 159, 174, 181, 188
Ukraine, 139, 155–6

Index 243

UN, 1, 35, 72, 80, 82–4, 86, 105–6, 186–7, 191
UN Charter, 105–6
UN Development Programme, see UNDP
UN Framework Convention on Climate Change, see UNFCCC
UN General Assembly, 82, 84, 118, 183, 202
UN High Commissioner for Refugees, see UNHCR
UN Security Council, 27, 68, 70, 76, 80, 82, 86–7, 91, 105–6, 145, 157, 170–1, 185, 187, 189, 199, 202
UNDP, 10, 22, 184–5, 187, 210n3

UNFCCC, 71, 73–4, 84–5, 87
UNHCR, 118, 130–6, 138, 141–2, 202
United Kingdom, see UK
United Nations, see UN

weapons of mass destruction, see WMD
WMD, 2, 11–12, 17, 22, 24, 69, 71, 85, 144–66, 182, 198–9, 201, 204, 207–8
 EU WMD Strategy, 145, 149–52, 154, 157, 159, 163–5

Yemen, 15, 88, 176, 183